FANFARE
FOR A
TIN HAT

FANFARE
FOR A
TIN HAT

A Third Essay in
Autobiography

ERIC LINKLATER

MACMILLAN

First published 1970 by
MACMILLAN AND CO LTD
London and Basingstoke
Associated companies in New York Toronto
Dublin Melbourne Johannesburg & Madras

SBN boards: 333

Printed in Great Britain by
WESTERN PRINTING SERVICES LTD
Bristol

0333 11705 0

To my grandson
ALEXANDER RAGNAR
who
at the age of two
may enjoy its flavour

List of Illustrations

1. Ship *Eurydice*: my maternal grandfather in
   command   32
2. My father, Robert Linklater   33
3. Elizabeth, my mother, with her first grandchild   64
4. Eric Linklater in 1921, from a drawing by
   W. J. Johnston   65
5. Marjorie MacIntyre, 1933   160
6. In Dalecarlia, Sweden   161
7. Merkister, Orkney   161
8. Eric Linklater in 1944, from a drawing by
   Michael Ayrton   192
9. Pitcalzean House, Easter Ross   193
10. The Pitcalzean Highlanders   193

Note

In 1947 I published a book of essays called *The Art of Adventure*, which has long been out of print. Included in this narrative are substantial parts of four of the essays, and fragments of one or two others, where they fall into place in the calendar of events. There are also two short extracts from a pamphlet called *The Atlantic Garrisons*, which the Stationery Office published in 1941.

❧ One

I HAVE already written two volumes of autobiography, and for reasons that seem to me sufficient – though my judgment is not unbiased – I now propose to write a third.

The first volume was called *The Man on My Back*, the second *A Year of Space*. In the latter I took advantage of two improbabilities, thrust upon me, to describe a voyage. I was asked to go to Korea, where there was a war of confused purpose, and to New Zealand, where I was required to lecture and hoped to catch some large trout. In an aeroplane flying from Europe to the Far East, from Japan to the Antipodes, time and space lose their separate identities, and I found it as easy to travel backwards in time as east or south in space. In the second volume there is, therefore, alternation between movement and memory, between the afterglow of days in an old calendar and the new horizons that dawn is uncovering. In spite of such violent deviation, however, *A Year of Space* is an accurate trustworthy chronicle; and that cannot be said of its predecessor.

In *The Man on My Back* there are chapters in which every statement is true to fact, and emotions are recorded that fit the occasion like a well-made glove. But parts of it are misleading – the final pattern was forced upon me – and I should, I think, explain what went wrong, and why.

The title, for a start: there were those who read into it a meaning I had not intended, and believed, in consequence, that I was laying claim to motives – to a character indeed – of quite implausible nobility. For that mistake, not I but my publisher was to blame. On a preliminary page of the manuscript I sent him there was a quotation from Montaigne which read, so far as I remember, something like this: 'It was said of So-and-so that, although he had travelled widely, his travels had neither improved his temper nor enlarged his understanding. For wherever he went he carried himself on his back, and the burden was too much.'

There lay a pretence to modesty, not to nobility of mood; but when my publisher or his printer lost that explanatory page there was no clue to the meaning or purpose of the title. It happened, moreover, that somewhere in the narrative I quoted an old Norse proverb: 'Bare is his back who has no brother' – and many, putting two and two together, assumed that I was posing and posturing as my brother's keeper. In 1941, when the book was published, the acceptance of un-welcome responsibilities had become common form; but I was not trying to win favour by a show of timely virtue. My simple purpose had been to identify a persistent handicap.

The final chapter, moreover, was dictated by circum-stance. I had intended a quite different conclusion – a rather elaborate *peripeteia* – but before the book was finished the war of 1939 had begun, and as a Territorial soldier I was mobilised in August. My income was drastically reduced, and I had to make a little money to supplement my pay and support a wife and two small children. So, for a conclusion unrelated to the original design, I described the manner of our mobilisation – our training was minimal, our resources were scanty – and found a perfunctory end on a small island at the southern entrance to Scapa Flow. Truthful though it was, that conclusion falsified my purpose, and for some years I have felt that I should correct an impression which the book, so misshapen, unintentionally created.

In it there were omissions which tact, if not tenderness, determined; and some of those gaps can now be closed. I want to add a little – but very little – to what I previously wrote of my service in the first Great War. In the first volume I was rigidly determined not to exaggerate my experience of war, because in comparison with so many of my near-contemporaries my service had been small and short and of no importance. I made light of a major emotional experience, and assumed a mannerly reticence which I regretted even while I admired it. By my resolute decision to avoid emotion and hyperbole I fell victim to the opposite fault of 'good form', and became guilty of another falsity.

It is too late now to recall emotion, and I shall not try. At the age of seventy I have lost all knowledge – real knowledge, that is – of the young man who went to France at the age of eighteen. I remember much of what happened to him, and I propose to relate one or two episodes which retain the acrid flavour of an experience that I might now find incredible if I had not substantial evidence of it. But I have no intention of trying to re-create the thoughts, the feelings, the fears and occasional bravado of someone so utterly remote from the septuagenarian into whom he has strangely grown. I shall not deny, however, that the title I have chosen for this – my third and concluding volume of autobiography – has been suggested by sentiment; and to prevent its being misunderstood, in the manner of an earlier title, I shall explain it.

The end of my four or five months of active service, as a private in the Black Watch, came when I was hit on the head by a German bullet. I fell unconscious on friendless ground, but quickly recovered. My fingers were numb, and I could not pull the little roll of lint or gauze – the dressing for a wound – from the cotton envelope which enclosed it. I pressed the whole envelope to my bleeding head, clapped my helmet on top, fastened it by the chin-strap, and with some difficulty made my way to a Regimental Aid Post. There I was encouraged to take a closer look at my helmet, for one of those in attendance at the R.A.P. loudly exclaimed, 'Here's a bloody good souvenir, if you can get away with it!' – 'It's mine,' I said, 'and I'm bloody well going to keep it.'

There was a neat little hole where the bullet had made its entrance; there was a large and jagged hole where the bullet, flattened and disappointed by the density of my Nordic skull, had forced an exit and gone off in the general direction of Ypres. With the determination of the slightly insane I kept possession of my helmet, and I still have it.

A few months ago it celebrated its jubilee: the fiftieth anniversary, that is, of the painful occasion when it was overtaken — for though I was running as fast as I could, the bullet came faster — and decisively punctured. Its survival, after so long a time, and in a century so troubled as ours has been, deserves, I feel, a little recognition; and, though this volume will not be published until the jubilee has receded into the backwardness of time, I want to record it in the large print of a title-page. In doing so, I shall bow to history rather than to vanity.

My narrative, from now on, will have gaps other than those which, as I have said, I hope to fill; for manifestly I must not repeat what I have written in the previous volumes. But I shall try to maintain the continuity necessary for easy comprehension, and recognition of the sequence of events; and the best way to ensure that is to start at the beginning.

In *The Man on My Back* I said something of the long holiday months of my childhood that were spent in Orkney; but what I wrote was brief — with a carefully measured brevity — because I was intent on giving the book a strict and orderly design within a series of compartments, each of them neatly closed, and none too large. But now, I feel, I should give myself more latitude, because in what I remember of my early years there are embedded fragments of a way of life — a temper, a habit of thought — that has wholly vanished even from our remotest islands; and what I remember of Orkney, in my earliest knowledge of it, has remained in memory because it was a land of story-tellers, and many of their stories I heard again and again.

Some of them, in later years, I learnt to discount, for gossip is an art, and sometimes the narrower sorts of truth have to be stretched to give congruity to a story and reality to a character. But the very fact that gossip was recognised and valued as an art — immensely valued — is a clue to the nature of that vanished habit of life, that landscape obliterated by progress and prosperity.

🦋 Two

My grandfather, Magnus Linklater, was an Orkney crofter with 'a coo's keeping': he had enough land, that is, to provide pasture and winter keep for a single cow and her followers, which might be a calf and a young bullock. As well as his cattle-beasts he certainly had a few sheep, some hens and a loudly crowing cock, and one or two Shetland ponies. His croft of Mossetter lay near the village of Dounby, in the middle of the West Mainland of Orkney. Not a stone of the little house now remains.

So small a property left him plenty of time for other interests, and an old flintlock gun was perhaps his most cherished possession: he was said to have been a good shot and to have shown great patience in the pursuit of game. There used also to be a story – the truth of which I cannot guarantee – that he was able to recite the tale of his ancestry back through sixteen generations. He was born, I think, in 1825, and if the span of sixteen generations can be estimated at four hundred years it is thinly possible that the story may be justified by the fact that my name first appears in a Norwegian document of 1426, or a little earlier, that records a 'Complaint of Orcadian Commons'. The name, at first sight, is unrecognisable, but the old spelling reveals its origin as a simple place-name. He who added his complaint to that of other 'goodmen' of the time was Cristi Aelingaklaet; and as *ling* means heather, and *klaet* a solitary rock – perhaps one of those monoliths that our remote predecessors raised for an unknown purpose – the original form of Linklater can be translated as 'at a stone in the heather': an address that suggests a spacious background, but certainly not a rich one.

Cristi, however, was a 'goodman', so called not to indicate his virtue, but his rank. A goodman was of necessity an odaller, which implies that he held land which had been in his family for at least five generations. Magnus, then, with his 'coo's keeping', was the much diminished and woefully impoverished descendant of a family established in Orkney by 1300, when the old Norse earldom was still a lively memory, and Norse blood had hardly been adulterated by Scotch addition. Storer Clouston, my friend of many years ago – a most erudite historian but a romantic genealogist – awarded me even more distant and much more distinguished ancestors than Goodman Cristi.

For several centuries the Linklaters owned parcels of land in the northerly parish of Sandwick, and by some association of ownership or inheritance which I have long forgotten he presumed their descent from a redoubtable man, conspicuously alive in 1136, called Sigurd of Westness, whose wife Ingibjorg was a great-granddaughter of Earl Thorfinn the Mighty, whose mother was a daughter of Malcolm II, King of Scots. There is nothing unlikely in that presumption; in a community so small and isolated as that of Orkney it is probable that everyone except recent arrivals – incomers of the last two or three hundred years – is descended from Thorfinn and the terrible earls who preceded him.

I can truthfully assert, however – and show evidence for the assertion – that I have never felt much confidence in the legitimacy of long genealogies. A quarter of a century ago, when my elder son existed only *in utero*, I began to write a narrative poem – long since disappeared – in which I tried to chronicle his descent and estimate the manner of his life-to-be. There remains in my memory only a single couplet, recurrent as a cynical refrain:

> But Cuckoos in a Family Tree
> Complicate Heredity.

Nor shall I pretend that a connexion with the terrible earls, even if its legitimacy could be established, would inspire any feeling of kinship with those grim rulers. What is real about my ancestry, and what – when I choose to think about it – can still waken genuine emotion, is the ability of some nearer generations to survive and maintain their sense of identity – their knowledge of long descent – in circumstances that never precluded winter hardship and were often wide open to a knowledge of hunger.

But the knowledge of his ancestry – if indeed he was so learned as to know it, or so ingenious as to invent it – may have helped my grandfather to get a witch for his wife. Initially, I suppose, his physical attraction prompted that exceptional alliance: in the parish of his birth, a countryside of low dark hills and dancing lakes under enormous skies, he was known among his neighbours as 'a bonny wee man'. He did not live long, but he never lacked a wife.

The witch, whose name was Mary Marwick, married him. That is to say, it was she who made marriage possible, and when she had disposed of her rivals sent for the minister to clinch it. It was, indeed, the manner in which she got rid of her predecessors in his bed that first gave her the name and reputation of a witch; and about that some explication is necessary. For what follows I rely, of course, on stories that I heard, again and again, when I was a small boy; but later in life I learnt something of the economy that lay behind them.

There was a time, about the middle of the nineteenth century, when young women in Orkney could make a few shillings a week by plaiting straw for ladies' bonnets. Leghorn bonnets they were called, and in Italy, where they originated, they were made of wheat-straw. But rye-grass served almost as well. The plaiting was done at home – the girls would have a pot of water beside them, to moisten the faded grass – and many a crofter found occupation, more agreeable than he had ever known before, in watching his wife and daughters at work under the shelter of his own roof. If they were diligent they could make enough money to reduce his own labour to an agreeable minimum.

My grandfather's first wife was a girl of eighteen or so, industrious and well behaved, whose nimble fingers brought

15

him a small but steady income, and she might have made more but for the untimely visiting of Mary Marwick. She, who was rather better off, had more liberty than most, and a restless temper. She would go from house to house, in Sandwick and the Hillside of Birsay, with no better purpose than to satisfy her curiosity about what her neighbours were saying, doing and thinking and to buy their confidence with the gossip she had already gathered.

In my grandfather's house she would listen by the hour to his tales of poverty and grandeur in the dead centuries of time, and all the while watch with black and staring eyes the slim figure of his young wife, whose fingers were busy in the moistened straw.

Well do I remember her eyes, for in my childhood they daunted me, and held me in a sort of frightened trance when I was taken to see her in the cottage that a generous son-in-law had built for her. There she was, sitting up in bed in her old age, her face as yellow as a lemon, a cap of Maltese lace on her head – my father gave it to her – and under her forehead two great pits of shadow in which burned, as it seemed, a blackness that had the nature of light: a sable light that shone and saw.

Those were the eyes which had unnerved, and frightened to her death, my grandfather's first wife more than half a century before. The poor girl grew limp and thin, her fingers lost their cunning, and when she took to her bed Mary Marwick continued to visit her, with the pretence of bringing her comfort and the gossip of the countryside; but would leave her lying weak and weeping to her pillow.

Within a few months of his marriage my grandfather was a widower, but still ignorant of his destiny. A year later he married again, but not Mary Marwick. His second wife was a little older than his first, a tall, strapping girl with a loud and ready laugh, and dazzlingly quick at straw-plaiting. A few weeks after the marriage, Mary Marwick resumed her visiting.

She enjoyed, as I have said, more freedom than most of her neighbours, and that she owed to the high wages that her father earned aboard the whaling ships that fished the Davis Straits and Baffin Bay. Until the middle of the nineteenth century the whalers from Dundee and Peterhead used always to call at Stromness to fill their water-butts and recruit their crews – as many as fifty ships might call there in the spring of the year – and the best of their harpooners was Mary's father. He made more money than any other of the Orkneymen, and when his ship came back to Stromness, before winter set in, it was known that he would take three days to walk the fourteen or fifteen miles between his harbour and his home.

In Stromness there were good inns, and every few miles along the road there was an ale-house where Marwick was expected to call. He was a strong man with a great breadth of shoulder – perhaps a little wild – and his eyes were as piercing as his daughter's. He had a good croft – better than most of them – but neglected it, for when the whalers took to going as far north as Baffin Bay it was usually past harvest-time before they returned. And what was the point of grubbing in wet fields to grow a few stooks of rough barley or poor, thin oats when a man had money in his pocket? Marwick usually had money enough to drink his fill, and last the winter; and Mary, his only child, was better dressed than other girls in the parish.

My grandfather's second wife made much of her to begin with, and would cry a warm welcome when Mary opened the door that let the cow into one end of the house and human beings into the other, which was no bigger, though a little more comfortable. She would sit on one stool, the young wife on another, and my grandfather in a high straw-backed chair with a hood to it that kept off the draughts. They would talk of country matters or my grandfather would tell tales of the hunger and famine that made Orkney a sorry country in the seventeenth century, and of the witchcraft that grew rife in the land.

He was, I am sure, an innocent creature, with no suspicion that witchcraft was a dangerous subject for debate. Mary Marwick would be watching his new wife with a sombre glitter in her dark eyes; and sometimes the girl would throw

17

up her hands with a cry – letting fall the wet straw they held – and say there was a numbness in her fingers, she could plait no more; and sometimes she would clutch her breast with a groan, and say she felt as if a great pin had been thrust in below the nipple.

She lasted longer than the first one, but died in childbed. Now by that time every woman in the parish, and most of the men, were looking askance at Mary Marwick, for nothing was hidden in those days, and what went on in one house was soon known to all its neighbours. The women had no doubt at all that Mary had ill-wished those two poor girls, and ill-wished them with the manifest intention of following them, as soon as she could, into my grandfather's house, poor though it was. Their menfolk were less outspoken, and said it might be better to wait and see what happened next; for there was no great profit, so far as they could tell, in marriage to Magnus Linklater. They were also unwilling to say anything that might offend Marwick the harpooner. Some of them had sailed with him to the Davis Straits, many had drunk with him on winter nights, and they knew that he was a dangerous man to cross.

Three people only – and two were in their graves – had never suspected or entertained a thought that there might be some source of malignity in Mary Marwick. My grandfather, I think, had an inexpugnable innocence, and his two wives must have yielded themselves so completely to the general power of the woman that they could conceive no dread of her specific, wicked influence. Charm is too weak a word to use, but it has to be admitted that she had some gift of fascination in which 'charm' must have had a facet. As a child I was unaware of it – I saw her only twice, and then I was too frightened to feel anything except a forbidden impulse to escape – but I am sure that my mother both recognised her fascination and responded to something that may be called her charm.

Some months after the death of the second wife, Marwick the harpooner came home from sea with his pockets full of money. They had found whales far to the north in Baffin

Bay, under the cliffs of western Greenland, and it was mid-November before he returned to Stromness. A few weeks later there was a wedding at his neglected croft, where dancing and drinking went on for three long nights, until the feasting was over, and the last ale-cask dry. Then Mary the witch went home to Mossetter with her 'bonny wee man'.

There they lived, in apparent contentment, for about fourteen years, during which time four sons and a daughter were born to them, all of whom survived the croups and catastrophes of childhood. Perhaps they got a little of the money that Marwick had made in icy northern seas, for the children grew up without any memory of hunger or privation. They knew nothing of luxury, of course, and probably never saw butcher's meat on the table. But they ate well enough – much better than poor people in towns – for a pair of lean black collies could usually catch a hare, and my grandfather's constant wealth was his old flintlock gun. He had neither taste nor talent for any regular kind of work, but he took great pleasure in long, furtive expeditions to the upland moors, where grouse were abundant, and in patiently stalking the grey geese that came in flocks to autumn fields. He would set night-lines for trout in the big loch, not far away, or spear them in the Hillside burn. Add to these plovers' eggs and gulls' eggs in their season, and young puffins and guillemots from the Birsay shore, and the bare scrubbed table at Mossetter may well have worn more than a sufficiency of flavour and variety to add to the milk and meal, the berebread and cheese, the kale and potatoes that were its daily furniture.

The sons of Magnus and the witch were John, William, Thomas, and Robert my father, in that order of birth; and Mary, the daughter, came between William and Thomas, I think. She grew up to be the prettiest girl in the parish, the image of her bonny wee father, and as sweet-tempered as she was pretty. She was the only one, except her father, who never quarrelled with her mother or showed any fear of her; and when the witch grew old and weary and weak in the legs Mary looked after her with patient care. She had married a handsome young farmer with a yellow beard, who dashingly rode a big grey pony that was thought to have Arab blood in it.

Magnus died in his early forties; not, as some said, untimely worn out, but of a rheumatic fever after walking home, drenched to the skin in bitter weather, from a field by the western cliffs with his old gun under his arm and a pair of grey geese over his shoulder. A little while before his death the oldest boy, John, had gone to Stromness, apprenticed to a boat-builder. He grew tall and strong, a black-avised youth who, both in temper and looks, took after his maternal grandfather. When he was nineteen or twenty he quarrelled bitterly with his mother and, running from home, was not heard of again for nearly forty years.

The cause of the quarrel was his coming home from Stromness to say that he was engaged to marry; and the consequences of that announcement were long remembered, and told, again and again, with infinite zest, convincing detail, and something very like awe. The witch flew into a temper, abused her son, vilified and ridiculed the girl – whom she did not know – and swore there would be no marriage without her consent. So John went back to his lodging in Stromness, that same night, supperless and walking through the dark, and the final row came a week later.

His apprenticeship finished, John was earning a decent wage, as wages were then accounted, and to his sweetheart he had given, as a pledge of their betrothal more useful than a ring, a gold watch. It did the poor girl no good, for Mary the witch discovered where she lived, and took it from her.

Later in the week, when John went to see his sweetheart, he found a frightened, woebegone creature who would scarcely speak to him. His mother had so terrified her that she had made up her mind to break off the engagement and never see John again.

When Saturday came, John walked out to Mossetter, and met his mother on the brigstones before the house. He was so angry that, for a little while, he could not speak; and she stood watching him with a grim and gloating look, convinced of her power and rejoicing in it.

Then, reaching into her pocket, she held out her hand and said, 'Here's your watch, and see that you take better care of it in future.'

Then the story – at this point it never varied – reached a new pitch of excitement; for John took the watch, and with all his strength threw it into the heather behind the house.

Still he said nothing, and she spoke little except to cry out against the wickedness of throwing a good watch away. But presently she said, 'You'd better come in and have your tea.'

'Not in this house,' he said. 'If I can't see her, you'll never see me again.' And turning on his heel he left her.

He kept his word, and she died without seeing him, or even hearing from him or of where he had gone. No word or whisper of him reached Orkney until 1918, when a private soldier in the uniform of a New Zealand Rifle regiment – a young man with a dark complexion under a big pinched and pointed khaki hat – arrived in Kirkwall and said he hoped to find some relations. His father's name was John Linklater.

A very different sort was the second son, my Uncle Willy. Him I remember – though I met him rarely, and only in childhood – as a plump and genial man with bright, healthy cheeks and a wandering mind. He was always immaculately dressed, when I saw him, in the whitest of linen and a trimly cut suit of dark blue serge. He wore a bowler hat and carried a malacca cane, and as we walked together he would utter small, indifferent noises and repeat his simple questions without listening for an answer.

'Woof, woof,' he would say. 'How old are you now, boy? Woof, woof. Heard from your father lately? Last I heard of him he was in Kobe. Kobe or Yokohama? Strange life, don't know how he sticks it. Woof, woof, woof. Wouldn't suit me. Woof, woof. Hard on your mother too. How is your mother?'

He had seen my mother an hour before. We were staying in Greenock with friends of hers, and that day we had gone to tea with Uncle Willy, his wife and only daughter. Then, very kindly, he had taken me for a walk along the Esplanade.

'Been to Orkney lately? Never go there myself. Not for

many a year. Woof, woof. Too far away. But your father built a house there, didn't he? Wonder why he did that. Woof, woof. What are you going to do when you grow up? Don't be a fool like your father, and go to sea. I told him not to, but he'd never listen to me. Never listen to anyone who didn't agree with him. Woof, woof. Where is he now? Kobe, isn't it? Or Yokohama?'

Uncle Willy lived all his grown-up life in Greenock – a town, much maligned but very handsomely situated, with which my mother and her parents had long association – and for many years he was employed, in what capacity I do not know, in a ship-building yard. He may have had a little more schooling than runaway Uncle John, but he must have started humbly enough, and then, by the evidence of his clothes and way of life, got gradual promotion to some position of limited but grave responsibility. He and my Uncle Tom married sisters, who were women, as I remember, of prim and starched demeanour, with angry tongues and vinegar in their veins. Each of them had but a single child: Willy a girl, and Tom a boy.

It is difficult to guess how much education they got from a village school so primitive in its economy that every boy, setting out in the morning, carried not only his bag of books, but a peat under his arm for the fireplace before which the master warmed his backside. Scotland was famous, in those days, for the education it afforded; and schoolmasters, who had considerable authority, wasted no time upon an egalitarian distribution of instruction. Dull boys they ignored, and bright boys they wooed into a love of learning, and beat with enthusiasm when their pupils – their few, favoured pupils – failed to use the faculties that God had given them. Uncle Tom and my father were bright boys, and Tom acquired enough learning – or a sufficient foundation for more learning – to let him do well for himself, until a mixture of stubborn pride and his wife's parsimony took him to a very cold, uncomfortable death.

He was apprenticed to the sea, and by the time of the Boer War was commanding a troopship carrying Canadian volunteers to South Africa. He may already have established some connexion with St John's in Newfoundland, but I rather think he settled there after that military traffic and in consequence of new friendships made in the course of it. By 1911 he was a director – or perhaps managing director – of a shipping company in St John's, and in that year came home to buy another vessel for the company's fleet. It was only a small fleet, of small ships, and if the company was not dominated by Uncle Tom it was accustomed to doing business in a very leisurely and lenient way. For he was able to combine his mission with a long holiday in Orkney, and he did not sail again for Newfoundland till the end of February 1912.

Before then my father had built a house, for our summer holidays, near the northern end of the big Loch of Harray in the West Mainland of Orkney; and Uncle Tom rented a farmhouse called Howan a couple of miles beyond Dounby and not much farther, across the fields, from the tumbled walls of the croft of Mossetter where he had spent his boyhood. With Uncle Tom were his ever-complaining wife and his small son, with whom I was not in sympathy.

My father, on leave from his ship – and, if I remember rightly, waiting for his next ship to be built – also spent some weeks in Orkney that summer, but except for one topic I have no memory at all of what my elders talked about; for I had a new, absorbing interest of my own. They may have had boyhood memories to barter: I do not know. They had ships to discuss, the buying or navigation of them – that is certain – but I had a boat of my own, and I was self-sufficient. My father had bought me a well-made, sweetly fashioned dinghy, ten feet of keel, the total price of which, with oars and a rudder, was £5 10s – I found the bill for it many years later – and I spent most of that summer afloat and alone, in a world of private contentment.

The one topic of grown-up conversation that lodged in my mind is pinned to memory by my father's loud and angry voice saying, 'You're a fool even to think of it, Tom!'

What Uncle Tom was proposing was not only to buy a ship – no harm in that, if the surveyors can be trusted – but

23

to sail her out himself, under his own command, to New-foundland. Tom's argument was that he, like my father, was a master mariner and able to take a ship from the Clyde to any port on the map; and in this – though now I rely on later talk, on what my mother subsequently told me – he was hotly supported by his unpleasant wife. She pointed out – and no one could deny the truth of what she said – that to hire another shipmaster, whose return fare would have to be paid, would be a large, additional expense; while to do what my father urged, and go by passenger ship – there would be three berths to pay for! – was wanton extravagance.

The argument continued, and I went fishing. My father returned to sea, and Tom and his family spent the winter in Greenock. He found a suitable ship, bought her, and such alterations, replenishments, or additions as were necessary for her new trade were completed early in the following year. From somewhere abroad my father wrote again, imploring Tom to engage a younger and more experienced man to take command – it was eight or nine years since Tom had been to sea – but Tom refused to listen to his younger brother, and by the end of February he and his wife and their only child, that poor little boy – how deeply I wished that I had been fond of him! – lay aboard the doomed ship at the Tail of the Bank.

The ship, called *Erna*, was small and old: about 3500 tons gross and built in 1890. She sailed on 28 February, with more than forty passengers aboard – most of them, I suppose, were emigrants, tempted by the offer of a cheap crossing – and, though she was expected to make the passage in ten days, she was never heard of again. There were, at that time, wild gales in the Atlantic, and arctic ice had been carried far to the south. She was probably caught and crushed among icebergs and floes off the Banks of New-foundland. A month later the dangers of the route were widely advertised by the loss, in similar circumstances, of the great ship *Titanic*.

❧ Three

Some of the disabilities of life a hundred years ago had compensations that have also vanished; and a village school might be able to enlarge instruction with help from a parish minister.

In my father's boyhood there was, in Orkney, an eccentric but gifted minister called David Johnston, who before graduating at St Andrews had attended classes at all four of the Scottish universities, but spent most of his time in scholarly idleness at Oxford. The local Presbytery objected to his continuing habit of taking long holidays, but he paid no attention to complaints. From 1868 until 1893 he ruled the parishes of Harray and Birsay from a church, perched on top of a hill, that commanded a broad and fertile landscape; and exercised an almost feudal authority with occasional diligence, a warm devotion to his people, an absolute assurance that he was always right – 'I shall never cry *Peccavi*,' he said – and an irritable disposition to write to the newspapers to correct social blunder or national error.

His scholarship was widely known, and in 1893 he was appointed to the Chair of Divinity and Biblical Criticism in the University of Aberdeen. He was totally unfitted for such an office – always unpunctual and absent-minded, his eccentricities had grown with the years – and the Aberdeen students who attended his lectures behaved with such riotous indiscipline that Dr Johnston – who would not resign, who never admitted he was wrong – had to be removed by Act of Parliament.

Long before that, Robert my father had emerged as the liveliest and brightest of the several score pupils at the village school in Dounby, and at the age of thirteen or fourteen was elevated by the master to subordinate authority as a pupil-teacher. His mother the witch and the Dounby schoolmaster persuaded themselves that he had academic abilities which deserved encouragement, and sought the help of Dr Johnston. That good man readily agreed to foster the education of a young parishioner, and offered his private tuition in Greek and Latin. Within a few months my father, who had no wish to become a teacher, began to feel imprisoned by the fearful implications of Caesar's Gallic War and Greek verbs, and wrote to his brother Tom, seeking help to escape. He was a stalwart boy, of exceptional strength, and on the horizon of his innocence scholarship looked like a dark, enclosing cloud.

His brother was sympathetic, sent him money, and paid for his indentures as apprentice in a sailing ship. Escaping from the benignity of Dr Johnston and the ill-advised ambitions of his mother, he went to sea and discovered his vocation. He was still very young when appointed second mate aboard a handsome clipper-ship sailing out of Greenock. She was either *Eurydice* or *Orpheus* – I have forgotten which – and her commander was James Young, Swedish by birth but naturalised by habit as a British sailor, who was accompanied by his English wife Sarah and their daughter Elizabeth.

Several years were to pass before Robert married Elizabeth. Their early meeting had no immediate consequences, and he went his own way to command, at the age of twenty-two, a very pretty little barquentine, the *Corisande*, engaged in the rough Newfoundland trade. He found his first wife in Orkney, and took her voyaging with him. But Atlantic gales and the violent movement of a little barquentine were too much for the poor girl, and she died of them. My father refused to let her be buried at sea. His passage was long delayed by contrary weather which no skill of seamanship, no artist's trimming of the sails could defeat; but he was obstinate and the crew turned angry. What really happened I do not know; but as a small boy I was told – and heard

26

the story more than once – that incipient mutiny was quietly and quickly quelled when the leading mutineer, coming aft to argue with my hot-tempered father, was felled by a judicious blow with a belaying-pin. Immediately the weather changed – or so the story had it – and before a favouring gale the *Corisande* came surging up the Firth of Clyde, and my father buried his young wife in the kindliness of Christian soil. My mother never spoke of her, and I know nothing more about her. But I still have a deftly painted water-colour of the barquentine.

The camaraderie of the sea brought Robert Linklater and Elizabeth Young together again, but when they decided on marriage they were faced with two decisions, both necessary, that neither relished. My father's last command in sail was a big, four-masted barque called *Celticburn*, and from her broad quarterdeck he had to transfer himself to a steamship's bridge. That was a transition which he and my grandfather, and all right-thinking men of their sort, regarded as a fearful degradation, but which young men could not avoid because sailing ships were no longer profitable, and steamships offered them the only livelihood for which they had been taught. The new firm by which Robert was employed owned ships that sailed from Bristol Channel ports – from Cardiff or Avonmouth – to East Africa and South Africa by way of the Mediterranean; and Elizabeth Young would have to leave the little town on the Clyde in which, when she was not at sea, she had spent her early years. She bitterly resented the migration, and her resentment had a curious effect on my childhood: I was led to believe that we were living in exile.

My mother had no drop of Scots blood in her – her father was Swedish, her mother English – but she was a woman of fierce and determined character who had arbitrarily decided that she was Scotch; and Scotch she remained when she went to live in South Wales.

I was born in Penarth, of which I have no memory, for while I was still an infant – or perhaps a little older – we removed to a new, protruding limb of the city of Cardiff. The limb was a benign and well-gardened series of public parks which modest rows of small houses accompanied. I have never returned to Cardiff since we left it in 1912 or 1913, but now, when town-planning is so highly regarded, I am inclined to think that, sixty years ago, it must have been in the vanguard of municipal progress. I was very happy there, despite my mother's insistence that our habitation was no more permanent than a gipsy's camp; but I was happier still when she took us to Orkney for long summer holidays. Of them I shall have more to say later. At the moment my topic is Cardiff.

Its principal pleasures, as my memory retains them, were bicycles, small rowing-boats, a series of plump, dark-haired little girls – most of them, I think, called Gwynneth – and food. Of food, that grave and splendid topic, I shall defer discussion. The boats were for hire on a large lake in one of the parks, and from an early age I had a season-ticket that let me take useful exercise and enjoy the unfailing pleasure of plank-thin proximity to water. The bicycles and the plump little girls were closely associated, and there were picnic parties as far afield as Caerphilly.

My education had its beginning – an unhelpful beginning – in a dames' school conducted by two tiny, fragile, grey-complexioned old ladies called the Misses Jennings, whose young assistant – a rosy, bouncing, pretty girl to whom I was perversely attached – clouded for many years my appre-hension of arithmetic by a system of instruction which – for me, at any rate – invested mere integers with the incompre-hensibility of Egyptian hieroglyphs before discovery of the Rosetta Stone. I doted on my rosy teacher, but quailed before the sinister nonsense of the little white sums she chalked on her blackboard.

Some time later I was entered at the curious nucleus of a school which has since become much respected as the Cardiff High School. It was then housed, in part, in tem-porary hutments of a sort which became familiar in times of war; and was known, without much appreciation of the emotional significance of names, as the Cardiff Intermediate School for Boys. We wore, on striped caps, badges which carried those unimpressive initials C.I.S.B. and twice or three times a week we played association football, hockey, or cricket. More freely, and without supervision, we also put on padded gloves to play fives in concrete courts which, in a building-programme, had been given priority over permanent classrooms.

I remember few of the boys who were my companions, but I can recall, very clearly, the appearance and habit of several of the masters. There was a splendid man, who taught Classics, called Mr Brace or Mr Bryce. He was an atheist who stood defiantly erect during morning prayers ostentatiously despising their unwarranted appeal. He had two sons, as gaunt and seemingly as under-nourished as their father; and he used to say that no one could call himself a gentleman who had no knowledge of Homer's Greek. There was Todger Evans, excessively Welsh, with a strange domestic smell, of whom I was very fond. There were one or two rank adventurers, flashy men who obviously were taking a job between jobs, to provide a living while they looked for something better. There was a delightful man – called, I think, Grieg – who took some of us to see Glamorgan play Gloucestershire at cricket and told us to watch, with close attention, everything that Gilbert Jessop did. 'Not only while he's batting! Anyone can enjoy Jessop's batting. He's got a wonderful eye, and scores very quickly. But watch him while he's fielding, and then you'll see the real artist that's in him.' And there was a master of a very different sort, a little, pursy, ill-tempered teacher of elementary science whom I met again, several years later, in improbable circumstances that I shall describe with much pleasure in a later chapter.

A contributory factor in my mother's aversion to Cardiff was David Lloyd George and the fact that he, like her neighbours, was Welsh. In the early years of this century there were many shipping companies whose mushroom enrichment owed something to gross neglect of the comfort and safety of their ships and ships' companies; and Lloyd George, as President of the Board of Trade, contributed to the dangers of seafaring by his decision to raise the Plimsoll

Mark, the permitted loading-line, and so, for ill-found and under-manned vessels, aggravated the risks of foundering in heavy weather. It was in 1876 that Samuel Plimsoll, 'the sailors' friend', persuaded Parliament to pass the Merchant Shipping Act which, among other statutory rules for safety, ordained a maximum load-line; and thirty years later, in a new Shipping Act, Lloyd George deepened the line and reduced the freeboard of too many unpainted tramps that lurched out of the Bristol Channel into the sudden storms of the Bay of Biscay. By seafaring men – and even more so, I fancy, by their wives – it was widely assumed that Lloyd George had been bribed by an unprincipled minority of Cardiff shipowners to introduce the Bill, and he and they were hotly denounced for their greed and irresponsibility.

I grew up in a house where there was little sympathy with Liberal measures, and none at all for Liberal leaders. It was, moreover, a temporary habitation. As soon as possible – as soon as my father should be transferred to a trade-route whose home ports were elsewhere than the Bristol Channel – we should go back to Scotland.

❧ Four

My English grandmother and my Swedish grandfather deserve the attention of a short chapter. They lived with us in Cardiff – where my mother had borne a second child, a daughter of much more forceful and resolute a character than mine – and of my grandparents I retain nothing but delightful memories and the most grateful affection. The old sailing-ship master was a lean, brown-faced, hawk-nosed man, infinitely patient with small children. With skilful hands he fashioned for our amusement wooden boats, accurately rigged, that would sail straight courses and stand up to flurries of wind; and tirelessly, in that almost open countryside, he took us for long walks to gather ragged bunches of wild flowers in spring, or pick blackberries in early autumn. He contributed, moreover, a monthly entertainment of which I never tired.

Punctually, every four weeks, a very large but empty barrel of beer was replaced by one ponderously full. A brewer's drayman – a man of huge stature, tall and full-bellied, with a moustache like a great brown waterfall – would drive his heavy horses into a lane behind the house, and on a sloping plank the new barrel was slowly and perilously brought down. It was trundled up the garden path, the plank was used again on rising steps, and now the drayman had to be helped by a short, stoutly built Welsh maid – sad of aspect but possibly contented – who served us faithfully for many years. It was pushed and handled to its final destination in a small, dark closet; dextrously the drayman tapped it, and was rewarded with a frothing pint; and there was great pleasure in watching him drink it off.

'My best respects, sir' – head back, a long, long swallow – 'and thank you kindly.' Tears came into his eyes, froth clung to his drooping moustache, and the empty cask went rolling away as if it weighed no more than a football.

As a boy my grandfather had run away to sea – it used to be a popular escapade – and I have said elsewhere that he probably owed his advancement to the fact that when the barque *Eugénie* was wrecked off the coast of Mauritius he with a rope swam ashore through heavy seas and all on board were saved. A son of one of the owners was aboard, and he and his father were probably grateful. But if my grandfather initially owed some success to favour, and the good fortune of being a strong swimmer, he subsequently earned it by his seamanship. Seventeen years after the wreck of the *Eugénie* he was in command of a new and very handsome clipper, the *Norval* of 1400 tons register, outward bound for Point de Galle. Caught in a hurricane a thousand miles from Mauritius, she was totally dismasted – decks swept, steering-gear and bulwarks carried away – and a minute or two before the last mast fell there were nineteen men out on a yard, trying to make a sail fast. My grandfather brought them down just in time – without a single casualty, without a hurt to any of them – and the masts were cut away. When the weather moderated jury masts were rigged, and slowly the voyage was completed. For that my grandfather received the thanks of underwriters in London, Liverpool, Manchester and Glasgow, and a cheque for £100.

In the small world of my boyhood, sailors were all-important: there was no doubt of that. People who lived ashore were not without merit, but Britain was an island, and without ships and sailors they could not survive: that was self-evident. Sailors belonged to a craft or mystery that set them apart, and of which they were intensely proud. They were, moreover, hearty, genial men, marvellously generous and possessed of extraordinary hands. I remember my grandfather's large, bony hands, cool to the touch and strong as iron: or so they seemed to a child. There were other old men who came to visit him – sailing-ship mates

1 Ship Eurydice: *my maternal grandfather in command*

2 My father, Robert Linklater

and masters – and their hands were the same. They were stiffer and stronger than other people's hands, and their fingers were never quite straight. In their apprentice days they had had to wrestle with royals and topgallant sails in a sudden squall, and wind and heavy canvas had shaped their hands to a heroic mould.

My grandfather lived till I was seven or eight years old, and his death was the first grief I knew. But my grandmother, who lived till the early 1920s, had a far deeper influence on my childhood, and preserved it from what might have been the ill effects of my mother's indifferent health, in those years, and her recurrent fugue into a neurotic incapacity. (There was a doctor in the Midlands whom she used to visit: he was called a nerve specialist in those simple days, and he may have been a proto-analyst.) But my grandmother had a sturdy, placid, English common-sense that was marvellously reassuring.

I did, however, acquire some reactionary or anti-social views from her. She was born, I think, in 1837, and in childhood learnt something of the Hungry Forties: but of the violence of those years rather than their suffering. Her father, Richard Dodd, was a substantial yeoman farmer on the Warwickshire border of Northamptonshire, where he worked several hundred acres of rich land between and about the villages of Braunston and Barby, and lived in considerable comfort in a tall, eighteenth-century house. The violent symptoms of distress, rather than distress itself, were his problem, and among the bedtime stories that my grandmother told, in her sweet and gentle voice, were some lurid tales.

'Often at dead of night,' she would say, 'my father would be called out to deal with rioting and fighting. He could summon, in emergency, a *posse* of special constables, and with them he would have to face an angry mob of men who were breaking into barns, and trying to set fire to haystacks, and all that sort of thing. Well, they were hungry, of course, and we did what we could to help them – their wives and children got soup and potatoes, and clothes too – but still

33

they were angry, though it wasn't our fault they were suffering, it was due to the Government. But it was my father and his constables who had to go out and save everything from being burnt to ashes.'

A one-sided view, of course, but not unnatural in her; and not unnaturally I caught, by infection of sympathy, an early prejudice against violence and the unruly expression of social unrest. There was a photograph of Farmer Dodd wearing a white hat and a look of grave benignity: it was impossible to believe that his actions were dictated by any rule other than justice, by any sentiment less agreeable than compassion. In his tall house there was a great, cool dairy, a vast wool-room for the fleeces of his six hundred sheep, a sweet-smelling apple-loft, a loudly cooing pigeon-loft, a jingling harness-room and saddle-room, a kitchen with an arched fire-place large enough to accommodate a pair of arm-chairs; and behind the house there was a paved courtyard surrounded by barns and stables and cart-sheds and cow-houses. He lived like a patriarch and looked like a patriarch. Farmer Dodd enlisted all my childish sympathy.

More innocently I acquired from my grandmother a decided preference for her old-fashioned pronunciation of such words as yellow, waistcoat, landscape, and bully as in bully-beef; which became yaller, weskit, lanskip, and *bouillé*. The name of Daventry, a town not far from her birthplace, I never heard pronounced as it is spelt until the B.B.C. so called it; she always spoke of it as Daintry. Of asparagus she would say, 'The village women called it sparrow-grass'; and ants she called pismires. She had, too, some scraps of historical gossip – that, I think, is their proper description – which can only have reached her by village tradition, the sort of storytelling which survived in communities long settled on their land, and seldom stirring from it.

The unfortunate Anne Boleyn was Nan Bullen in her memory, and no sympathy was given her. 'A slut if ever there was one,' she would say. 'No need to waste tears on her.' And of the Gunpowder Plot she had a curiously circumscribed and belittling idea. 'There was very little *plot*,' she said. 'There was a man called Catesby, ill-conditioned from the start and always dissatisfied; and he persuaded some others, as cross-grained as himself – one was called Winter, and another Jack Wright – to go to London and blow up the Houses of Parliament. But, as you would expect, it came to nothing.' Now Catesby was a Warwickshireman, and it is conceivable, I suppose, that some local memory may have survived in a community that, from the seventeenth to the nineteenth century, seldom travelled far from home; and local memories are often partial and prejudiced.

Of her far voyaging in the tall clippers that her husband commanded, my grandmother said nothing that I remember except, with firmness in her voice, 'No, I *never* liked the sea.' She owed her acquaintance with him to a most unhappy family quarrel. Farmer Dodd, at the age of twenty-one, married a Miss Russell, younger than himself, and quickly begot upon her eight or nine children, of whom several died. Then Miss Russell died, and Farmer Dodd married her sister, who by then was the Widow Davies. With his second wife my grandmother quarrelled bitterly, and leaving home in a state of great indignation went to employment as 'a lady's companion' with friends or relatives – I cannot remember which – in Liverpool. The friends or relatives had some connexion with the sea or shipping, and in their house she met the Swedish sailor who had Anglified his name as James Young; and it pleases me to record that when she took him into Northamptonshire, to show him off, there was a family reconciliation, welcome to both sides, that endured until the death of Great-grandfather Dodd.

What I must also record is that my grandmother, in her youth, was soundly instructed in the major domestic art of cooking, and when she lived with us in Cardiff she enriched my childhood by her constant satisfaction of my always voracious and increasingly judicious appetite. In several ways my life has been extraordinarily fortunate, and for most of it – not all of it, but for most of it – I have had the solid satisfaction of eating well. But I have analysed memory with all possible care — I have considered with scrupulous differentiation meals that I have eaten in various parts of the world — and I can say with total assurance that I have never eaten better than in the days when my grandmother cooked for us, and seldom so well.

Her pastry was superlative — feathery flakes that swiftly dissolved in the mouth and enclosed, in a richly flavoured gravy, fragments of tender steak and succulent, taut kidney; or encircled, in little tarts, her home-made strawberry, black-currant, or gooseberry jam. I remember with gratitude deep sirloins of beef, dripping red under a cornice of fat, and Welsh mutton redolent of hill pasture; dark, sombre Christmas puddings full of impacted opulence, and plump mince-pies bursting their frail encasement. Lemon-hued suet-puddings, light and friable under sweet-sour sauces, and ponderous beef-steak puddings in their fast-melting cover-lets. Fish? No, I think Northamptonshire gave her little experience with fish, and I have no recollection of fish from my grandmother's kitchen to compare with Dover sole in Aberdeen, Orkney lobsters, or fresh herring, freshly kippered in July, in Shetland. But she kept a larder full of jams and jewel-clear jelly; there were Gloucester cheese and creamy Caerphilly; and the air was scented with her raspberry vinegar. Heather-honey from Orkney, and haunches of yellow-hided bacon — oh, food! Most happily it colours and delights my earliest memories, and for that abundance of pleasure I am chiefly indebted to my dear grandmother.

Five

I n his autobiography, *The Story and the Fable*, Edwin Muir tells something of his childhood on the little island of Wyre, which lies east of the West Mainland of Orkney and south of the dark hills of Rousay. He writes with the clarity of northern light and a grave simplicity; and in the life of the islands, as he knew them, he discovers a vanished order and a quality of innocence that he describes without sentimentality and verifies by scrupulous detail. 'There was no great distinction between the ordinary and the fabulous,' he writes. 'The lives of living men turned into legend.' He was brought up, he says, in the midst of a life 'which had still the mediaeval communal feeling. We had heard and read of something called "competition", but it never came into our experience. Our life was an order.' 'Ordained,' he might have said.

Edwin Muir knew Orkney and its old manner of life better than I did – he grew up there, I was only a summer visitor – but I share his belief that the islands, until the eruption of war in 1914, retained a vestigial happiness that seemed to have survived from an age whose lost beatitudes no historian has noticed. Not, of course, an age of gold; but possibly silver. They had long forgotten the tyrannous misrule of their Stewart earls in the sixteenth century; they had recovered from the poverty that followed, when the fear of witchcraft darkened men's minds; they had acquired, by hard work and sober living, a small and modest prosperity, though narrow circumstances still persuaded many of their young men and women to look for a fuller livelihood in Canada or New Zealand. There were few people who could be called rich, but the majority – though money was scarce – were well fed by the richness of their fields, the natural abundance of their lochs and nearby sea; and a tradition of hospitality was substantiated by the fullness with which they spread their tables. Edwin's belief that they knew nothing of 'competition' is not quite accurate, for at the annual cattle-shows there was eager desire to win a first prize for the best Clydesdale mare or black Angus bull; but competition went little further than that. And in a pervasive innocence there was a widespread feeling that children – by the mere fact of their childhood – were entitled to the kindness of untiring patience. Orkney, to a child, offered not only freedom, but the astonishing pleasure of finding, for its small, impertinent voice, an indulgent hearing.

I was, I think, only seven when my mother first took my sister and me to the islands she so warmly remembered, and for the eight weeks of our holiday it rained every day. That, however, did not impair our enjoyment. Near the house where we lodged there was a little loch, with reedy, bird-quick edges, where we fell in as often as we went down to it. We would, as often, have got wet through though the sun had shone incessantly. That year, and the next, our summer home was a farmhouse whose geniality could not be clouded even by its lugubrious name; which was Moan.

The farmer, Johnny of Moan, was an easy-going bachelor, a constant prey to the demands of travelling tinkers and a few native vagrants, of eccentric habit but mannerly temper, who lived rough but idle and seemingly contented lives in what was, in effect, an uncovenanted, unadministered welfare state. Johnny had two sisters, a laughing, gossiping, energetic woman with a humorous squint in one eye, called Maggie; and a rosy, bouncing girl of fourteen or fifteen who could milk cows with exuberant speed, drive a young horse with dashing confidence, and was always willing to run down to the loch to rescue us from drowning or row us about in a small, roughly made boat that needed paint. With Jessie Ann of Moan I fell deeply in love, and some forty-five years later, when I met her again in New Zealand, we warmly embraced and cried happily to remember the days of an enchanted past. She was then the mistress – the widowed owner – of a large, architecturally fenced, and richly inhabited sheep-farm in the southern parts of the South Island; but still she remembered with undiminished affection – as, indeed, did I – the farmhouse whose front windows looked out to a small hillside azured over with wild lupins, and whose back door had a view of the little loch with foxgloves and yellow irises to colour its shore, with dunlins, black-headed gulls, snipe, redshanks and ring-plover to make a chorus for the breeze.

My knowledge of Orkney – the love of Orkney which dominated and perhaps distorted so much of my life – I owe, not to my Orkney-born father, but to my neurotic, frequently exasperating, and ultimately decisive mother. The distance between Cardiff, in South Wales, and Orkney, beyond the Pentland Firth, is considerable; but when she had made up her mind that her children should learn something of their father's native islands, the length of the journey was no deterrent. The migration, however, was a formidable undertaking that began with an overloaded four-wheeler to the railway station, and a train – trains were better then – which throughout the night and part of the following day bisected most of Britain – Crewe, Carlisle, Carstairs, Perth and Aberdeen – and there left us to face a voyage that was often stormy and never comfortable.

The ships that ran between Aberdeen and Kirkwall were primarily designed for the carriage of sheep and cattle. They stank of wet wool, ordure, vomit and vile cooking. But the crew and the stewards were friendly, and if we were lucky the voyage would last no longer than twelve hours. In rough weather we would have time to add to the accumulated sour odour of sickness, and sometimes we lay becalmed in a sinister fog and looked out at an oily sea closely circumscribed by a wet, white invisibility. The ships that serve that traffic today are fast, clean and well maintained; but sixty years ago the Board of Trade regulations about safety at sea were not always as closely observed as they should have been. I sometimes watched sailors painting the lifeboats without raising them from the chocks in which they stood; and once – when I had grown old enough to be inquisitive – I asked a sailor with whom I was friendly if it was wise to cement a boat to its chocks by repeated coats of paint. 'If we tried to lift it,' he said, 'the keel would come away.'

However unpleasant the voyage might be, there was always the thrill of going on deck to see the steep-sided island of Copinsay and its neighbouring islet the Horse – then the tidal passage called The String, with land on either side – and so into Kirkwall Bay, and there above the little town, in the twilight of a long evening or the harsh dawn of another day, was the brooding splendour of the cathedral that Earl Rognvald built, in the burly days of the twelfth century, to give honour to his sanctified uncle, Earl Magnus. The long journey had reached its end. All that remained was the pleasure of being driven, in darkness undisturbed by the dim oil-lamps of a gig, or in the crescent light of morning, over fourteen miles of familiar roads behind the warm smell – a sweet scent after the vile odours of the ship – of a strongly trotting pony.

I was ten, I think, when I made a discovery which, as it were, consummated the instant attachment to Orkney which our first summer in the farm of Moan had established. I had always known that my mother, soon after her marriage, had spent some months in Orkney with my father; and lately I had acquired some deeply exciting information about the human condition and the curious exercises on which humanity depended for its continuance. I had overcome my original estrangement from arithmetic, and a simple calculation proved beyond doubt that I had been conceived in Orkney. The discovery gave me great pleasure, and I feel pretty sure that my mother's extraordinary affection for the islands owed much to the fact that she had given being to a man-child there. She was a woman of strong emotions, and unashamed of sentiment.

The foothold we had found became a stronghold when, in

1909, my father yielded to my mother's insistence that we must have a house of our own in Orkney, and acquired an acre of land, overlooking a delectable bay, at the north-eastern corner of the Harray Loch. That house, and the boat my father gave me, were a major influence in my life for a very long time; and a year or two after the house was built my mother triumphed again and completed her purpose. My father was posted to employment on a Far Eastern trade route, and thereafter sailed regularly to Hong Kong, Shanghai, Korea and Japan. From those longer voyages he returned to London, the frequency of his homecoming was reduced, and the attraction of Cardiff, as a home port, vanished. My mother was free, at last, to return to Scotland, and promptly she set out to find a house in Aberdeen. The advantages of Aberdeen were obvious. It had good schools for a growing family, a university of its own, and between it and Orkney lay only a few miles of rough sea.

❦ Six

Sixty years ago Aberdeen was a handsomer city than it is today, and much more compact. It was blemished by some small, revolting slums, which have long since disappeared, but the greater part of it had a solid decency, a shining, adamantine precision. It was all granite, and it shone with intrinsic brilliance as soon as the bright northern sun came out to illumine the glittering streets that rain had lately washed. I was fascinated by its jewelled domestic walls.

It lay between two noble rivers, it faced the crashing onset of the North Sea, and its back windows looked out on a hinterland that gradually rose to Lochnagar and the high plateaux of the Cairngorms. It was a splendid city to which we had removed, and with exemplary decision I became an Aberdonian as well as an Orkneyman. The migration was, indeed, an event of major importance in my life, and the Aberdeen–Orkney axis was a trapeze on which I swung contentedly until appetite demanded wider arcs, and experience decorated them with new pleasures.

I remember only one fear on entering my granitic environment, and that was soon dispelled. My mother, with her sentimental belief in the dominating virtues of Scotland, had told me that Scottish schools were far superior to those in other parts of Britain; and that had filled me with unease when I thought of a new desk, a darker blackboard, and sterner masters. But, to my great comfort, I found that her pious belief had little substance in fact. With no apparent trouble I got a place in the Grammar School which had a presumed descent from a cathedral school of the thirteenth century, and there I discovered that in the mathematic classes – in algebra, trigonometry, geometry: subjects that have given me no reward – I was well ahead of my Scottish companions; that I knew more French than they did – I had, from Cardiff, a prize for French: Molière in red calf – and in Latin I had precociously read Ovid while they struggled with Livy. But I lagged far behind in the Scottish exercise known as 'versions'.

In Scotland, it was harshly made known to me, Latin was taught by translating, into the Roman tongue, passages from Burke, Clarendon, or Macaulay: the graces of the language were less regarded than its grammar; it was still thought of, in almost a medieval fashion, as a language that would be useful to us when we went abroad. We ignored the literature of Rome, and were taught, not to appreciate Latin, but to write it: a much more strenuous discipline.

English, moreover – still a new subject in Scotland – was taught as if it had become, in the ever-widening influence of the British Empire, a modern substitute for Latin. It had to be useful, it had to be precise, it had to preserve the decorum of an imperial tongue. We were firmly guided into an exact knowledge of all its tropes and ornaments, such as irony, synecdoche, meiosis, and hendiadys; but tedium was relieved by a sort of birthday book of quotations chosen – with a nice perception and often amusingly – to illustrate these necessary figures of speech. It was part of a general text-book written by William Murison, the senior English master, who instructed us with acid insistence and a thinly voiced, old-maidish attention to detail. As Latin was taught by translating Burke and Clarendon and Macaulay, so the practice of writing English was encouraged by compression into a précis of some passage from Addison, Temple or Ruskin. When, in a later year, I went to Bombay as assistant editor and a leader-writer on *The Times of India*, I was profoundly grateful for that discipline: it had taught me how to gut a Blue Book or White Paper in no time at all.

The Grammar School of Aberdeen was, I think, better than Cardiff's High School in one respect: its masters were men of more solidity, of a more impressive character. The

Rector, Morland Simpson, was a Yorkshireman who had adopted Scotland and made it his own country. He taught the Classical Sixth and persuaded us that the Punic Wars were more interesting than the Wars of the Roses or England's recurrent conflict with France. He suggested – to those who paid attention – that Horace was not merely a topic for examination, and Rome, the imperial city, had known excitements better than those common to a contemporary police-court. Primarily, of course, Julius Caesar was a great general, a superlative though ruthless administrator; but also – a deliberate leer would crease and corrupt the narrow shape of the Rector's scholarly features – he was, in the divorce cases that often agitated Rome's upper classes, by far the most popular co-respondent.

The senior Classics master was a limping, dedicated man called Middleton, whose obvious nickname had been imposed by a facial resemblance to Julius. He was tiresomely addicted – like a butterfly-hunter to the rarer lepidoptera – to the most intractable of Greek verbs, but could easily be persuaded to talk of the arcane differences between the Ionic, Aeolic and Doric dialects – to which one felt no need to pay attention – or to sonorous self-indulgence if we asked him to read, as it should be read, a passage from the *Iliad* that was much too difficult to translate.

Caesar Middleton was an extraordinarily kind man, and being distressed by my backwardness in Greek he compelled me to go, for private tuition, to his own house, where a maiden sister looked after him; and there, after an hour of Euripides, he would sometimes try to engage my interest in the further reaches of scholarship by telling me – and demonstrating its difficulties – of his own continuing study of Sanskrit. Like my father, however, I was alarmed by the threat of too deep an academic involvement, and in pure scholarship there was, at that time, a certain unreality. We were at war with the Kaiser's Germany, and neither skill at confecting Greek verses nor proficiency at mathematics would add anything to one's expectation of life in a regiment of Highland infantry. I am ashamed to remember how little

I appreciated Caesar's kindness and concern for my welfare – how poorly I responded to it – but I can truthfully say that I remember, more vividly than most people I have known, his voice, his limping walk, his imperial profile; and all my memories are charged with affection and respect. That, perhaps, is the restricted immortality which good schoolmasters earn.

War – the Kaiser's war – grossly interfered with the good, useful education that the Grammar School could have given me. I had enlisted in a Territorial battalion of the Gordon Highlanders, and in August 1914 I was called up, and promptly humiliated. My youth was too obvious – I was a rather narrow-shouldered fifteen – and, worse than that, I was short-sighted, I wore spectacles. Now in those proud days spectacled soldiers did not exist – spectacles in the infantry would have been as indecent as drawers under a kilt – so back to school I went, deeply hurt and sadly out of temper.

Nowadays it is difficult to believe that Rupert Brooke, with a voice suddenly inspired, spoke for a whole generation; and young people deride the mere thought of it. Truth, however, is independent of belief, and derision might be silenced if Rupert Brooke's old-fashioned patriotism were given a modern name. If, for example, it were called 'protest'. Nowadays, in schools and universities, there is widespread protest against the forms and conventions of our own society; and protest is regarded as a contemporary phenomenon. But in 1914 protest was louder, more general, and much angrier than it is today. It was, however, all directed against the insufferable pretensions of the German Emperor and the brutal behaviour of his marching armies. Indignation was fierce and popular, and everyone was delighted when Brooke, raising it to a higher plane, identified it with patriotism, and simultaneously made patriotism righteous. In the summer of 1914 I had already anticipated the mood that Brooke made popular a few months later, and for a day or two it had been exhilarating to wear a brand-new kilt and a khaki tunic that was rather too big for me. It was correspondingly depressing to be stripped of one's uniform and returned to the useless study of trigonometry and irregular verbs. More than once I tried to escape my humiliation and re-enlist, and more than once – almost in tears – I was again rejected.

There were, however, compensations. Youth is the time when disappointment lurks round every corner, and from every second window compensation lifts a curtain. The liveliest, most dashing and accomplished young men had all left Aberdeen to train for war at Bedford, and be killed in war at Neuve Chapelle or Loos, and in their absence there was a surplus of unattended young women who, deprived of escorts of the proper age, did not always despise the attention of mere schoolboys. But their condescension contributed little to our experience, for they were as virtuous as we were innocent. The formation of a tennis club was, perhaps, the most conspicuous example, in our social orbit, of the licence and moral laxity which go with war. Our stern Yorkshire Rector respected cricket, tolerated rugby, and would have nothing to do with tennis: he called it 'pat-ball' and preached against it. But a tennis club was formed, the Rector was defied, and admitted his defeat.

On the whole, however, we were a docile lot. We had lost our natural leaders – the tallest and the best of the Classical Sixth were in the Gordon Highlanders – and there was neither spirit nor sparkle in the school. Examinations were still compulsory, but otherwise had lost reality. It is a tribute to our masters – unnoticed at the time, but now it seems extraordinary – that we did, in fact, work hard enough to pass the statutory examinations, and few went out from the Grammar School, to die on the Hindenburg Line, without a decent quota of what would now be called 'O' or 'A' levels.

From time to time – one is thankful to remember – naked comedy intruded on our handsome, hidden city. Before the Government of those days admitted the necessity of conscription to maintain its battered divisions in France, there were convulsive efforts to encourage the flow of volunteers. The incentive might be a straightforward appeal to patriotism, or plump and lubricious invitation from the music-hall stage. It might even masquerade as an appeal to self-interest.

In Aberdeen we were flattered, and richly entertained, by that fat prince of mountebanks, Horatio Bottomley. It was not for him to describe the country's desperate need of men. According to Bottomley there were new divisions, ready to embark, on every quayside from Sydney to the Clyde; and munition-workers, toiling heroically, were turning out more shells than even our enormously reinforced artillery could fire. Victory was not far off, and unless we, the remnant manhood of Britain, made haste to put on khaki, the war would be won without us, and we would live the rest of our lives in bitter shame. That was Bottomley's message, and generously he told an unhappy minority – the few who were forbidden to join the forces – how to save soul and honour though they stayed at home. Let them contribute, he said, every shilling they could lay their hands on to the new War Loan that was being floated. He himself would guarantee that Loan.

Bottomley was superb, his blatant lies were delivered with booming assurance, and by his Aberdeen audience he was vociferously applauded. Never, I think, have I seen a more excited, nor heard a noisier demonstration of that 'willing suspension of disbelief' which, says Coleridge, 'constitutes poetic faith'. Bottomley – short, plump, a richly attired tub of vitality – was an impure genius who had found an enviable freedom, and considerable wealth, by the simple act of delivering himself from any obligation to truth.

A few months later came even richer comedy when Clara Butt arrived to sing 'Land of Hope and Glory' in that voice to which only an organ approximated. Her figure was impressive – in her bosom was the capacity for a resonance that shook the roof, her splendid abdomen rose like a bellows to maintain the pressure in her gigantic lungs – and it was thrilling, almost beyond endurance, to hear her promise of a glorious future that could not fail to materialise if the organ-voice continued to sing and recruits came forward to fill the ranks that Loos had emptied. But then, as if to puncture the soaring balloon of our enthusiasm, there advanced to the front of the stage her accompanist – was he also her husband? – Mr Kennerley Rumford.

In a full-throated, emotional baritone Mr Rumford sang a song which began:

> What will you lack, sonny, what will you lack,
>   When the girls line up the street,
> Shouting their love to the lads come back
>   From the foe they rushed to beat. . . .

Miserable indeed would be the fate of laggards who shunned the call to duty. You may live to cheer the victors – so Mr Rumford implied – but what comfort will that be when you see your mate go by 'with a girl who cuts you dead'?

The song progressed to even more searching questions:

> Where will you look, sonny, where will you look,
>   When your children yet to be
> Clamour to learn of the part you took
>   In the war that set men free. . . .

My own children have never incited me, even in a whisper, to tell them of the part I took in a war that disappointed all expectations; but Mr Rumford was uninhibited by any acquaintance with the facts of life, and sang, with confidence unimpaired:

> How will you fare, sonny, how will you fare
>   On that far-off winter night,
> When you sit by the fire in an old man's chair,
>   And your neighbours talk of the fight. . . .

He wore evening clothes of excellent cut: an abundance of white tie, gleaming white shirt, opulent waistcoat, and a perfectly fitted tail-coat. Never was moral inquisitor better dressed, and superbly incongruous were his final question and the ideal answer he returned:

> Will you shrink away, as it were from a blow,
>   Your old head shamed and bent,
> Or say 'I was not with the first to go,
>   But I went, thank God, I went!'

Then, to double our delight, Mr Rumford went superbly to and fro upon the stage, marching as though a drill-sergeant were beside him with a pacing-stick, and repeated in stentorian tones the last two lines of the song. My young friends and I cheered him with loud and vulgar pleasure; and it may be that we were grateful to him for release from an emotion that, when Dame Clara was singing, had threatened to become embarrassing.

I remember too – but now with shame – another occasion that provoked laughter almost as boisterous, and with far less cause. Its date is firmly fixed in history – it was 23 April 1916 – and the newly appointed Professor to the Chair of English Literature and Language at the University had been persuaded to deliver, to the boys of the Grammar School, an address in celebration of the tercentenary of Shakespeare's death. In later years Professor Jack – Alfred Adolphus Jack, of an academic family well known in Glasgow – became my mentor and my master, and earned the devotion I gave him; but in 1916 he was still a stranger in Aberdeen, and both his appearance and his voice emphasised a strangeness that I and my rascally companions found risible beyond restraint.

He was a highly coloured man with a thick growth of hair, the hue of oranges, a bright pink face, and brilliantly protruding blue eyes. He had, moreover, been trained to an outmoded rhetorical style – reminiscent of Victorian drama – and he was in love with his subject.

To express that love he advanced slowly to the rostrum that had been set up for him – he leaned forward across the lectern – and in a voice whose high-pitched peculiarity was aggravated by his inability to pronounce the letter *r*, he slowly declaimed, with a measured pause between his words, 'Fwee – hundwed – years – ago today – SHAKESPEARE – *died*!'

The effect was extraordinary. We collapsed in laughter with that spontaneous companionship in laughter which is one of youth's most enviable – though often to be deplored – capacities. Even our sternly dominating Rector found it difficult to bring us back to some semblance of humanity – to a false and shallow pretence of good manners – and I recall, with admiration, that Professor Jack – having recovered from a bewilderment equal to our own – delivered his carefully prepared lecture with unperturbed goodwill. I remember the occasion with shame; and that I have said before. But I wish I could laugh as whole-heartedly now.

In those years, however, much happened that provoked grief as extreme as laughter, and not long after Shakespeare's tercentenary I admitted a sentiment that was perfectly valid but undeniably absurd. News came that my father had died in consequence of an engagement, in the South Atlantic, with a U-boat. He had already delivered, to Vladivostok, a cargo of the munitions of war; and now, for our Russian allies, he was delivering another to that distant, improbable port. He commanded an armed merchantman, and its old 4.7 guns kept the U-boat at a distance. But my father, exhausted by exposure and the strain of two years' active service in hostile waters, fell ill and was put ashore in Colombo to die of pneumonia.

In my youth I shared, with enthusiasm, the high romanticism that Rupert Brooke made popular – a romanticism which I now remember as a fact, though distance has eroded all familiarity with it – and my father's death reinforced my determination to get into the army – the army which had shown no desire for my assistance – for the simple, blissfully absurd reason that I had determined to exact payment for him. I forget how many lives I wanted to take – it was more than I achieved – but I was devoted to my father – a little frightened of him, loving him for his generosity, the robustness of his mind and body, the romantic circumstance of a life that made the seven seas his highway – and in the mood of youth a desire for revenge was a natural reaction to the sorrow I suffered.

A few months before his death my father was on leave, and spent some days with us in Aberdeen. We lived in the western part of the city, which then had easy access to open country, and on a Sunday afternoon – after church in the morning – he said to me, 'Let us go for a walk.' I remember my pleasure, and extreme discomfort. I was wearing new shoes and a bowler hat, and neither fitted very well. For some time we walked in silence, and then my father said, 'How old are you now, boy?' – 'Nearly seventeen,' I said. – He hesitated for a while before revealing his embarrassing train of thought, but finally, with manifest reluctance, said, 'That's an age when, if you're normal, you must be taking some interest in girls – and it's not impossible that some girls are taking an interest in you. Well, what I want to say to you is this: make up your mind that you'll never take more from a girl than she's willing to give you.'

I was deeply impressed. I had never supposed I had any talent for seduction, and now a regretted disability was hallowed by my father's wisdom. But then he spoiled the effect – the splendid effect – by muttering to himself – I heard a murmured self-communing – 'And if you take all she's willing to give you, you'll have more on your plate than you know what to do with.'

We walked for a long time. In glossy, tight new shoes my feet were sore, under the pressure of an ill-fitting bowler-hat my forehead was sore; but I was happy to be with my unpredictable father. I deplored his literary tastes – he preferred Marie Corelli to Conrad, but I was ignorant, then, of the high esteem in which Marie Corelli was held by Gladstone and Queen Victoria – and I was prepared to be lenient in judgment when I remembered that he had given me a good rowing-boat when I was ten, that he never came home from sea without lavish gifts, and that I was slightly afraid of him. That walk, on a Sunday afternoon, was, in effect, the last time I saw and spoke with him; and to let him go unavenged would have been stark poltroonery.

But I had to wait for almost another year before I found the opportunity I needed; and now, with long-remembered gratitude, I record the name of Captain James Stewart of the Royal Army Medical Corps. Jimmy Stewart had gone to France early in the war, and served arduously in its initial battles and lamentable defeats. Then he was posted to garrison duty, a quiet interlude at Castlehill Barracks, where he soon attracted the disapproving eye of the local Provost Marshal. He was found guilty of unmilitary behaviour in that he had been seen walking abroad without gloves, and, in Union Street, smoking a pipe while in uniform.

Jimmy Stewart, in consequence, had lost patience with authority and its regulations, and after calling me a bloody fool – 'You don't know what the infantry have to put up with, but I do, and my advice is to stay out of it' – he pleasantly agreed to do what I wanted. 'Come along to the Barracks at eight o'clock on Monday morning, before my masters arrive,' he said, 'and I'll pass you fit for home service. Then, if you're still determined to go to France, you can cook your own claim to a passage. But don't blame me when you discover how damned silly you've been.'

Jimmy Stewart was the friend I needed, and with his help I slipped into a dismounted battalion of the Fife and Forfar Yeomanry, and after a few unhappy weeks – of utter bewilderment in a rude world of which I had no previous knowledge – I accommodated myself to new surroundings, and presently found marvellous enjoyment in a life of purely physical activity for which I discovered unsuspected abilities. Then came the opportunity for which I was waiting.

The Fife and Forfar Yeomanry were sending a small draft to the Black Watch in France. I was Orderly Corporal, and the draft was short of one man, either sick or absent without leave. Hastily I made adjustments to my medical record – I improved the quality of my eyesight and added a year to my age – and with all the authority of an Orderly Corporal appended my name to the detail.

❧ Seven

Musketry and drill were the major elements of a soldier's education in that war. We spent many hours a week on exercises to build, in hand and arm, a firm and steady bed for the rifles that we cleaned and oiled and cosseted with a religious devotion. We fired innumerable practices that culminated in a great trial of skill, the acme of which was firing fifteen aimed shots – gentle pressure on the trigger, bolt-action clean and decisive after each shot, dextrous reloading – within forty-five seconds. There were other, more boisterous tests, in which one had to charge from trench to trench over encumbered ground, bayonet-stab some grossly inviting sandbags, and then, quite breathless, engage an elusive target; but 'the mad minute' of rapid fire – so, romantically, it was called – was what proved or disproved one's ability. I, having suffered the humiliation of wearing spectacles, obeyed the prediction that any self-taught psychologist would have made, and became a very good shot. Twice or more I fired that final trial, using both the standard Short Magazine Lee-Enfield and the more elegant Ross rifle, which the army refused to sanction; and on each occasion I made a marksman's score, and proudly put on my sleeve a brass badge of crossed rifles. But drill, perhaps, was even more important than musketry.

It was a small draft – not more than thirty or forty – with which I crossed to France in grey December weather. Most of us were N.C.O.s and our drill was impeccable. One of the simple manœuvres, on which weeks of time were wasted, was an exercise called 'At the halt on the right (or, with equal lack of purpose, on the left) form platoon.' It had been useful in the Sudanese desert when a marching column, without loss of time, had had to move into a hollow square to repel a charge of furious fuzzy-wuzzies; but in trench warfare it was totally irrelevant. We still practised it, however – practised it assiduously – and in the Fife and Forfar Yeomanry we had given an almost balletic gaiety to changing direction, half-left or half-right, with a beautifully executed kick-step.

We landed in Boulogne, and the commander of our draft, to keep us out of mischief, proceeded to drill us on a bleak parade-ground. Right or left, we formed platoon with exquisite precision, and a staff officer, benignly watching, admired our kick-step. 'Most interesting,' he said. 'I think General Whatnot would like to see that.' So, for another twenty-four hours, our advance into the freezing mud of Passchendaele was deferred until we had performed again our balletic manœuvres for the pleasure and instruction of General Whatnot. The war – in which no one had ever been called on to form a hollow square – was then in its fourth year.

The long and frightful battle had perished, of inanition, before we arrived, but Passchendaele was still a landscape of incommunicable horror, so stark a denial of life that nowadays I sometimes wonder, not why, but how we endured such insufferable discomfort. Our forward positions were holes in the mud. Shell-holes deepened and extended to give cover to a section of ten or a dozen men. They were water-logged craters in which we were never dry. Our feet and our arses were sodden-wet, and we seldom got enough to eat because ration parties on their way up the line were usually shot at, and lost not only several men but much of what they carried. A loaf among ten was not an uncommon division of bread, and often it happened that all our good bully-beef had gone, and nothing was left but that abominable contribution of our American allies who were already establishing their hegemony of wealth by selling us thousands of tons of 'pork and beans' in tins that contained a sliver of pig-fat on a muddy concentrate of nature's most repulsive vegetable.

For a few weeks I sat in cold mud – water above my boots – or endured the fatigue of maintaining access to the forward shell-holes by carrying up duckboards and rations. Daily, or nightly, the duckboards were shelled and destroyed, and the ration-carriers, because rations seldom arrived intact, were abused for their incompetence. I was, I think, more frightened of my fellow-soldiers in the Black Watch than of the Germans, of whom, for a month or more, I never saw a single specimen. But if, from an occupied shell-hole, one raised an inquisitive head above the deliquescent parapet, the hard rattle of a machine-gun revealed their presence a hundred yards away.

We lived in a discomfort that was both gross and grotesque. How we endured it I do not know, but why we endured it is perfectly clear. No reasonable person – even in 1917 – could conceive the possibility of Britain's defeat, and to maintain Britain in the field was therefore a natural and realistic function. Sooner or later the Germans would have to admit their initial mistake and the ultimate defeat it had invited.

To the Germans we gave a grudging respect – they were good soldiers – but we had no such feeling for our French allies. In our opinion – the stubborn opinion of private soldiers – they were dirty and totally unreliable. They were grasping, mean and deplorably casual in their disposal of the dead. There was a widely held belief that the French Government insisted on being paid ground-rent for the trenches we occupied; and that, we said angrily, is typical of French greed and Westminster's ineptitude. We had, indeed, little respect for our own Government. Like all infantry, kilted or trousered – enislanded within the emotional coastline of their own regiments – we were as narrow-minded as religious sectaries of the seventeenth century. Virtue resided in us – that was incontestable, for we were its living proof – and we admitted its companionable existence in the Brigade of Guards and the Australians; but we saw little sign of it elsewhere.

We left Passchendaele as a sudden thaw began – iron frost

had succeeded some weeks of rain, and now rain was returning – and as we departed from that furious desolation we
presented – if observers had been there to see it – a bizarre
appearance. A highly intelligent company commander had
told us to take off our kilts and wear them as capes about our
shoulders. So we said good-bye to Passchendaele with a
flutter of grey shirt-tails dancing behind our bums; and
forty-eight hours later, when the thaw had created a vast
quagmire in which fierce streams ran wild, the battalion that
relieved us lost a score of men, not from shell-fire, but by
drowning.

From the Salient about Ypres we removed to the Somme.
In that war there was little variety – the mud of the Somme
was a paler, more sympathetic mud than the dark and evil
mud of the Salient – and in comparison with Hitler's war –
which ranged the world from Normandy to Rangoon – it
was flatly monotonous. It enjoyed, however, a natural richness – and suffered equivalent sorrow – from a condition of
its management that was absent from the unnecessary but
more intelligently conducted conflict which began in 1939.

In the war of 1914 guns went into action behind pulling
horses, and there was an extraordinary realism – the realism
of tragic drama – in the spectacle of eighteen-pounders
moving forward – horses straining, drivers urgent, gunners
on the limbers – that the gun-tractors of the Second War
never reproduced. All transport depended on horses, and the
smell of horse-lines was a rich, invigorating and delightful
smell that did much to dispel the hot stench of battle, the
sour and dispiriting odours – in areas which the French had
occupied – of death. But in conflict with that warm, good
smell there was the occasional sight of gun-teams running
into shell-fire, and the scream of wounded horses was more
painful by far, and seemed more pitiable, than the quiet and
decent complaint of a dying man. Mules – those intractable, anarchic creatures – could take dreadful wounds and
gallop on; horses showed a tragic susceptibility to pain.

Somewhere I have read that the weight of fodder for
our horses, carried from England to France, was greater

56

than the tonnage of ammunition so transported. I do not know if that is true, but certainly there was fodder enough to create, in the horse-lines that stood a little way behind the battle areas, a rich and comforting air that seemed to naturalise – almost to domesticate – the destruction of war. It was the ancient smell of the farmyard, where the midden rises as the year increases, and dung is the promise of health for another season.

It was a revolutionary change that eliminated horses from war, and war was impoverished – before nuclear fission and fusion declared its bankruptcy – by the disappearance from it of the arm which had given it its most spectacular fame. In 1939 the Polish Lancers charged, unavailingly, the inhuman efficiency, the steel-sided brutality, of German tanks; and cavalry joined the dodo and the brontosaurus in extinction. I am glad to remember the gallop of horses in action, and the farmyard comfort of their picketed lines.

In *The Man on My Back* I wrote, as I have said, of my brief, undistinguished introduction to war with a mannerly reticence which was too mannered to be true. In a novel called *The Impregnable Women*, however – a novel inspired by angry revulsion against the prospect of war's renewal – I imagined a situation, created by Britannic tergiversation, in which we found ourselves, in alliance with Germany, fighting against France and her allies on ground familiar to me – though I had faced the other way – in 1918. There, protected by the good mask of fiction, I was less restrained, and now, when I open the novel, I can find some passages in which I recognise a very respectable approximation to the truth.

As, for example:

Rain was falling on the flooded battlefields. It came on whirling gusts of wind and beat upon shelving trenches and a myriad dark lagoons and the hooded soldiers. When the frost went the earth had collapsed as though its ribs were melting. Soil and sandbags, losing their rocky form and crisp security, had resolved into shapeless puddings and a soft floor of mud. In tiny holes and crannies the water gathered, and overflowed their crumbling edges, and ran in turbid little rills to fill a larger pool or join a deeper rivulet. The grey lids of ice dissolved, that had covered shell-hole and hoof-mark, and opened filthy tarns and innumerable small brown puddles. The soggy earth was pocked with water-holes that filled from subterranean springs and over-filled with rain. Duck-boards that had been frozen to the hard earth now lost their hold, and slewed in the yielding mud, or moved uneasily in rising water, while the straight sides of deep-dug trenches, flattened from the clouds, bulged weakly out and their diminished strength let parapets collapse and scarps fall suddenly.

The dead were yielding to corruption now. They no longer lay gaunt and rigid, but huddled softly in the mud. When the frost melted in their flesh the starkness of their last agony had relaxed and the icy preservation of their youth dissolved. They no longer showed how young they had been, nor any likeness to any of the ages of man, but buried their faces or let the rain fill their mouths like any puddle of the fields. Sometimes when a shell struck a flooded crater a dead arm would rise, like that of a drowning man, or a body heave slowly into sight. But that was all that suggested they had once known strength and movement. They were no more to be recognised as the sons of men, but as parcels of the troubled earth.

The battalion, moving out, marches for several miles to a hutted camp, but finds little comfort there, for the camp is still within range of the German guns.

The ground between the huts was a water-logged marsh, spanned and intersected by duckboards. Eliot, who had been writing to Lysistrata when the iron walls of the camp were shaken by the first explosion, stumbled along one of these slippery tracks with the half-finished letter in his hand. He had found a few sullen and disdainful men still in their beds, and ordered them out. He turned a corner and dimly saw a figure struggling in the mud and trying to haul something out of a slimy pool. He thrust the letter into his pocket and went quickly to help.

His boots slithered and sank in the soft earth. He stooped, and putting a hand into the filthy pool felt a cold and naked limb. He re-pressed his nausea. 'Who is it?' he demanded.

The young soldier beside him, hauling away and sobbing with the effort he was making said tearfully, 'It isn't a who, sir. It's rations.'

'What do you mean?'

'I was carrying it from the Quartermaster's store, sir, and when that whizz-bang came over I got a bit of a fright, and let it fall. It's beef, the 'ind-leg of a cow, and if I leave it 'ere I'll be crimed for losing it.'

Eliot, in a violent revulsion of feeling, began to laugh, but the boy was still serious. He had a clean crime-sheet, and his only military ambition was to keep it clean. The loss of a quarter of beef would be a serious offence, and he was most reluctant to abandon it. Eliot spoke sharply to him, but the boy answered triumphantly, 'I've got it now, sir!' and dragged the lump of filthy meat on to the duckboard.

I feel, now, no sensation of self-pity, nor am I playing for sympathy. But the novel spoke more truthfully than my well-mannered autobiography, and that boy – though I did not speak as he did – was, undeniably, me.

✾ Eight

On the Somme we moved into deep trenches, too broad for safety, that had been carelessly dug, and left in a very untidy state, by the South African Scottish. Immediately we set to work to improve them, and for some time – we were in the near neighbourhood of Gouzeaucourt – we were troubled only by light and occasional shell-fire. I have to admit, however, that my memory of the next few months is imperfect. After I was hit, at the end of April, I had, for a few days, no memory at all. My sight was like a troubled television-screen, and of the recent past I recalled only the dismembered pieces of a jigsaw puzzle that I could not put together again. For some weeks I lived in a state of subdued bewilderment – subdued and alleviated by the kindness and charm of the American nurses who staffed a large hospital in Boulogne – and only gradually did I recover memory in an orderly sequence. And that sequence, though vividly reminiscent of particular scenes – vivid even now – never recaptured, in full, a day-to-day, time-tabled memory.

I have, for example, a clearly focused picture of French seventy-fives coming into action with marvellous dash and celerity, and almost I can hear the rhythmic din that followed: *la rafale des soixante-quinzes* was a stirring and distinctive tune. They were close beside us, but the guns pointed away to our right flank – and where were we? Somewhere between Ypres and Kemmel Hill, I think, when, on our side of Kemmel, the massive strength of a German assault was repelled with punctual assurance. I cannot pinpoint our position nor recall the date of that spirited performance, but the seventy-fives, I remember, were up and away – as soon as they had completed their task – with the drilled precision of their arrival.

I cannot – in consequence of my disrupted memory – put a date to a very odd coincidence that let me meet again, in ludicrous circumstances, the only master in my Cardiff school whom I had really disliked, and disliked with good reason. By the early months of 1918, of course, we were scraping the barrel to find manpower, and Mr W. – that bitterly sneering, bitingly sarcastic teacher of elementary physics – was manifestly not what would have been recognised as 'officer material' in 1915. But he – small and fat and no longer young – came to us on the Somme, and in some interval from the front line I saw him, at embarrassingly close quarters, in a village estaminet.

I was sitting, drinking red wine, with half a dozen sergeants. I had been summoned to that exalted company because I spoke adequate French, and they, who had no skill in languages, admitted to their table a private who happened to be capable of asking, without effort, for another bottle of the same, or – for the quartermaster – that redoubtable mixture, a *café à quatre cognacs*. I was well pleased to be with the sergeants, who were brave and hardy men from the slums of Dundee or such dismal mining villages as Cowdenbeath and Lochgelly, and to impress them I had been talking with some fluency to the amiable woman whose absent husband owned the estaminet. But then, from another room, came a sound of argument – an out-of-temper dispute – and from that door, running, came our plump hostess closely pursued by a small, thick-set and elderly second lieutenant. His excitement was obvious, for the front of his kilt was held aloft by an intemperate erection that raised it as if on the ridge-pole of a marquee; and our hostess fled before him with squeals of terror that may or may not have been genuine. But our rugged sergeants were truly incensed by such behaviour in an officer of their regiment. They, having drunk a bottle apiece, and an occasional *café à quatre cognacs*, held their liquor with propriety; they had no sympathy for an officer of inferior capacity.

61

Now a few days later – or a few weeks later, for my memory is still at fault – we were suffering, in those trenches near the Somme, a bombardment by heavy trench-mortars – called, in the lingo of those days, Jack Johnsons – that created darkly erupting, earth-shaking explosions. I happened to be going from one bay to another, in our now tightly walled trench, when I saw, crouching by the fire-step, a small, stoutly built man, and going towards him – for I thought he had been hit – I recognised the randy Mr W. It was, perhaps, the first time he had encountered Jack Johnsons, for he was paralysed by fear; as I would be nowadays. I remember, with shame, that some old scar, scratched by his sarcasm on the tenderness of my youth, must have revived in my subconscious mind a forgotten pain, for I patted him on the shoulder and shouted, 'Don't worry, Mr W. We've all forgiven you.' I never saw him again, and he may not have survived to torment other schoolboys with his rodent humour.

Our leisurely occupation of the Somme trenches came to an end when Ludendorff, with sixty-two divisions, suddenly launched his massive attack against the Fifth Army in the early morning of 21 March. By marvellous good fortune I escaped the first onslaught, for a couple of weeks earlier I had become distressingly lousy. Daily we scorched the folds of our kilts with a lighted candle; at long intervals we were marched to some steamily disgusting bath-house, where we were given shirts that had been washed in evil-smelling water; but the lice survived both flame and chemicals. They survived and multiplied, and when their numbers became excessive their host developed trench-fever. My temperature soared to a tropical height, and I was removed to a hospital in Rouen. I soon recovered, and on the twenty-first I was in Calais, awaiting orders. Before going up the line again I was caught in a savage and very frightening little battle between some angry Canadians and the red-capped Military Police. What had upset the Canadians I do not know, but about thirty or forty of them spread out, lay down, and began seriously to shoot it out with a large number of the Police who had mysteriously appeared in camp, presumably to deal with threatened violence. I, returning from the canteen, was caught between the two sides, and hurriedly dropped into a shelter-trench. One of the Canadians kindly shouted to me, 'Keep your head down and stay out of this. It's got nothing to do with you.' Fervently I agreed with him, and presently the battle, becoming fluid, moved away. 'They're trigger-happy' was all the explanation I ever heard of that curious affair, but I was given no time to be inquisitive. On the following day, with a few other temporary invalids, I was on my way back to the battalion.

It was already sadly depleted – I rejoined, I think, on the twenty-third – but we attempted a small counter-attack, and moving to a flank took, without much trouble, the required position. A battalion of young soldiers, newly arrived from home and pitiably under-trained, was then supposed to go through and forward from us to gain a dominating ridge about two hundred yards away. Their leading company advanced, and ran into fire. It was not unduly heavy – no heavier than we had faced – but they were raw, they had never been shot over – they had worn uniform for only eight or ten weeks – and they broke and fled. It was a singularly unpleasant and dispiriting sight; and we, the mere remnant of a battalion, also had to withdraw and continue our retreat.

That night we were almost surrounded. There was a dramatic order – whispered, not shouted – to move by sections, at speed, but with all possible quietness. There was a brooding, tense excitement till the sky lightened and we saw, in the dimness of dawn, what seemed to be open, unoccupied and unperturbed fields in front of us. But immediately ahead lay a sunken road, and the first men who tried to cross it were shot down by fire from two German machine-guns whose gunners lay on the road perhaps a hundred yards away, to the right.

There was, momentarily, some consternation. But suddenly a dark-haired, thin-faced little corporal – his name I forget, but I shall call him Alexander – jumped down to the road with a Lewis gun, and opened counter-fire with his lighter weapon. His nerve was steadier than the Germans', he found a better aim, and killed or disabled both their gun-crews. Hastily, behind him, we crossed that treacherous road, and for an hour or two continued, unimpeded, our retreat.

I have written elsewhere of an action near Bray-sur-Somme, and a day of astonishing comedy when a warrant officer of the South Irish Horse mustered several fragments of broken battalions, and, for as long as daylight lasted, fought with Aldershot precision a battle of fire-and-movement against German troops supported by small, motor-drawn guns: his motive being to win experience, for his remnant of Irish troopers, for their culminating war against England. To his inflamed but still orderly mind the World War in which we were engaged was merely a dress rehearsal for Ireland's supreme and necessary battle.

It was, I think, on the night before the Irish rehearsal that some forty or fifty of us slept, not uncomfortably, in a grave-yard. Between the simpler graves – bare hummocks of turf, unmarked by stony pavement or marble edges – there was shelter from a prowling wind, and apart from hunger we had little cause for complaint. But the retreat, of course, had separated us from the normal sources of bread and bacon, of bully-beef and plum-and-apple jam, and the deserted vil-lages through which we passed had been stripped clean. I remember the pleasure with which I found a big jar of green plum jam, and the greed with which I ate it. But there was no plum jam in the graveyard, and when gun-fire woke us we were very hungry indeed.

It was, then, with envious and eager interest that we saw a man – a soldier unknown to us – coming from the ruins of the village with a long French loaf in one hand. There was, perhaps, a baker's shop in the village – in what had been a village – and most of my neighbours were already afoot when, in quick succession, two shells burst in the graveyard and filled the air with fragments of angels' wings and shattered crosses. The man who had found bread was killed, and the long loaf he had carried lay beside him. Half was soaked in blood, but the other half looked clean enough, and

3 Elizabeth, my mother, with her first grandchild

4 *Eric Linklater in 1921, from a drawing by W. J. Johnston*

beside me a meagrely built man – who may have been used to hunger – pulled out his jack-knife, ran forward and knelt to cut the loaf in two. A third shell landed, not far away, and the thin man either leapt or was blown back towards us. He got up, shouting his pain and anger, for he had lost the bread and one side of his face was hidden in a waterfall of blood.

A sergeant gave him first-aid, tied a field dressing over the wound, and tried to comfort him. 'You're all right,' he said. 'You've lost a bloody ear, that's all.' But then the thin man lost self-control as well as his ear. 'My ear, my bloody ear!' he shouted. 'Where's my bloody ear?' And like a retriever seeking a dead grouse in the heather he went down on hands and knees to search for it. We were, by then, in a hurry to leave, and presently we found a ration dump. It was after we had eaten, perhaps, and were in a better mood, that the Irish bandmaster took us in hand and drilled us, through a long day, to fight with Aldershot precision for his own private purpose.

The long retreat was, indeed, no 'bug-out' – as the Americans called their ill-disciplined flight from the Yalu River in 1950 – but a rearguard action, often stiffly contested, which, though our own front dissolved and we went back for many miles, inflicted on Ludendorff's sixty-two divisions more losses than he could afford. We of the 4th/5th Black Watch had been reduced, by the end of the month, to between thirty and forty men and one wounded second lieutenant, whom we had mounted on a grey farm-horse. The regimental history says there were thirty-one survivors, but I think we were a few more than that.

Then, after resting for one day, we went back to the Salient as part of a composite battalion formed from remnants of the 60th Rifles, Sussex and Cheshires and South Wales Borderers; in which, with details gathered from here and there, there may have been almost a full company of the Black Watch. In the line again – a line with no cohesion at all, for the Germans were pressing on to the Channel ports and our defences had been opened by the sudden defection of our Portuguese allies – my first job was as company runner. We had, at first, no Signallers to lay their lines between one isolated position and another, and urgent messages had to be carried by hand. My companion runner – for obvious reasons the message was duplicated – was a sturdy, cocky little boy from Dundee, and the first time we went out – taking cover where we could find it – he startled me by stopping, a hundred yards short of our precarious destination, and saying, 'Now, look here. I've been on this lark before, and you'll do what I tell you. It makes a very good impression if you come in looking cool and casual, and the way to do that is to smoke a cigarette – dangling from your lips – and the last fifty yards you just *stroll*. It makes a very good impression!'

Was it for the sake of bravado? I think not. I believe he was moved by an obscure respect for good manners. The people awaiting our message would be reassured if they saw us, not sweatily running towards them, but leisuredly strolling. So, choosing cover in which to strike a match, my cocky little friend and I used to light our cigarettes and, with rifles slung, amiably talking, we deliberately loitered for the last fifty or a hundred yards – then briskly pulled to attention, gravely saluted and loudly exclaimed, 'From Captain McOstrich, "B" Company, Sir!' For a couple of days it was exhilarating and nervously amusing, but then the Signallers arrived, and I found different employment. I remembered the crossed rifles I had once worn on my sleeve, and when an orderly sergeant called for marksmen I became a sniper.

Some months ago a young woman, a journalist, came to talk to me, with the object of finding material to fill her weekly gossip-column. She hoped, I suppose, that I would utter some startlingly unpopular opinion that would give her sub-editor a briskly attractive headline, and in the course of conversation she asked, 'Is it true that in the First War you were a sniper?' – 'It is,' I said. – 'But how could you reconcile that with even elementary morality? Wasn't a sniper merely a murderer? Like an assassin waiting for President Kennedy?'

It was, however, nothing like that. For the three weeks in

which I lived an almost solitary life, remote from my platoon, my sniping, against an ever-probing and often advancing enemy, was much more like a succession of deliberately invited duels in which I had, admittedly, the initial advantage of choosing my position, and the inherent advantage of being a better shot – as things turned out – than most of the Prussian Guards who opposed us. We thought, or pretended, they were Prussian Guards, but they may, in fact, have been Saxons or Bavarians. Whoever they were, they were very active, and more numerous than we. But, whether Prussians or Bavarians, their musketry was not of the highest class.

It is a mistake to suppose that war did not become intellectually intolerable – as well as economically destructive and socially atrocious – until after the dropping of that epoch-changing bomb on Hiroshima. It became insufferable, though sufferance continued, when Napoleon summoned his *levée en masse*, and more evidently when the Germans first used poison-gas. The massive slaughter that modern weapons made possible in 1916 and 1917 destroyed all lingering notions that war retained a romantic appeal which could balance its brutality and multitudinous grief. By 1917 war had become an outrage against common sense, as well as against humanity; but we, by then, were more deeply committed to it than the German aggressors. They would have been willing to temper their aggression, and make terms that allowed them to retain some reward for their effort; but we had decided to fight, *à outrance*, against aggression, and I, a microscopic projection of general insanity, shared to the full its insensate purpose, and with a robust perversion enjoyed the brief remnant of my active service. My few weeks as a sniper gave to my life an excitement, an intensity, which I have never known since. I have, on the whole, had a happy life, and I have known much pleasure. But in my nineteenth year I lived at a high pitch of purpose, a continuous physical and mental alertness, that has never again suffused my brain and body – and which, in later years, my body and brain could not have sustained.

Abominable though war may be — abominable though total war is bound to be — it is impossible to deny that the fortunate individual who emerges from a period of incessant danger — from activities, apparently for the public good, that deliberately invited danger — may survive with a memory that has nothing to do with social right or wrong, with moral purpose or lack of purpose, but simply with the knowledge that, for a little while, he lived in an air as remote and perilous — and perhaps as rewarding — as the frozen winds that beat about the awful top of Everest.

Continuous excitement, however, did not exclude cautious consideration and a judicious estimate of the precarious situation in which we lived. Out of a battalion that had numbered about seven hundred some thirty or forty of us had survived the March retreat, and now the Germans, intent on reaching the Channel ports, appeared to have an equal chance of repeating their success. I was friendly, at that time, with a solidly built, serious young man from Ayrshire. Before joining the army he had been a Boy Scout of high rank: a Rover Scout, perhaps. It was with great surprise that I learnt, one day, that he had been collecting maps. I, in the dishevelled state of the country through which we had been passing, had amassed a large number of good French maps, and I discovered — or we discovered — that we had an identical purpose.

It was about the time when General Haig declared we were now fighting with our backs to the wall, and though we all thought highly of Haig — he was an honest man, starkly opposed to the chicanery of Lloyd George — we laughed loudly at his message, for behind us there was nothing so substantial as a wall. My friend the Rover Scout and I had both come to the conclusion that if Ludendorff broke through to the coast — as he had broken through to the market-gardens of Amiens — there would be no sense in waiting to be taken prisoner, but a prudent and practical policy would be to break away while there was time — quietly at nightfall — and begin to make our way south to the Spanish frontier, and so to Gibraltar. When we put our maps together we were able to decide on a likely route, circuitous but avoiding military centres, that would take us as far as Bordeaux; and we agreed to go together. We had both been storing emergency rations, such as stale bread and the hard, rather bitter slabs of chocolate which could still be bought here and there.

Before that dread emergency came about, however, I enjoyed – and lived to remember with sorrow – another meeting with the heroic Corporal Alexander who had let us cross a sunken road that German machine-gunners dominated. We were in the very extremity of a broken trench-system that had first been dug two or three years before – it protruded, absurdly, into no-man's-land – and the previous afternoon we had beaten off a German attack that came in from the wrong direction – towards the parados, or back door, not the parapet, or front door – and at night I and two companions – one of them the cocky little boy from Dundee, with whom for two days I had been a company runner – took shelter in a dug-out which was a condemned slum of a dug-out, and bore the ill-written notice: 'Keep out. Dangerous.'

It was, indeed, obviously falling down upon its dilapidated foundations, but it offered some protection against the rain which had begun to fall; and soon after we had decided to sleep there we were pleasantly surprised by a visit from Corporal Alexander. We were doubly pleased when he produced a water-bottle full of rum, and in a very short time we were all loudly singing. To begin with, I fancy, we sang that splendid revolutionary song – it threatened a revolution that no one wanted, and relieved our feelings – which began: 'Have you seen the officer? I know where he is – down in the deep dug-out I seen him' – and after slandering, with equal lack of justification, both sergeant-major and sergeant, went on, with an impressive aggrandisement of disillusion and melancholy, to the defunctive concluding verse:

Have you seen the private? I know where he is,
I know where he is, I know where he is –

Hangin' on the old barbed wire I seen him,
Hangin' on the old barbed wire!

That, sung by four hearty, rum-impelled, well-blended voices, was most enjoyable; and then came unexpected reward, for Corporal Alexander – that most gallant man, to whom we all owed our liberty, if not our lives – sang in his sweet and melodious voice a couple of songs we had never heard before, but made haste to learn.

One was a rollicking lyric which, in several versions, has now become well known; but I think it proper – in the sense that duty is proper – to set down the first verse and the chorus, as, for the first time, I heard them in that dissolving dug-out:

As I was a-passing Reilly's farm,
    Who should I see but Reilly's daughter?
Suddenly the thought came to my mind,
    Like to screw old Reilly's daughter,

Yiddy-i-yay, yiddy-i-yay,
    Yiddy-i-yay to the one-eyed Reilly,
Rub-a-dub-dub, balls and all,
    Jig-a-jig-a-jig, très bon.

Then came a song – little known in comparison with 'Reilly's Farm' – which I found immediately appealing because it went to a bumping, simple waltz tune:

Oh, my true-love's a soldier and gone to the war
    And the badge that he wore was a bright shining
    star,
He's as bold as a lion and as black as a coon,
    And he fell deep in love with me old mush-a-room.

We sang them over and over again, until we had learnt the words, and then – the rum finished – Corporal Alexander went out to the trench that intruded into a vacancy broader and more fearful than no-man's-land. A minute or two later we heard a single shot, and hurrying out, in alarm, we found him whimpering under the rain, on a floor of wet black mud, and thickly bleeding from one ankle. He had tied a sandbag round his leg, and shot himself above the right foot. He had endured and suffered as much as he could, and after singing to us, in that dissolving dug-out, he must have said, 'This is the end, for I can take no more. There's no more rum, and my spirit is spent.' In my little experience of active war, Corporal Alexander was the only man I knew who escaped from the trenches by so dire a method; and except for a reckless, medal-seeking company commander and some dourly resistant sergeants, I met no one braver. But because he was gay and lively his spirit, perhaps, had the sort of strength that tunes a fiddle-string – and when the string is screwed too taut it snaps.

Many weeks later I heard that a court of enquiry had decided to ignore the statutory demand for a court-martial. For a self-inflicted wound the punishment was severe but the court balanced the account by cancelling the award of the D.C.M. previously recommended to Corporal Alexander for his gallant and successful action against German machine-gunners in the long retreat. That decision may seem un-generous; but against the standards of military discipline, as then enforced, it was compassionate.

A few days, or perhaps a week after that, there was a hurly-burly of fairly close fighting in and about the miser-ably ruined village of Voormezeele. We were driven out, we recaptured it, and again were thrown back. I was hit, and my friend the Rover Scout was beside me at the time. The German advance had been checked, if not halted, and with some regret we had cancelled our romantic notion of an independent retreat to the Spanish frontier. He, country born and bred – accustomed to the formal violence of country pursuits – told me, when in Scotland we met again, that my response to a German bullet was exactly that of a rabbit when it is shot in the head. A rabbit, in that moment of death, leaps high in the air; and so – there was something like admiration in his voice – so, he said, did I.

I thought I had lost touch with that young soldier – who

used to be me, and no longer is – but a little while ago he almost came to life again, in this room where I am writing, as a neglected legacy from my mother. She, who lived into her ninety-first year and was unashamedly sentimental, had kept every letter I wrote to her, and after her death my sister sent them to me in a large, untidy bundle. I put it away, embarrassed by the thought of reading what had been written by someone who was a virtual stranger; and not until I was driven by a recurrent need to empty overcrowded drawers and cupboards did I intrude, before destroying them, on those forgotten pages.

The earliest, scribbled in pencil on rough scraps of paper, had been written in France and told very little because censorship prevented soldiers from relating anything but trivialities. But a day or two after I had been wounded and carried into hospital in Boulogne I showed – in a way that now elicits my admiration – the good manners which I then possessed. I wrote to my mother with the single purpose of calming her fears. 'There is no need to worry,' I said. 'I was hit on the head, but though the bullet pierced my helmet it travelled idly round my skull and went off again.' The pencilling had grown faint with time, but my purpose remained clear, and my manners were impeccable. A week or two later – after a painful operation – I was light-hearted and even facetious about my misfortune. My mother had told me how despondent she felt when a War Office telegram announced that I had been 'S' wounded – she did not know whether 'S' stood for slight or severe – and I replied, again with a dim pencil, 'I am sorry that the news you got fluttered your dovecote, but I have to admit that I too felt slightly fluttered when I fell.'

Within the next few weeks I endured a second and more serious operation, in a dismal hospital in the far east of London, and before it and after it I lay within easy distance of death; but in none of my letters was there any trace of self-pity. It is true, of course, that in that war no one who found himself, still alive, in a hospital bed, felt much impulse to self-pity – for all but the most painful of beds were preferable to the trenches – but my distant relation, the young man who was my predecessor, deserves a little credit for reticence. He was facetious, in a manner I found embarrassing as I tore up his letters, but he never asked for sympathy. Sometimes he demanded money and cigarettes, but never pity.

✣ Nine

In *The Man on My Back* I wrote as much as was advisable of
what I suffered and enjoyed during my several months in
hospital, and there is nothing I want to add to that account
except some belated words in praise of the nurses – both
professional and *amatrice* – who showed such fortitude,
patience and tenderness in their care of men revoltingly
wounded, pale in the shadow of death, and indecently
boisterous in the new strength of convalescence. There were
exceptions, of course – among *amatrices* the unaccustomed
exercise of command sometimes released an intemperate
despotism – and in no profession or institution are there
doors so close-fitting as to exclude stupidity. But in a general
memory nurses are wrapt in that rosy sentimental devotion
that Victorian poets thought proper for all womanhood; and,
unlike all women, they in their specific function deserved it.

Before my twice-channelled head had properly healed I
was returned to duty – in consequence of female displeasure
and some small misdemeanour in a narrowly disciplined
hospital – and I owe my first acquaintance with Edinburgh
to the fact that the Reserve Battalion of the Black Watch was
stationed in the Castle. Residence there was unpleasantly
cold and comfortless, but extremely interesting.

In the back end of 1918 Edinburgh could show something of the squalor of the eighteenth century, and more,
perhaps, of the lightly sleeping tendency to violence so
characteristic of its earlier history. The Old Town could still
erupt in turbulence, and the people who lived in its stinking
courts wore clothes that were ragged and drab and evil-
smelling. At the end of the week, on a Friday or Saturday

night, there was always trouble in the High Street and the Lawnmarket, and it may have been a Saturday soon after the Armistice that I remember for the roaring, drunken commotion that filled both Lawnmarket and High Street. Some extreme emotion had emptied the tall houses, and out of them had trooped a rout of wild humanity. There were girls and women – shouting girls and blowsy women – with men disabled by war – more patched and tattered than the poorest of men today – and among them soldiers exultant in their new freedom, kilted or flamboyant in the tightly cut, wing-spread breeches of the Field Gunners and the slouch-hats of six-foot high Australians, all at one in a raucous camaraderie of drunken excitement. Had revolution been in the air, it was such a mob as revolution might have spouted in obscene and purposeless display; but the deafening noise it made was, on the whole, a friendly noise. Here and there hilarity was dominant. Here and there a sentimental chorus drowned the scream and counter-scream of domestic argument.

Across the lower end of the Esplanade that leads to the Castle there was a line of Military Police to contain the turbulence beyond it; and as one approached one had to shove and shoulder a way through a packed and contrarious throng, some of it singing, some punching, some passing half-bottles of whisky. I saw a young soldier, no older than myself – yellow-haired and pink of cheek – struggling to escape from an old, grey, horribly grimacing woman who was trying to bribe him with a packet of Gold Flake – twenty for a shilling – to go home with her; and both of us, with a convulsive effort, reached safety beyond the Red Caps. Then I heard a cry for help, and turning round I saw a man, to whom I was infinitely indebted, wrestling with a couple of young women, bold and exigent creatures, flaunting their attractions and manifestly drunk.

With great reluctance I went back into the hurly-burly, and there was a prolonged and heated dispute before we persuaded the young women to be reasonable. They were sisters, the one married, the other a spinster; and my friend

Private Macmillan had, I think, made love to both of them; but perhaps more ardently to her who was married, and so wakened in her sister a fury of jealousy. Some such domestic complication was the reason of their quarrel, but my main concern was to rescue an old friend, and as we reached the Esplanade, through the line of Military Police, I remembered a previous occasion when, with a great shout, he had demanded my attention and saved my life.

I was, at that time, at the far end of a trench where I was bowling grenades at a pack of Germans who had come too close for comfort. I was intent upon my task – I was no hero, I was an artist committed to his design – and I had failed to notice the retreat, or tactical withdrawal, recommended to the rest of my platoon; and Macmillan, very bravely, had come back to shout 'Hey, you! We're getting out!'

Then, in a great hurry, I had joined them; and now, from the way in which he spoke of the jealous unmarried sister from whom I had rescued him, it appeared that I had saved him from a situation almost as dangerous as that from which he had extricated me.

Warmly we congratulated each other, but as we approached the Castle we heard another sound of tumult. In the Guard Room – so a sentry told us – there were twelve Australians, all over six feet tall and exceedingly drunk. In that war, or so it seemed, every Australian had the stature of a giant and a strong addiction, when inflamed by drink, to violence that occasionally won a Victoria Cross. We listened, gravely critical, to their language, and presently climbed the steep road to the chill austerity of our barrack-room. There, though there was little comfort, we found peace. Some of our fellow-privates may have drunk as much as the Australians, but exhibitionism was discouraged in our grim fortress. Discipline ruled the Castle, and it was a pleasure to come home out of chaos.

That, for me, was the beginning of a long and rewarding acquaintance with Scotland's capital; but in 1918 it was only an interlude without consequence. Soon after the Armistice we were despatched to Fort George, on the Moray Firth – a fort of great architectural interest, more like collegiate than military buildings, but even colder and more uncomfortable than the Castle – and from there, early in 1919, I returned to civil life and became a medical student at the University of Aberdeen.

It was soon apparent that I had chosen the wrong profession, but I was reluctant to admit my mistake. Students who had been in the armed services were rewarded with a small grant of money, but the grant was dependent on a punctual ability to pass statutory examinations, and when, after a term or two, I failed to do so, I was deprived for ever of public assistance. But I remained at the University for rather more than five years. Like Bernard Shaw I can say, 'I never threw myself into the battle of life. I threw my mother into it.'

She, though always kind and deeply affectionate, had been, in my youth, neurotic, and fanciful or resolute by a change of temper that was quite unpredictable. But after my father's death she accepted, with a fortitude that was calmly assured, responsibility for her family, and never rebuked me for my dismal lack of academic success. In later life I have often felt that my warm regard for my father – I mourned him for many years – might not have survived if he had survived. He had a stern, old-fashioned notion of duty, and – had he lived – would certainly have thought it was my duty to pass examinations. How long would I have retained my love for him if he – explosively, as was his habit – had shown his disapproval of me? We would have quarrelled bitterly – that I now realise – but my mother was marvellously long-suffering, and between us there was no dispute except on those occasions when I said, 'I'll have to find something else to do. I know So-and-so and So-and-so – I can get a job, I think, as a tea-planter in Assam or Ceylon – .' Then she would say – she who was so reverent of a traditional Scottish education – 'You will not leave Aberdeen until you have taken your degree.'

I am infinitely grateful to her, and equally grateful to Aberdeen; for I enjoyed my extended years at its University.

In the early 1920s its University was still a small, provincial entity, hardly troubled by the new ideas that were blowing about the world – mildly indifferent to external conflict – but comfortable in its own society where everyone knew everyone else. Our numbers never, I think, exceeded 1500, and in the academic village that lay between King's College and Marischal our professors were members of an aristocracy that could afford to be eccentric because it was so well rooted.

The Principal and Vice-Chancellor, Sir George Adam Smith, had in his earlier years survived a charge of heresy brought against him by the Free Church of Scotland, but more lately had acquired a large and solid fame founded on his magisterial *Historical Geography of the Holy Land*: General Allenby had used it as a text-book for the campaign that culminated in his sweeping advance through the plain of Esdraelon to Damascus and Aleppo. It was in the pulpit of King's College Chapel, however, that George Adam Smith made manifest his real authority. When he preached from a text in Isaiah he left the curious impression that he was contemporary with the prophet. By the passage of time, of course, his mind had been sophisticated, but they shared a common domain of knowledge.

Then there were the Harrowers. He, Professor of Greek, was unassailable in his dignity, and his dignity was reinforced by the fact that Blanche, his wife, was the daughter of a previous principal. Typical of our academic village was the fact that everyone knew Mrs Harrower's Christian name, though she was by no means an easily approachable woman. She could, indeed, be frostily remote. But sometimes she condescended to amuse, and would tell her story of an early, long-defunct dramatic society's production of a Restoration comedy. 'It was very well produced, and *very* funny. Two tall and beautiful young men, superbly dressed in oyster-coloured satin, came out, and one said to the other, "Eh, Rrochester, Ah've lost ma purrrse!" That glorious Buchan accent supervening on Restoration costume made an unforgettable occasion!' Self-conscious laughter used to follow her anecdote, for the Buchan accent was common enough in the corridors of King's and Marischal.

But the Harrowers were genuinely interested in amateur dramatics and the theatre, and for three years he, with professional help, produced Greek plays in his own translation. Well-designed costumes encouraged some charmingly pretty girls to enlist in his choruses, and in my vain pursuit of one or more of them I suffered deeply. I joined the cast of an ambitious *Oedipus Tyrannus*, and wore a violet-bordered grey himation. There were two girls who, in peplos and chiton, acquired a beauty, an unfamiliar attraction, that far exceeded their everyday appearance; and I may have let my mind stray beyond the Sophoclean dialogue. I played the dullish part of Creon, and advancing to the foremost edge of a promontory intruding into the audience exclaimed, 'Hear me, men of Thebes' – and in that loneliness, a loneliness beyond help, forgot the message I had to deliver. I stood there, mute and miserable, for three, five, seven seconds before memory returned. Later in the evening I was congratulated on the unexpected emotion I had given to my speech. In my agony my forehead was bedewed with sweat that glistened very prettily. Or so I was told.

Older than the Harrowers was Charlie Niven, Professor of Natural Philosophy. Anarchy invaded his lecture-room, but anarchy never became coarse or vulgar because Charlie Niven, aged and gentle, enjoyed a general affection though little respect. It was known that he, a good many years before, had demonstrated the possibility of wireless telegraphy, and for the amusement of himself and his friends had constructed, in places a mile or more distant, the necessary apparatus for transmission and reception. But when an upstart Italian, called Marconi, discovered a wider and more practical use for airborne communication Charlie Niven was indignant at the commercial exploitation of an interesting little scientific experiment.

The most distinguished of our professors was the least loved. He was Frederick Soddy, soon to become a Nobel Prizeman. A man of cold and haughty demeanour – with,

79

perhaps, a native aversion to Scotland or contempt of teaching – he did not conceal his dislike of ex-servicemen, and on one occasion was so offensive that his whole class rose and walked out. It was an orderly protest, and he was civilly informed that his absent students would return as soon as he was ready to apologise. What he said to offend them I do not know, for I was not there. I found his lectures uninteresting, and seldom attended them. I failed in my first attempt to pass his degree examination, but was unexpectedly successful the second time. A laboratory assistant, who was no fonder of his professor than I was, kindly gave me a proof copy of the paper he had set, and by sitting up all night I acquired a fund of knowledge sufficient to deal with it. Almost immediately after that, Soddy left us and was given his Nobel Prize. Later in life he showed a dislike of money – or of the theories that governed the flow and expenditure of money – as extreme as his distaste for ex-servicemen.

On the medical side our teachers, with hardly an exception, were the most genial of men. There was the ebullient Sir Henry Gray, whose operating-theatre sometimes resembled a miniature battlefield, but whose surgical skill often contradicted a fatal diagnosis. The Professor of Surgery was John Marnoch, and he was so neat and dextrous that his operations were almost bloodless. Once, being honoured by an invitation to dine with him, I watched him carve a couple of pheasants – holding a slim carving-knife as if it were a scalpel – and saw with admiration his dissection of six – or was it eight? – transparent slices from each side of a breast.

The Professor of Midwifery, McKerron, was the last of an old school. His academic qualifications were slight, but he was marvellously shrewd, his practical experience vast, and his knowledge of human nature profound. An exchange of thought between him and Gray was happily remembered. 'She'll need a Caesarean,' said McKerron, and Gray palpated the woman's swollen belly with his thick fingers that looked so clumsy and were so clever. 'No trouble about that,' said Gray. 'The child's lying like this: the head here, a haunch there, and that's a shoulder. To all intents I can see it!' – 'Just so, just so,' said McKerron. 'Tell me, Gray, is it a boy or a girl?'

He who, at that time, had most certainly established Aberdeen as a clinical school was the Professor of Medicine, Sir Ashley Macintosh. With unfailing firmness and pure benevolence he devoted himself equally to the welfare of his patients and his students. Before I decided to abandon the study of medicine – anticipating, by a moment only, the Dean of the Faculty's decision – Ashley asked me where I had spent some long week-end of holiday. 'In the farthest, uppermost parts of Donside,' I said, 'with Dr Howie.' – 'Oh, you could learn a lot from him! He's one of our very few G.P.s whose diagnoses I accept without any question. He has such advantages, you see. He has been there all his life, and now he's looking after the grandchildren of his first patients. Nowadays so few doctors stay anywhere long enough to profit by experience.'

It was a kindly village in which we lived, and it escaped the narrower bounds of provincialism by the experience of war – which, however deplorable, is far from narrow – that the majority of our students had brought to it. Twenty years after I graduated – in Arts, not in Medicine – I resumed, not altogether happily, a connexion with the University when I was elected its Rector: the temper of the students who came back, in 1945 and 1946, was altogether different from the temper of those who returned from the First War. Not all, but the majority of ex-service students in 1945 and 1946 were inclined to complain of a wasteful and unnecessary interruption of the studies that, if unimpeded, would already have advanced them to positions of modest affluence in which they might have found themselves contentedly married and enjoying an almost sufficient income. In 1919 and 1920, however, those who had escaped inclusion in the fearful casualty-lists of the First War were suffused with a sense of gratitude – to God or good luck – that inclined them to a sheer and simple enjoyment of life which often became exuberant. We were thankful for dawn and sunset, and always ready to enjoy the louder pleasures of Saturday night.

The pleasure of survival was not unclouded, however. The after-effects of war were still with us. Long after their apparent recovery from gun-shot wounds there were those who died of gas-gangrene, and I remember a black day in 1922 when I said, 'Now I have shot my load of grief, and I'll give death no more attention.' My father had died in 1916, the nearest and dearest of my schoolboy-friends had been killed in our last, victorious advance in 1918, two of my closest companions had slowly died of poisoned chest-wounds, and others to whom I had been warmly though briefly attached had been killed before my eyes – and I resolved to banish pity and turn away from sorrow. My resolution was permeable, of course, but I raised a palisade of pretended indifference and for some years tried to live within it.

It is remarkable, I think, that we who had suffered the pains of military service felt no dislike of uniform. By 1921 we had re-formed the old University Company of the 4th Gordon Highlanders, and when in camp with them I was taught new notions of decorum. I became a sergeant, and in the Sergeants' Mess, especially at the week-end when wives and sweethearts were admitted, there was such politeness as daunted me. The sergeants' ladies drank port-and-lemon, the sergeants – many decorated for gallantry – drank, as if the taste were strange and new to them, half-pints of beer or small whiskies-and-water; and never a vulgar word was uttered. The Officers' Mess to which I was later promoted enjoyed a much larger freedom.

Then Sir George Adam Smith, whose two elder sons had been killed in the war, got authority to establish an Officers' Training Corps, and I transferred to it, as Company Sergeant-Major in the Infantry contingent, under the redoubtable command of John Boyd Orr. He, who had won a D.S.O. in the Navy and an M.C. in the Army – and was also a Fellow of the Royal Society – was very properly awarded the Nobel Peace Prize in 1949, and later became

Lord Boyd Orr. In 1923 he was a commanding officer whom anyone with a modicum of intelligence – and all who could judge and appreciate character – were delighted to serve. He had the quietness, the ease of manner, that so often go with innate authority, and from under brows ferociously umbrageous he looked at you through eyes of disconcerting intelligence. No one has ever had a better commanding officer, and as his Company Sergeant-Major I learnt a lesson of abiding value.

He gave me almost complete freedom, and I enjoyed that near-absolute command which a C.S.M. can exercise. As a drill-sergeant I was good – my prize drill-squad won a silver cup for the staccato brilliance of its rifle-slapping, the synchronised percussion of their blackly gleaming boots – but, having both exercised and enjoyed the experience of command, I exhausted my taste for it. It was not what I wanted from life. I had no real wish to dominate, no appetite for power. I had been seduced by the mere novelty of what I was offered, and having inspected my new domain – having appreciated all it contained – I asked no more of it. Only once, in later years, have I felt any desire for power, or pleasure in possession of it.

I shall, however, describe a very happy occasion when I used a temporary and accidental power to good purpose. With the O.T.C.s of several other universities we had gone to Scarborough for our summer camp. We were to be inspected by General Sir George Milne, then Chief of the Imperial General Staff, whom we in Aberdeen called Georgie Milne; for he too – by origin at least – was an Aberdonian. In charge of the camp there was a small staff of uncommonly stupid regulars, and it was they who made arrangements for the parade. By their maladroit direction we marched off, and took up our positions, an hour and a half before the expected arrival of Georgie Milne. It was a day of blistering heat – a brazen sun shone naked in a windless sky – and within half an hour there were casualties among the amateur soldiers who surrounded the broad inspection-area.

Standing motionless 'at ease', a dozen or more toppled over, white-faced, across their falling rifles; and I – who by then had been advanced to the rank of second lieutenant – looked anxiously behind me at the hundred and twenty for whom I was responsible. My senior officers, in the manner of senior officers, were walking leisurely to and fro, remote from the tension of those they had left behind them, and in my docile, unmoving ranks there were two or three warn-ingly pale faces.

I turned about – the sun was incandescent – and pulled my company to attention. 'Ground arms!' I ordered. They laid their rifles down, and resumed an upright pose. 'Now pay attention,' I said, 'and do exactly what I do.'

I turned to my front, and spreading my legs far apart I leaned forward, head to ground, until my Glengarry cap touched the turf and my view was restricted to the dark penumbra of my kilt. Then, rising, I said to my company, 'Do that, and tell me what you see.'

They were well-brought-up young men, and unwilling to utter a reply which, in those days, was considered rude and improper. 'Tell me what you see!' I shouted, and two or three answered as I wished. 'Louder, much louder,' I commanded, and 'Say it again!' I exclaimed. Then, in a great chorus only slightly muted by their kilts, came the response I wanted, and 'Balls!' they cried. 'Balls to Georgie Milne!'

It was unfair to him, but an appropriate comment on the mishandling of our great parade; and when I had restored them to their state of stand-easy, every face was healthily flushed and there was no danger that any of my company would faint before the C.I.G.S. arrived and came slowly and majestically to pace before us.

But an amateur militarism occupied only part of my time – I had much time to spare, because I attended so few classes – and I edited a weekly paper called *Alma Mater*, I became President of the Union, and I helped to inaugurate the first Gala Week – for the endowment of voluntary hospitals – which instituted a practice that still continues. I

was, too, one of a clique – a coterie or faction – that engin-
eered the election of a woman as President of the Students'
Representative Council. She was the first woman to hold
that office, and in the Scottish universities no woman has
held it since. Our campaign roused bitter feeling and angry
opposition, but Mary Esslemont, our candidate, was a young
woman of uncommon ability, of great strength of character,
and her elevation was only a prelude to the lifetime of
service she has since given to Aberdeen.

I began to work on my own account – in pursuit of my
own interests – when I removed from Marischal to King's
College, and read English Literature under Alfred Adolphus
Jack, the newly arrived Professor whom, on 23 April 1916,
we had received so rudely in the great hall of the Grammar
School. I soon became one of his most grateful students. He
had a devotion to literature which, though limited, was
absolute within its limitations; and his devotion was in-
fectious. His conspicuous and rather absurd appearance –
the orange mane of hair, bright pink face, proptosed blue
eyes – seemed to emphasise the intensity of his interest in the
meaning of words and the relevance of prosody, and from
the problems of Shakespearean speech to the academic
absolutism of Matthew Arnold we explored, under his
direction, the more obvious glories of English writing. But
beyond Matthew Arnold we did not trespass. English
literature came to an end with him – and a very good
terminus, I now think. For the current practice of assessing,
in terms of literature, contemporary or recent writing is
condemned to failure or fatuity because content, carried by
sociological tides above expression, will usually give content
an apparent superiority over expression; but in the measured
judgment of history expression will count for more.

For a year we were much occupied with textual criticism,
and Jack was as interested and ingenious in his elucidation
of Shakespearean verbiage as Simenon in the explication of
crime in Le Havre. But he was also a passionate Words-
worthian, and one of his amiable weaknesses was a habit of
interrupting a well-organised lecture to quote a suddenly

remembered phrase or passage that let Wordsworth's panoptic vision illumine the matter in hand. He was absurdly fond of the little Lucy poems, and again and again he would pause, for pure enjoyment, to recite one or other of them. But the effect of his recitation was often spoiled by his inability to pronounce the letter *r*, and more than once I heard him intone, with deep feeling:

> No motion has she now, no force,
> She neither hears nor sees,
> Wolled wound in earth's diurnal course
> With wocks, and stones, and *twees*!

His recitation excited laughter, but laughter never embarrassed him. I doubt if he heard it. And modern opinion moved him no more. He had in his department a young lecturer, Claud Colleer Abbott, a scholar and a good minor poet, who was aware of strange happenings in the south, and rebel movements in literature. Abbott, a highly intelligent and rather nervous incomer to Aberdeen, used to entertain one to beer and plum-cake, and read the brand-new verses of T. S. Eliot. At first hearing they meant little to me, and less than that to Adolphus Jack. Some years after Eliot published *The Sacred Wood*, Jack asked me, 'Have you read it?' – 'Yes,' I replied. – 'It's very nicely *said*, of course, but is there anything in it that you or I didn't know already?' – 'Very little,' I discreetly answered. – 'Nothing at all!' he declared.

It was a village, closely circumscribed, in which we lived; and within its circumscription there lingered a curious or stubborn innocence. I am convinced, for example, that in the early 1920s homosexuality was virtually unknown in Aberdeen. 'Bugger' and 'buggery' existed in any normal vocabulary, but not in fact. One knew about Oscar Wilde, of course, but he had no more relevance, and little more reality, than a character in the Arabian Nights. I remember, indeed, a curious occurrence which suggests that even the police had little knowledge of practices long established among our richer neighbours in South Britain.

86

In all the Scottish universities we were much inclined to party-giving and mutual entertainment. Conferences and athletic meetings regularly occurred, and whenever we went to Glasgow, or Glasgow came to Aberdeen, there was a celebration that left both universities limp for several days. It was, I think, after the visit of some Glasgow athletic teams, and a dinner which lasted till three o'clock in the morning, that I found myself walking home – between the granite faces of Union Street, the more genial graces of Albyn Place – with a friend, a little older than myself in years and much older in experience, who had been teaching for some years in Vienna. Or was it Paris? Was it Dresden? He had a fund of engaging talk, he was a friendly, entertaining man who made no attempt to assert his superior knowledge of the world with reminiscence of the Left Bank or sweet-smelling cafés in the Ringstrasse; and with a sufficiency of strong drink in him he could be as noisily cheerful as his juniors. As we walked westward through broad streets we were, indeed, singing; and from moon-shadow on the other side there came a policeman.

He was a very young policeman, good-looking, with the fresh complexion of country birth and nurture. He told us, very politely, that we were making too much noise – in stiff shirts, high starched collars, and dinner-jackets we were protected against rude remonstrance – and my reply was equally civil. But my friend went further. He left civility far behind, and became wantonly affectionate.

'Oh, constable,' he exclaimed, 'what a lovely voice you have! Tell me where you come from – but no, let me guess. Deeside or Donside? It's Donside, I'm sure. Somewhere beyond Alford, I think. It's my favourite part of the country! And those pretty buttons you wear – those pretty silver buttons! Do you think I could unfasten them? Just a few –'

The constable, deeply alarmed but too astonished for speech, pushed him away, and I, even more frightened, took my besotted friend roughly by the arm and dragged him off. He staggered slightly – he had, perhaps, drunk more than I had – and having initiated movement I increased our speed, and with a shouted good-night to the policeman we left him – mouth agape, consternation plain upon his moon-lit face – manifestly bewildered by an emotional impact of a sort hitherto quite unknown to him. My unhappy friend babbled of the beauty of young, country-bred policemen, complained bitterly of my unkindness, and began to cry.

Of the girls who came up to the university the majority were chaste, and chastity was still regarded as a normal temper and condition for the young. There were, however, a few sub-marital pairs whose association, by long continuance, had acquired respectability. So far as I remember it seldom lasted after one or the other had been liberated by graduation, and its social effect was narrowing: they were inclined to withdraw from the crowd and live in each other's pockets. I knew a girl – Dido was bright, competent, good-looking – who lived to regret the pocketing, the confinement, of two wasted years, and I remember with admiration the tough acceptance with which she announced its conclusion. 'You know,' she said, 'that I've broken with Willy?' – 'I'm sorry.' – 'Oh, it was inevitable. I was good enough for him in Aberdeen, but Willy is Dr Willy now, and off to London. He'll need something better there, and all I regret is that if it hadn't been for me he'd never have passed his finals. It was I who made him work, and if he hadn't worked I'd still have him.'

A sturdy realism was characteristic of Aberdeen, and still is. I spoke, not long ago, to the Supervisor of Women Students and asked her, 'What are your problems this year?' – 'I'm finding it difficult', she said, 'to keep the girls from bringing their carry-cots into the Union.' *Autre temps autres mœurs*, but carry-cots in the Union suggest an acceptance of the facts of life that may be compared with Dido's resignation when Dr Willy went off to London.

The bright light of realism colours one of my last student memories. In an undistinguished year I had taken my degree and decorated it with several prizes. That gratified my mother, but when I met Professor McKerron in Broad Street he beckoned to me from the other pavement, and as I crossed the road he shouted, 'Clever fellow, aren't you, Linklater? You stay here till there's no competition left – all the good ones have gone – so you walk in and scoop the pool. Well, well, good luck to you. There's a lot of art in good timing.'

🜊 Ten

W HEN, taller by a degree, I left Aberdeen and went to Bombay, my promised salary as an assistant editor of *The Times of India* was 600 rupees a month or £540 a year. In Aberdeen, in 1925, that was regarded as an extravagant reward, but in Bombay I found it less than sufficient to keep me in reasonable comfort, and from my letters – that my mother so carefully preserved – I have discovered that within a very short time after my arrival I was impatiently engaged in a demand for higher pay that my employers – I thought them a parsimonious, cheese-paring crew – stubbornly resisted. But I soon made myself useful, for I was a fluent writer and enjoyed, when I was young, a self-confidence that let me compose two-thirds of a column on any subject suggested to me. Within a few months, moreover, my status was enhanced by sickness and death, which in India have always been the shortest way to preferment for those who survive.

The editorial staff was sadly reduced, our proprietors were unwilling to reinforce it, and we who remained could no longer be refused the larger salaries for which we asked. I found agreeable quarters in a flat that I shared with two other men, and in the habit of that age we employed seven or eight servants who attended, punctually and efficiently, to our domestic needs. It was notorious that bachelor establishments enjoyed better service than most married couples; for wives, having little else to do, showed an interest in the detail of household accounts that their servants found exasperating.

In a surprisingly short time I was able to live very comfortably indeed, but I had to work hard for my comfort, and in eighteen months I was out of Bombay only twice: on each occasion for a short week-end. With unsparing clarity my letters show that a constitutional aversion from regular toil was greatly aggravated by a daily burden that a prolonged hot weather made still heavier, and the belief with which I had left home – that I might find a vocation in India – did not survive a twelvemonth there. But the strange, the odd and improbable thing is that even today I read news of India with an emotion that no other part of the world – outside our own bewildered islands – can elicit.

I think it true that no one who has lived and worked in India can remember it without a troubled affection and a sense – perhaps absurd – of responsibility mishandled. Indians, of all sorts and conditions, had a feminine ability to rouse affection, and a perverse, extraordinary gift for stirring exasperation: a gift that was fortified by a hostile climate. I had no sense of guilt about our presence in India when I went to Bombay; I thought then, as I do now, that if a balance-sheet could be struck – beginning in the years when Robert Clive defeated the vast ambition of Dupleix, and robbed the French of the eastern empire he had promised them – the account would show that we had given India more than we took from her. But having seen something of the way in which we behaved in India – of the insensate pretence to superiority that white people, of no intrinsic distinction, exhibited in their dealings with Indians – I left Bombay with a feeling of uneasiness, related to guilt, of which I had been innocent when I landed there.

Snobbery, of course, was indigenous long before we arrived. The caste system is snobbery enforced and justified by religious or pseudo-religious sanctions, and no English snobbery – even in the embroidered years that the great Whig families dominated – has ever been so extreme. We, perhaps, were the only people who ignored the caste system and spoke with some civility to the wretched creatures – sweepers and the like – who lived beyond or beneath its cruel divisions; but we spoke too little and too seldom.

91

In India one had to acquire a protective insensibility, a sort of social blindness, that let one ignore the fearful evidence of a poverty beyond help. I do not believe that any power, however wise and charitable and well intended, could have done much to heal the misery of Bombay and Calcutta, and in the villages there could be little progress in husbandry while superfluous cattle lived safe but hungry within the pale of Hinduism.

Hinduism prevented good husbandry and degraded human beings, but Hinduism had to be accepted, and to those who accepted it as their heritage and their faith we might have shown more courtesy than we did. Had I been born a Hindu I would have found utterly insufferable — totally beyond endurance — the vulgar indifference to my faith, the blatant incomprehension of my gods and my philosophy, that were exhibited by all but one in a thousand of English and Scotch businessmen and their wives. Only in the Indian army, whose junior officers were outstandingly intelligent, did I find any real sympathy with, and knowledge of, the natives of the country in which we had elected to work. But even the soldiers had no intention of living permanently in India; it was only their professional residence.

The Portuguese had chosen to live there, to settle down and marry into the coastal districts they had bought or conquered; and the ruins of the great black forts they built remained as memorials to their vain endeavour. We may have been right to avoid entanglements, but we did wrong in creating a new and alien caste which had no relation, other than a proclaimed superiority, to the original castes that, few in number to begin with, had a solid base in history and originally, perhaps, a social justification.

In India *sunt lacrimae rerum*; but it would be wrong to suppose that I spent most of my time there — or even much of it — in tears or complaint or demanding another 200 rupees a month. My long-forgotten letters reveal a pattern of life that was broad enough to include friendships, pleasure, even gaiety, and — to my surprise — a good deal of physical activity. I used to swim before breakfast, or row with the Bombay Rowing Club, and occasionally there was a primitive sort of golf on the maidan. At the week-end we often went to the long beach at Juhu, some miles north of the city, which now, I believe, is a popular and crowded resort, but then was a vacancy of sand and sea in front of a few dozen native huts and their planting of coco-palms that waved above a green and swampy land.

There was one considerable house there, built by our generous friend Naoroji. He, a Parsi whose relation with *The Times of India* was mysterious, had a deeply rooted, most engaging habit of hospitality, and through him – whose close connexion with some native states was also unexplained – we met occasional nobilities or notabilities from Gujerat and Rajputana, and suffered dinners of inordinate length where the curry was always cold and the champagne warm. Naoroji, who distrusted architects, had designed his own house, and not until its walls had risen some eight or ten feet did he remember the necessity for a staircase. Unperturbed, he built an outside stair, which was serviceable enough, and a little while later, to repair another omission, added an independent block which consisted of bathrooms and water-closets. He was a very good friend, and though we sponged off him our sponging was excused by the fact that it gave him pleasure to introduce his young British friends to grandees from Udaipur.

I made friends also with people who sailed on the great inland sea of Bombay's harbour: not with rich men whose immaculate boats lay at anchor below the terrace of the Yacht Club, but with those who liked to hire, for half a day, the long, clumsy, bunder-boats that carried a huge lateen sail and a crew of six or seven to hoist it; or with men who sailed cheaply, and often excitingly – their boats leaked, their gear was rotten – to far, unknown corners of the harbour, and back under a starry sky to the corona of lights that illumined Bombay with a promise that daylight did not fulfil.

I had no social ambition, nor ever burdened myself with the convention of leaving cards where cards should be left, and dining in consequence at tables where the silver might be heavy and conversation would match it. I was once told, indeed, that a lady – seated at such a table – had remarked, with disapproval in her voice: 'Mr Linklater? The most Bolshevik young man I've ever met. Now I understand why the tone of the leaders in *The Times* has been so deplorable of late.'

That, I think, must have been in 1926, at the time of the General Strike in England. We professed unpopular opinions, and supported the strikers. As well as writing leaders I had to fill a gossip column, and sometimes decorated it with light verse. As, for example:

RED BRITAIN

(On Saturday there was a football match at Plymouth between Strikers and Police. The Strikers won.)

Said Mr Winston Churchill to Sir William Joynson Hicks,
'I dreamt of Cook* again last night – confound his knavish tricks!
The country's going to the dogs!' – and faintly answered Jix,
'I always dream of *blood*, I'm so *afeard* of Bolsheviks.'

The wicked Baron Banbury went to the House of Lords,
And said he wanted action, and called aloud for swords.
Said wicked Baron Banbury, 'We'll confiscate their hoards
Of Moscow-tainted bullion, and we'll beat them to the boards!'

And Trotsky on his samovar grinned evilly and said,
'I see the Dawn arising, and the Dawn looks very Red.
The bourgeois blood of Bloomsbury will bubble when it's shed,

* The miners' leader.

94

And there'll be an Upper Abattoir where all the
Lords have bled.'

And Revolution started — when we heard the
whistle blow —
And sternly fought the Royalists, and sternly
fought the Foe,
And Trotsky claimed the victory from Joynson
Hicks and Co.,
For the Strikers beat the Coppers in their match
on Plymouth Hoe.

That, I suppose, might have explained the annoyance of
the lady at the dinner-table; but fortunately it didn't deprive
me of other friends, and from careless memory my letters
have resurrected two girls of uncommon attractiveness, the
one called Lucille, the other Jo, whose natural influence was
such that an Inspector of the Indian Police — I think that was
his rank — could sometimes be persuaded to provide us
with a launch, belonging to the Police, from which we
practised an elementary sort of water-skiing. A simple
plank was hauled astern, on which one stood erect if one
could, and the launch made no great speed; but to the
pleasure of the game was added a factitious excitement when
we discovered sharks in the harbour. 'The shark-infested
waters of Bombay' we called that dancing blue expanse, but
the sharks, in fact, were small and harmless.

Lucille was a Canadian, a teacher of gymnastics, lucent
and lovely; Jo, a red-head, had been born into the power and
splendour of the *raj* — her father had commanded his
regiment of Sikhs or Punjabi Mussulmans — but now made
a thin and precarious living as somebody's secretary. Both
these girls thought highly of horses, and exaggerated the
pleasure of riding them.

Circuses in Bombay were a recurrent entertainment, and
to us, in my second cold weather, came an American company of clowns and acrobats that included a rousing rodeo to
which ambitious young soldiers contributed a nightly drama
when they challenged the rough-coated, snorting broncos

and were invariably defeated by them. One evening, after dinner, I took Jo and Lucille to the circus. They were enraptured by the rodeo, and demanded an introduction to the tall, lean man, of commanding presence, who ruled it. He was called Red Cannon, and I, as a journalist who could give him half a column of free publicity, was *persona grata* with him and others in the company. I took the girls down, and within a few minutes they and Red Cannon had established an easy friendship. Both wanted to ride his bucking broncos, but very sensibly thought it prudent to get the feel of an American saddle before riding in public. 'Sure,' said Red Cannon. 'Nothing easier. Can you bring 'em along? Around seven tomorrow morning? O.K., I'll be seeing you.'

That was my early morning exercise for most of the next week, but I saw no more of Jo and Lucille until the Saturday night which concluded the circus's visit to Bombay. Then again I gave them dinner, and Lucille, radiant as ever, was talkative and excited; but Jo was silent, her face tight and determined. Red Cannon had told Lucille, 'No, you're not good enough, but Jo – well, maybe she's got a chance. No more than a chance, but she may get a break.' So at dinner – small and slender under a copper crown of hair – Jo was quiet and withdrawn, still resolute but very frightened.

It was a gala occasion, for the Governor and other dignitaries were there, and with growing impatience we waited for the issue of the nightly challenge. Then Jo left us, and after three or four soldiers and other adventurers had been thrown from indignant horses she appeared with Red Cannon – she had found opportunity to exchange her frock for jodhpurs – and he, in a voice that carved the expectant air, declared that for the first time a lady had accepted his challenge, and would try to ride one of his unconquered, unconquerable broncos. 'So give her a big hand now, or maybe you won't get another chance!'

Minute on the agitated back of a shaggy chestnut, Jo left the gate and plunged forward, floating, as it seemed, above its arching body, and when she reached the turn was confident enough to take off her hat – a wide-brimmed western hat – and wave it to the crowd. A vibration of cheering rewarded her, and then, as silence fell – for the bronco had become vicious again – there came from somewhere in the throng, now all afoot, a high-pitched yell, learnt in the immensity of Texas, and the appropriate injunction: 'Ride 'im, cowboy! Ride 'im!' And that is what she did. She rode him, she survived the twist and heave of his back, the shock of his forelegs coming stiffly down, the supple swerve of his hindquarters, the anger of his plunging head and returned to the starting-gate and the welcome arrival of two horses that enclosed her snorting animal and let Red Cannon, mounted on one of them, lift her down.

After the great tent had emptied – it was still hot with enthusiasm and the smell of sweating horse-flesh – there was a party, there was some devotional drinking to Jo's success and, though Red Cannon's help was not ignored, it was warmly agreed – by a party that still added to its numbers – that nothing could better Jo's horsemanship except her simple pluck. She was a modest girl, too poor to ride regularly. 'I wish I could,' she said, 'though never again on a horse like that. Thank goodness tomorrow's Sunday! I couldn't sit on an office chair, and I couldn't use a typewriter. Look at my hands!'

Of another uncommon occasion, of some slight historical importance, I have been reminded by rereading *The Watery Maze*, Bernard Fergusson's compendious account of Combined Operations. To one of the rare, and perhaps the earliest of amphibious exercises, which had no successor for many years, he gives a line and a quarter: 'in India a thousand troops were put ashore in boats at Kasid, 30 miles south of Bombay' – and with them, unnoticed by Fergusson, went I.

In the guise of a war correspondent I escaped from the office for three days, and put to sea in H.M.S. *Emerald* of the East Indies Cruiser Squadron. The exercise was by no means easy, for after steaming south we anchored a couple of miles off-shore and in gross darkness transferred several hundred Indian soldiers from the *Emerald* into cutters that rose and fell, with distracting suddenness, on a lumpy sea. To the sepoys the *kali pani* – the black water – was a truly hostile element, and, though most of them mastered their fear, there were a few who had to be lifted, by a couple of ratings built like heavy-weight wrestlers, and passed down to others, as burly, in a rising boat.

I spent four or five roughish hours in a motor-launch, towing cutters to the distant beach, and then went ashore and slept for an hour on warm sand. I had a swim and was given breakfast by a beach-party. By then the assault troops had all disappeared, and when I set off to follow them I was soon lost in dense jungle. They, in darkness, had all found their way forward at great speed, but I, in daylight, was trapped in a thickly overgrown nullah with steep, crumbling sides, and had some difficulty in finding my way out again. But then, on higher, almost open ground, I was rewarded by a noble view: cruisers lean and immaculate on a bright blue sea; inland the troops advancing in a long, extended line; to the north the great ruins of an old Mahratta fort; and all ahead lay the vast emptiness, brown and green, of an India that I hardly knew, an India more enticing by far than the hotly crowded streets of Bombay.

We had an arduous day – a red-faced, sweaty day – but I slept in comfort aboard a ship of the Royal Indian Mail Line, and the following morning disembarked again to climb a jungle-clad hill at the other end of the Janjira peninsula. The whole exercise was acclaimed as a great success: in a manœuvre of a sort virtually unknown, *nothing went wrong*, and that could rarely be said of even the most conventional manœuvres. But there was no further experiment in combined operations until after the war of 1939 began, when amphibious assault became necessary: at first to deny the apparent defeat we suffered, and later to essay the reconquest of Fortress Europe. I had had the good luck to share in an intelligently conducted but almost solitary anticipation of a mode of warfare that became obligatory fourteen or fifteen years later.

I lived, on the whole, an abstemious life, as did most of the people I knew; for work was a discipline that all but a very few accepted. There was, however, occasional relaxation, and I have been astonished to find that I was once a guest of the Bombay Grenadiers at a smoking-concert: the period flavour of 'a smoking-concert' is irresistible, and forbids suppression of the fact that it must have led to heavy drinking, for I sang, to loud applause, the rumbustious ballad of 'Samuel Hall'. The Grenadiers were a voluntary organisation of the Territorial sort, whose drill did not match the pride and pomp of their name; and I had musical friends of a sort superior to them.

I remember listening to Bach and Brahms, on a gramophone, while an exquisite young man expatiated on what he called 'the lacy bits'; and in the house of a scholarly Moslem lady, the Atiya Begum, I heard, without much pleasure, a good deal of Indian music. The Begum lived on Malabar Hill in an imposing mansion built of Agra stone by masons brought down from Agra. The architect was her husband, in his own province of the arts as erudite as she, and from Fyzee-Rahamin I learnt something of the niceties of Moghul painting, whose masters used paint with the precision of jewellers. Even in Bombay the fine arts had their place, but the commoner accidents of life prevailed.

Another of my colleagues died, very painfully, of pneumonia, and a day or two later someone said to me, 'He wouldn't have had so large a funeral if his club bills had been smaller.' His extravagance, indeed, had led him into that most dismal of *culs-de-sac*, embezzlement; as I soon discovered. My dying colleague, on his deathbed, had asked me to be his executor, and brief investigation showed that he had spent, not only his salary, but most of the Provident Fund to which we all contributed. He left a widow and one small child, who had lately gone home; and I, on their behalf, had to engage in a new debate with my employers, and with the Masonic Lodge of which my culpable poor friend was a Previous Grand Master, or some such high official. I persuaded my employers that the Provident Fund had been negligently administered, and the negligence was theirs; and the Masonic Lodge acknowledged some responsibility for its late Grand Master's widow and child. It was my first, my only acquaintance with what must be the saddest of all crimes, for embezzlement brings its own punishment to lives that, for the most part, are separated from ours only by a larger ineptitude, a more pervasive weakness. I had sat with him as he died, choking for breath; and remembering his innocent pleasure in life, his uncalculating extravagance, I found it difficult to blame him for a dishonesty that had its origin – as so often it has in the politicians who govern our lives – in a sheer inability to recognise facts.

India gave me a lot of experience, of a sort unknown to me before, and I might have stayed there longer if my life had been less closely confined. I had been promised opportunities to travel, but I was imprisoned in Bombay, and Bombay was not enough. I could see, moreover – as a mere will o' the wisp far away – a prospect of America, and in our half-century no one has been able to resist even a will o' the wisp's invitation to New York, New Orleans, San Francisco and the immensities between them. Also stirring in my mind was a growing wish to write something larger and with a life more lasting than leading articles which died like butterflies, and seldom showed a butterfly's iridescence. Daily work moreover – punctual, regular work – was something of which I had had no previous knowledge, which I did not like, and from which I wanted to escape. Sheer honesty compels the admission that an unfriendly commentator might describe me as an early example of what is now so graphically called 'a drop-out'.

I gave three months' notice of my resignation, and made preparation for a journey, aimed approximately at Scotland, which would take me through Persia and across the Caspian Sea to the Caucasus. That journey I have described elsewhere – it was hilarious as well as hazardous – and for the next year I found, by sheer good luck, employment in Aberdeen under my old professor. That led me – the will o' the wisp lighthouse proving true – to a couple of years' handsomely subsidised freedom in the United States.

✤ Eleven

THE seeming respectability of a university appointment –
minimal though it was in dignity and duration – was a useful
base from which to apply for a Commonwealth Fellowship,
and when my application succeeded I rejected the obvious
allure of Yale and Harvard and said I wanted to go to
Cornell. I knew nothing of Cornell, but I thought it would
be more explicitly, more natively American than the older
institutions which owed something to English models; and
from a map I had discovered that it lay in open, unsullied
country, divided and illumined by long lakes that would
reflect the sky.

I was fortunate in my choice, for the University of
Cornell – neighbourly with a little town called Ithaca – was
built about a large and handsome campus, and surrounding
it lay a vast, generous landscape that, as autumn advanced,
exposed the bold red hues of ripening maple and sumach,
and between its low hills were the long and narrow waters of
Lake Cayuga. Good fortune, moreover, was reinforced by
my supervisor, who bore the distinguished name of Quincy
Adams. Scion of a family which had given his country its
second and sixth presidents, he was a bachelor of kindly
temper who, most sensibly, had no wish to enlarge his
responsibilities. He was well pleased when I told him that I
would not trespass on his time, but could, I thought, do the
work I intended without much recourse to him for help. He
readily agreed to a suggestion that my attendance at lectures
would be unnecessary, and his supervision was restricted to
an occasional invitation to lunch with him on a Sunday, or
drive on a fine afternoon to see the country.

Unlike most of his contemporaries, he deplored the ever-growing reticulation of well-made roads, and looked for rough tracks that shook his sturdy Chevrolet as if he were navigating a fretful sea; and I saw something of a countryside still unconquered – dominated but not vanquished – by man and his profitable ingenuities. Here were the old hunting-grounds of the Iroquois, that redoubtable confederacy of Mohawks, Onondagos, Senecas, Oneidas, Cayugas, and Tuscaroras; and it was hardly possible to look at those scarlet hills and pale blue waters without deploring the onslaught of history – without abominating the zeals of civilisation – and sadly mourning the Redskins' unhappy end.

In those years we were often told, by our American friends, that our continuing presence in India was shameless and disgraceful – that the British *raj* should immediately be dissolved – and no purpose was served by pointing out, however tactfully, that our Indians still lived in India: that they had neither been exterminated nor pushed into reserves in Nepal or Tibet. We were wanton oppressors – that remained obvious – but our American cousins had removed the Iroquois in virtuous obedience to the demands of a progressive society. The Iroquois had been an obstacle to progress, and obstacles could not be tolerated.

There was, in the United States, a notable difference between its history and its people. Its history – the record of its government – had been clumsy, intractable, and covetous; its people – or those whom one met – were congenial, broad-minded (except on the topic of India), and generous beyond measure. Lincoln, the most agreeable of men in private life, had, as President, waged war at the cost of a million lives to preserve a democratic union which denied freedom of decision to the states of the union; and his successors in Washington, while deploring Britannic imperialism, had for their own profit established financial controls in South America, and expelled the remnant power of Spain from Cuba and the Philippines, as their predecessors had ousted Mexico from Texas and California. Like all other governments, Washington made its own rules and concealed policy under a heavy disguise of righteousness; but the people of America – or those with whom one became friendly – were honourable men, blissfully indiscreet, and lenient to error with the leniency of native magnanimity.

It may be, of course, that any government is preferable to the anarchy of no government. In 1928, however, the Government of the United States seemed intent on discrediting itself by its vain attempts to enforce the Eighteenth Amendment to the Constitution. That inordinate prohibition was enacted in 1920, remained as law until 1932, and forbade the brewing and distilling of ale and spirits and all trade in them. For eight years after the enactment the United States enjoyed unexampled and growing prosperity, and the Eighteenth Amendment was bitterly resented by a host of people, many of them young, who had never been in the habit of drinking gin and corn-liquor till gin and corn-liquor were made illegal. No one felt bound by the Amendment, and the consequence was that a new criminal class appeared to supply honest Republicans and God-fearing Democrats with the strong waters that freedom demanded and their government forbade them to buy. Crime became a new industry – a major industry – and, because America could afford both the anarchy of crime and the expensive bottles which its new criminals supplied, America entered a romantic period in which money, bootleg-whisky, and blood flowed freely, and a new mythology was created that replaced the old mythology of the Frontier and the vanishing West. In the new mythology I found material for the novel which allowed me to set myself up as a novelist and live in relative freedom; and though I disliked the government of the United States – its history and continuing practice – I should not reprehend it; for it was my great and permanent benefactor. Writers, it may be, have always owed more to bad governments than to good ones.

In Aberdeen, in the year that stretched like a bridge between India and America, I had written a novel called *White-Maa's Saga* which had some of the virtues of green things and a naïve enthusiasm, and most of the faults of inexperience. It relied, like many first novels, on an auto-biographical substratum which had to be raised, falsified, and decorated to make a good story; and when I sailed to New York its untidily typewritten pages, growing shabby in transit, were still looking for a publisher. At Cornell I found cheap lodgings in a rooming-house designed and conducted for students, and having made amicable arrangements with Professor Quincy Adams I settled down to a quiet and pleasantly industrious regimen. During much of the day I read widely, in an excellent library, and made notes for a thesis I proposed to write; and in the evenings – which began early, because I usually ate in a cafeteria which served its last meal at six o'clock – I wrote, with a total though not grave commitment, my second novel.

It was pure fiction, the sheer product of invention, and I wrote it as an exercise from which I hoped to learn something of the strategy and tactics necessary, as I believed, for the construction of a novel. I finished it early in 1929, and called it *Poet's Pub*. It was duly published, and made a little more money than my first: the advance on royalties was £100 as against £30 or £40 for *White-Maa's Saga*. Some years later, however, *Poet's Pub* began a long life in a new uniform when Allen Lane introduced his paper-backed Penguins – sixpence a copy, a farthing for the author – and chose *Poet's Pub* as one of his first ten titles.

Before I finished it – in my comfortless lodging-house in Cornell – its predecessor had been accepted by Jonathan Cape, and I had made a decision of some importance: of importance to me, that is, in my private world. I had arrived in America with the intention of writing about the development of urban, realistic comedy in the late Elizabethan and early Jacobean theatre: the sort of study that might recommend me for employment in a provincial or Canadian university. But I had already turned my back on a journalistic career in India, and now I dismissed all thought of a scholarly future. I determined to be a novelist; and the material for my third novel lay broadly spread before me in forty-eight united states.

In the late autumn of 1928, however, that enterprise – manifestly more ambitious than its precursors – lay far ahead, and my immediate task was the apprentice work of *Poet's Pub*. I did not abandon my daily reading in the library, but its purpose became less academic, and I admitted that my primary interest was elsewhere. For two or three months I lived soberly, dutifully, and gave myself small liberty until I had written some 40,000 words and won the satisfying feeling that my carefully induced pregnancy would proceed to a live birth. Then I allowed myself a little freedom, and began to acquire friends.

Everyone of Britannic origin, who has lived in America, has declared his delighted surprise at finding in his new neighbours a genial, open-armed, embracing hospitality that wholly transcends the cautious, wary, and restricted friendliness so typical of our own islands. I found their tales to be true, and became a recurrent guest, in houses and motor-cars and speakeasies, of newly acquired acquaintances who immediately made known their protective interest in an obviously underprivileged immigrant from the homeland their fathers or forefathers had so thankfully abandoned, and whose memory they so illogically treasured.

Rich friends and poor friends were united by a common generosity. Poor friends gave one abominable liquor that had been brewed or concocted, distilled and confected, in domestic laboratories; and rich friends, on whose walls hung a genuine Rubens or Velasquez, made one free of cellars providentially filled before the blight of Prohibition fell upon them. And wherever one went there were always girls, more animated and better dressed than those I had known in Scotland, and perhaps a little more vapid. Young women – or so it seemed to me – rarely discovered individuality until they had been married for a year or two, then thankfully divorced. Girls of university age had an artificial vivacity and mannerisms identically packaged. But one never knew them long enough to complain that their talk was stereotyped, their personality a product of time and circumstance rather than of character.

'Necking' and 'petting' had become a national entertainment that was widely advertised and much debated. They were, in the 1920s, a social innovation; or, perhaps more accurately, indulgence in them had become more open – flauntingly open – and in the publicity that young people already attracted they became a phenomenon, a feature of the age, that deeply perturbed an older generation whose youth had been circumscribed by a still vigorous Puritanism. Prohibition, and a general prosperity, had popularised bootleg whisky and bathtub gin; illicit liquor relaxed old norms and standards of behaviour; and defiance of the Eighteenth Amendment led inevitably to a discard of prohibitions more native to New England. But in our present climate, forty years later, the gaiety of the late 1920s – so untrammelled as it seemed to the critics of those years – wears now, in memory, an engaging innocence, the green hue of vanished Aprils.

There were, it is true, some parties where decorum winced and exuberance ruled; and there may have been others from which decorum fled. But I think it true that in 1928 – when, for a party, we still wore by habit the stiff uniform of a starched shirt and a black tie – the reticence of Puritanism retained a lot of authority, and the rebels against Puritanism had not yet won the freedom of revolution. In that slim, slight novel of the period, *The Great Gatsby* – so much over-rated – Scott Fitzgerald is awe-struck by the excitement of rebellion, and in its liveliest chapter hilariously re-creates the licence of a drunken party; but even at an extravagantly drunken party there are known rules – rules may be broken, but have not been abolished – and when Gatsby quite unnecessarily is killed his death can only be explained as a symbol of Fitzgerald's moral disapproval of a partially permissive society whose laxity he himself guiltily enjoyed.

I remember an admirable party at a country club in the respectability of Connecticut. A daughter of my host had become engaged to marry, and the party was in her honour. It was large and lavish, and on the ballroom floor decorum maintained absolute rule. I danced with my hostess, and she told me how very gratified she was by the good behaviour of her guests. 'Nowadays,' she said, 'you never know what's going to happen. So many young people drink too much – just because drink's forbidden – and I've seen many a party where a few people have spoiled the enjoyment of everyone else. But here – well, look around – everyone's sober and well behaved, and that I take as a tribute to my daughter, whom they respect!' Warmly I agreed with her, for her daughter was a very beautiful girl; but when I went down to the locker-room for a drink I saw ten or a dozen young men comatose on the benches, and a few others, too exuberant for a hostess's pleasure, were being forcibly prevented from returning to the upper floor. Law existed, rules were recognised, and should not be flagrantly broken.

In so large a country, however, there was room for different interpretations of the law of the land, and the rules to which society was obedient. I remember the newspaper report of a card-party – in Dallas, I think – at which a woman shot her husband across the table – shot him dead – because he doubled her bid of five spades. The judge listened patiently to the evidence, and then asked the surviving members of the party to reconstruct their hands. He assembled the remnant cards, and asked the mourning widow, 'Is this the hand on which he doubled five spades?'

'It certainly is,' she said.

'And when he laid it out, and you saw what he'd got, you shot him?'

'That's right.'

'I think you were justified. To double five spades with a hand like that was to offer provocation beyond endurance. The case is dismissed.'

The law of the land is the same in Texas as in Connecticut, but in Dallas the rules may differ from those accepted in New Haven; and the great size of the American land-mass, that makes possible such a difference, is one of the major difficulties that confront the European visitor or immigrant. He knows, because he has read it, that the United States cover almost three million square miles, but he hasn't the imagination to grasp and accommodate even the thought of so vast a magnitude. Yet there is no possibility of understanding the United States – its history and its people – without some appreciation of the bulk and variety of a single country so vast that it reaches from the Atlantic to the Pacific, from the Gulf of Mexico to the frosty edge of Canada.

You may look at a map, but maps flatten and delude – no one can see what a cartographer pretends to have seen – and nowadays, if you fly headlong across the continent, speed will destroy the reality of its magnitude. I was lucky in that I travelled widely, and travelled often by trains that gave one time to learn, by pure sensation, the distance between Washington and New Orleans, between New Orleans and Houston, between New York and San Francisco. After a train journey through the Middle West it was easy to believe in the reality, the natural emotions, of American isolationism; what was difficult was to accept the fact that America was already breaking the bonds of its isolation, and might escape them altogether. Kansas City was remote from the Atlantic, separated by mountain ranges from the Pacific, fatly contented with its own immeasurable environment, a periphery that gave it lands like an ocean to enisle it from the world. What inducement could it find to join a world so divided by hatred, hostility and a clamant poverty as the old world of Europe and Asia?

The self-sufficient magnitude of the United States was something we learnt by a tactile experience of it; and I doubt if it can properly be learnt in any other way. But another thing we learnt was the enchanting variety of that great country. I have said something of the Iroquois' old hunting-grounds, and a few hundred miles south of them are the enormous shores of Chesapeake Bay, where an ocean comes in to rape a continent and leave on blazing beaches the sunlit scars of its assault; and south of the Bay remains evidence that the native Indians of those parts, bloody though their practice may have been, were gourmets whose taste we must respect; for here and there, along the beach, are tall heaps of oyster shells left in reverent memory of the gluttonous feasting they enjoyed. I went south to the Carolinas, and the balconied elegance of Charleston, aflame in their season with roses and magnolia, camellias and jasmine. Tree-lined streets, colonial architecture, verandahs full of flowers, and old ladies with a proud and delicate memory of their ancestors: that was Charleston, and I added myself to the majority who have fallen in love with it.

A few miles inland, on one of its enclosing streams, are the Ashley River gardens: many broad acres coloured by a riot of coral-pink, crimson, and pale guinea-gold azaleas that reflect their brilliance in jade-green water. To the north, over another few miles, is the Gothic gloom of enormous trees, live oaks and cypresses, that rise in stilly shadow from the swamps of the Santee River, and bear from their branches great curtains of Spanish moss. That water-borne forest harbours white egrets – magnolia-hued but fiercely shaped – and larger herons, blue or white, with here and there – conspicuously aloof – a sea-eagle bred proudly for supremacy. At some time the delta of the Santee was dammed to make peninsulas of firm, dry land, and on one of them stood the cottages of a negro hamlet; where we went ashore.

Our leader – commander of a fleet of three narrow canoes – was Josephine Pinckney, a poet, young and tremulous amidst the constant perils, the sensational, unexpected rewards of life. She was, I think, the last offspring of a long ancestry of plantation-owners, settled in the early seventeenth century, and when the grandsons and granddaughters of her grandfather's slaves recognised her, they came rushing towards her in a radiance of delight that was like the brightness of egrets in the swamp. They shouted and laughed, they cried and kissed her skirts, they surrounded her with a doting affection. I had been told, more than once, that plantation-owners and slave-owners in South Carolina never sold their people down the river. Commerce of that sort had soiled relations in Georgia and Mississippi, but in South Carolina surplus slaves had been manumitted. I do not know if that is true, but Josephine's reception seemed to substantiate the stories I had heard. It seemed to echo a persistent memory of kindliness – and for her it must have been some consolation for a tragical disaster of the previous evening.

There had been, in Charleston, a party; and by ten o'clock – because uninvited guests had arrived – all the drink was drunk. Drink, in those years, was more precious than money; and in Charleston no one was rich; most, indeed, were poor. Josephine was poor, but admitted her possession of a bottle of whisky. A single, precious bottle that she had been keeping for some great occasion. Generously she decided that this was a sufficient occasion, and I went with her to get it. She would not let me carry it. 'Men are so clumsy,' she said. But she herself was trembling with excitement, with the joy of giving, and at the door of the house where the party waited she let the bottle fall. She burst into tears, and sobbed against my shoulder.

She is dead now, but before her death her shyness was startled by the loud success of a novel she wrote, and her poverty, I believe, vanished overnight. I owe my memory of her – my brief and delighted acquaintance with her – to a friendship that coloured and enriched much of my two years in America, and still continues. It began – we were all young enough for horse-play – in a wild game of leap-frog aboard the ship in which we sailed to New York. I, from the top of a jump, was violently thrown backwards, and momentarily lost consciousness when my head hit the deck. Hamilton, quick to my rescue, felt the gully in my head that a German bullet had made, and thought I was fatally wounded by my fall. He denied, a little while afterwards, that he had fainted from the shock, but admitted his need of strong drink; in which I, quickly recovering, gladly joined him.

Hamilton Gilkyson was one of those Americans – a diminishing minority – who resembled Abraham Lincoln rather than Herbert Hoover. His interests and affections were those of a world most comfortably civilised, but he looked like a man born and bred to meet the challenge of the frontier: in the stern but deluding lines of his face there was nothing that remotely resembled the growing complacency of American faces — fat, insensitive, overconfident — that Hoover had seemed to initiate and popularise. He had a sense of humour that was never loud, never obvious, but seemed to be a constitutional leakage. He was constantly funny, recurrently witty, and his jokes and witticisms leaked out of a body that was taut and trim, athletically made, and had no other weaknesses. Sometimes he raised a surprised eyelid at his jokes; he never drew more overt attention to them.

He and Phoebe his wife, with several young children, lived some twenty or thirty miles from Philadelphia in a large, old-fashioned house that had been built, a century before, during the youthful growth of the eastern states. Phoebe was red-haired, vivacious with the natural vivacity of a warm April, easily talented — she wrote for, and edited, a small family-owned newspaper — and she and Hamilton had their being at the centre of a large concourse of friends and gifted or eccentric acquaintances.

In their house I met Joseph Hergesheimer, one of the most loudly admired lions in the literary zoo of those days: a plump, pursy man of genial, rather vulgar appearance. During the afternoon he was disappointing, but after dinner — and eleven mint-juleps, it was said — he roared very amusingly. At some earlier hour of the day a girl of great charm and few inhibitions, sitting beside me, said loudly, 'Who's that on your other side? Hergesheimer or Mencken?' And a moment later, almost as loudly, 'Well, I don't think much of either of them, anyway.' Today, I suppose, Hergesheimer is little remembered, even in the United States, but for a good many years such novels as *Three Black Pennies*, *Java Head* and *The Bright Shawl* were highly regarded, and in some lunar phase of literary criticism — which is inconstant as the moon — may well be lighted again by passing favour.

The Gilkysons took me to Richmond, to call on James

Branch Cabell. Like many at that time I had a great admiration for *Jurgen*, and it was interesting, though slightly disconcerting, to find that Cabell – a short, squarely built man of a slowly moving, ponderous sort – had withdrawn from the world, as if into Jurgen's Poictesme, and surrounded himself with an almost impermeable rampart of silence. It was, I think, on a later visit to America that I met Owen Wister, author of *The Virginian*. He, with patrician manners and a most genial temper, may have left a name no better remembered than the others, but to the American scene he bequeathed an enduring hero: it was Owen Wister who first described the slow and purposive approach, along the otherwise deserted street of a shanty-built western town, of two gunmen, virtue on the one side, villainy on the other, and equally armed. That great invention converted the early magnates of the cinema to a Manichean view of life, and since their time the television box has a thousand times presented as protagonists of Good and Bad – different as night from day, but alike in fortitude and dexterity – the Two Fastest Guns of the West. Owen Wister – or so one felt – had lived through violence unperturbed – observed the factitious heroisms of the Wild West with a genial scepticism – but retained his youthful affection for the ardours of life on an extending frontier and the brash, open-eyed but unseeing creatures who peopled it. He was a most likeable man.

Another of the Gilkysons' friends was Emily Balch, who at one time had edited a little magazine that gathered between its covers all the poets and short-story writers of the Southern States. Then she married a rich man, who, after a few years, obligingly made her a wealthy widow and a patron of the impoverished poets she had previously encouraged. Carl van Vechten, who wrote enthusiastically about Harlem, had flatteringly described her as 'by a leopard out of Sarah Bernhardt', but when I knew her she was plump and less dangerous than that. She offered, when we were both in New York, to introduce me to Sinclair Lewis, whose Nobel Prize, in 1930, had roused much controversy and earned him the unforgiving wrath of Theodore Dreiser, than whom no more ungainly a writer – even in America – ever published a book. We dined, as a preliminary, at Jack and Charlie's, the famous speakeasy which became the more famous restaurant called Twenty-one: in the last year or so of Prohibition the Eighteenth Amendment was a dead letter, and Jack and Charlie made no attempt to conceal their expensive service.

We had a very good dinner, which lasted a long time, and it was late before Emily left me to pay the bill. This happened on my second visit to America, when there was more money in my pocket than I had had as a Commonwealth Fellow: enough, I hoped, to satisfy Jack and Charlie. But their wine was dear, and we had, perhaps, drunk a little brandy. The bill was more like an appropriation for the armed forces than the *addition* for dinner for two. Nervously I added, from waistcoat-pockets, some casual notes to what was in my wallet, and found I could pay it. But only just. A single dollar remained, and now I was confronted by waiter and wine-waiter, maître d'hôtel, bus-boys and their captain – all those attentive *serviteurs* who, in New York, are accustomed to lavish disbursement. But I must have drunk more than a little brandy, for I hid my panic and ran the gauntlet with a desperate aplomb.

I stood up, waving my solitary dollar bill, and walked slowly towards the door, loudly bestowing compliment and gracious thanks – now to this side, now to that – until I reached the end of the line, and to him who stood there I presented, with a flourish, the smallest tip ever seen in Twenty-one. Emily emerged from the powder-room. 'Quickly, come quickly,' I said. 'You will have to pay for the taxi.'

Sinclair Lewis was at that time married to Dorothy Thompson, a renowned and formidable journalist. We realised that it was now very late, but rang the bell again, and when the door was opened we saw, under the light, an angry woman who looked as if she had found comfort against a wasted evening, but was in no mood to welcome visitors.

She let us in, however, and with deep resentment hardening her voice told us how earnestly she had tried – but tried in vain – to keep Red Lewis sober. Then, as vainly, to keep him awake. But an hour ago she had put him to bed, and now the Nobel Prizewinner was fast asleep. 'And so,' she said – now with triumph in her voice – 'you've come for nothing!'

'Indeed we have not!' said Emily in her sugar-cured Southern tones. 'It was you we came to visit with, it wasn't Red!'

From then on a pleasant but ill-governed evening again became pleasant, and anger, mollified by judicious flattery, vanished to make room for hospitality. . . .

It's true, all true, but I have been seduced by gossip. I admit my fault, but do not much blame myself – for gossip was grafted onto the stock of English writing when Chaucer wrote a prologue to his Canterbury tales; Jane Austen gave the novel a new, pellucid distinction by distilling, into a fine art, the common brew of gossip; and Joyce, the Irish demiurge, compounded of Dublin gossip the heroic and comic nonesuch of our century. If gossip is good gossip there is much to be said for it. If the proper study of mankind is man, there is something to be learnt by following him after dark or listening to his *obiter dicta*. But my present mistake is to have lost sight of the topic about which I began to write, and which deserves attention.

In Britain and in Europe we all know a great deal – much of it inaccurate – about American social problems, about crime in Chicago and racial discrimination in Mississippi, but few of us know anything at all about the extravagant beauty of great areas that maps label with ringing and romantic names. True, there is much that is dull and merely profitable in the middle parts. True, one can grow tired – looking through the windows of a slow train – of the sun-dazed plains of Alabama, variegated only by poor-white families blinking on a bleached front porch, by negroes, mules, and little unpainted towns baking in summer's heat. But New England has a charm that oddly consorts with sturdiness, and New Orleans an elegance that survives a summer climate as frightful as Calcutta's. Go west and south-west, and there a desert rises to sculptured magnificence, or harshly descends to the oven-depths of the Grand Canyon: it should be seen by moonlight and the rising sun from a stream called the Bright Angel that joins the Colorado far below the reddish cliffs of the canyon. North-west of it are the heights of the Sierra Nevada, domesticated for holiday-makers and hill-walkers by the Yosemite National Park.

If the United States were less important to the world it could sell its scenery as Ireland and Norway do. Much of its scenery is majestic, much of it – in New England, for example – gently or elegantly attractive. But scenery, as a national adjunct, is reserved for small countries, and the world, which ruefully acknowledges the intrusive power of the United States, is generally unaware of the manifold pleasure they offer to the eye.

Even forty years ago Los Angeles was an urban calamity and now, I believe, it offends the perceptive mind even more than it displeases the physical senses. But the fretted coastline of California, white under Pacific surf, stretches in splendour to the great harbour of San Francisco. How noble and unfettered that harbour was before a bridge diminished the Golden Gate! North again there was the Columbia river, there was Seattle with a harbour more intricate and decorative than its neighbour. The world, I used to think, should know more of what we, who were Commonwealth Fellows, could see for ourselves: that behind the physical force of the United States – which to many was irksome – there were native beauties, landscapes of baroque magnificence, which they would find alluring. Were I asked to speak for America – or so I thought – I would not bludgeon the world with statistics about my wealth; I would woo it with the exposure of my secret valleys and unreported pleasances.

The shoguns of the Commonwealth Foundation were displeased with me when I wrote *Juan in America*, because in it I showed too little respect for the United States and its institutions. But they could not complain that I had failed to enjoy their country, and I have become increasingly aware of my extraordinary good fortune in having lived there, for almost two years, when the majority of its people were showing their pleasure in the sudden florescence of their strength and affluence. The organised crime that the Eighteenth Amendment fomented could be construed as a romantic protest against an intolerable invasion of personal liberty, and the Wall Street crash did not immediately darken a continent. On the Pacific side the national euphory was unimpaired for another year or two, and the students of Berkeley put on no mourning for what, to them, seemed merely a local mishap.

Both the universities I attended – Cornell for a start, then Berkeley – have in recent years erupted in hatred of a materialist society that either demanded too much from them or gave them too small a share of its wealth. But in my time the campus above Ithaca, and the campus that looked westward to the Golden Gate, were unperturbed by injustices that the world has always suffered, and consoled inevitable disappointment – the natural disasters of youth – with bootleg whisky and bathtub gin.

During my terms at Cornell there was no breach of academic peace worse than fire in a fraternity house, and what was then known as a 'panty raid'. The fire that consumed the fraternity house was much enjoyed: in the depths of winter the flames were brilliant against a field of snow, and trees were splendidly illumined by pendent icicles that took on the hue of frozen claret: runlets of Pontet Canet and Haut Brion stationary among the elms' bare branches. The 'panty raid' was an assault on a women's dormitory, from which female underclothes were carried off as trophies. The young ladies who lost their knickers appeared to be as well pleased by the publicity they earned as the young men who had – so to speak – rifled their drawers.

At Berkeley there was a more elaborate interruption of the term's routine, but it was quite uncoloured by social protest. Prowess in rowing was much esteemed, and the Berkeley eight was about to meet a crew of exceptional strength from Oregon or Washington. It was rumoured that the visiting

crew were endowed with consummate skill as well as uncommon muscle, but it was assumed that they were rustic
creatures unaccustomed to the sophisticated pleasures of a
great city. For their accommodation rooms were booked on
the fourteenth floor of a San Francisco hotel, and on the
fourteenth floor of a hotel on the opposite side of the street
were established the chorus girls of a musical comedy then
playing at a nearby theatre. They were told to leave their
windows uncurtained, when bed-time came, and to undress
– not, of course, with improper ostentation – but without
unnecessary haste. On the following morning the Berkeley
eight, leading all the way, rowed to an easy victory, and no
one doubted that their success was due, in part at least, to
stratagem. But who could seriously object to subversive
tactics of so genial a sort? There was no ill temper of the kind
that Black Power would later unleash; and nowhere on the
campus was there protest against a system under which
degrees were awarded only to those who had passed the
statutory examinations.

In Berkeley I lived comfortably in a well-furnished flat
with a landlady of the kindliest sort who supplied me with an
abundance of local gossip. She had a bright eye for detail,
and a keen interest in death. She frequently attended
funerals – her friends appeared to live precarious lives – and
with simple admiration she would describe their handsome
presence as they lay encoffined in their party clothes,
smoothly coiffured, plumped and painted by the embalmer
as if for holiday. It was Evelyn Waugh who first found, in the
mortician's art and practice, the subject for a novelette; but
I nearly anticipated him with a minor character, in *Juan in
America*, who was an undertaker and advertised his services
with the inviting slogan: 'Why Go Around Half-Dead
When We Can Bury You For $39.50?'

There were several Commonwealth Fellows, all of amiable
temper, who lived nearby, and with them, for the only time
in my life, I became, with the regularity of a pious church-
goer, a communicant of the cinema; for that was a historic
year in the film world. We used to cross the bay to San

Francisco by ferry-boat – a charming and exhilarating little voyage – and in that steeply climbing city saw the last of the old silent movies, and some of the tentative first talkies; in which sound emerged as a breath-consuming squawk. I remember Garbo in an enchanting film – was it called *The Kiss?* – and the next time I saw her, a year or two later, she was no longer beautiful in a loneliness of beauty that had no need of language, but must let the hoarse emotion of her voice impair perfection with O'Neill's clumsy dialogue in *Anna Cristie*. Garbo survived the transition, but many of the speechless stars fell like cinders when the splendour of their appearance – virile dignity, female grace and loveliness – were betrayed by scrannel voices. It is a pity, perhaps, that the inventors who have plagued our age made talkies possible, for the silent film was developing an art which lost both purity and power when it had to make room for words. No spoken comedy can rival the exuberant invention of Chaplin's early masterpieces, and none of the great spectacular films ever suffered from the lack of dialogue or was enlarged by the addition of speech.

At Berkeley, as at Cornell, I attended no lectures, for my new novel occupied much of my time and most of my energy. I wrote several chapters with growing confidence, and then progress was interrupted by a gnawing discomfort in my guts. Even in my small circle of friends there were others afflicted in a like manner, for ulcers, either gastric or duodenal, were already beginning to question or contradict the national assertion of well-being. Stress and strain, or rodent anxiety, was a common and respectable cause, but my ulcer had a less reputable origin. It could be traced, I think, to a party I attended in Washington when Herbert Hoover was installed as President. By a friend at Cornell, a rather wild young man, I was driven for several hundred miles over snow-covered mountains where a succession of mishaps so delayed us that it was nearly midnight before we arrived at the friendly house where we had been invited to dine. We had little need to apologise, however, for the party was still in progress. It had, in fact, hardly begun, and went on for day after day. We watched the great parade – how badly the Americans march! – and as the original stock of liquor was exhausted, and replenishments went the same way, we grew a little careless in our choice of a bootlegger, and eventually were drinking some very bad whisky. When I fell ill at Berkeley I regarded my duodenal ulcer as a medal awarded for service at Hoover's enthronement.

Generous as ever, the Commonwealth Foundation gave me a bed in a very good nursing home in San Francisco, where I learnt something of the thoroughness and scientific scepticism of American medicine. I was examined and questioned with minute and laborious particularity. No one believed my simple explanation of how I got my ulcer, but my whole life and the health and longevity of my parents and grandparents had to be investigated. I had never, I said, suffered any venereal disease except love, but my thumbs were pricked, my veins were breached, to give my inquisitors large quantities of blood; and though their findings were as negative as my own reply, their final judgment in paragraph twenty-seven of a report that covered three foolscap pages, was merely 'Denied'. When I admitted that I had had malaria in India, they drew more blood and sent for specialists to examine it. They were inquisitive about my spleen, which was frequently palpated; and a supplementary report was added to the original. I had never, I said, had blackwater fever and trypanosomiasis was unknown in Bombay. 'Denied,' they wrote.

They treated me, however, with care and patient sympathy, and the nurses were courteous, kindly and abrim with interesting gossip about their alcoholic patients, of whom several were in residence; it was the sort of nursing home that attracted rich and fashionable invalids.

Convalescence was made tedious by my doctor's insistence that, for some weeks to come, I must drink, at two-hourly intervals, two ounces of milk and two ounces of an alkaline medicine, which compelled me – even when going to a cinema – to burden my waistcoat pockets with small, unappetising bottles. Life was very dull, but my kindly landlady took pleasure in succouring me with egg-whisks and milk-puddings, and I stayed at home and worked. During my second summer in America I was almost as industrious as in my earliest months there, and my new novel passed the halfway mark.

Early in June 1930, I packed my books – I had more books than clothes – and boarded a ship bound for New York by way of the Panama Canal and Cuba. Dick, my travelling companion, was a young man of hilarious temper, who at Oxford had won a Blue for his speed in running a quarter of a mile, and whose intellectual interests, in 1930, seemed to be confined to Proust and the more blood-boltered periods in the history of Mexico. We travelled steerage, for cheapness, and our fellow passengers gave us constant entertainment: in chapter fifteen of *The Man on My Back* there is an account of the voyage in which Dick is called Dick Etive.

On the Atlantic side I spent a few days with my friends the Gilkysons, a day or two in New York, and rejoined Dick in a small ship called *American Farmer*, which crossed to Liverpool in a leisurely ten days. For a year or two after our return Dick and I saw each other occasionally, and maintained our friendship. Then I lost sight of him until a year or two ago, when he emerged from vocational secrecy in what must, I feel, be called a blaze of publicity. Some enquiry into the recent activities of our security service, or services, opened a door hitherto locked and guarded, and seated in the room within was Dick Etive. As Sir Dick White he had risen to be Head of M.I.5.

❧ Twelve

My landlady in Berkeley – she whose social life often introduced her to funeral parlours – had told me of two young friends of hers, newly married, who had taken a furnished apartment in Oakland and found, in a chest of drawers, a dozen new shirts, a pile of female underclothes lately bought and never worn, a sheaf of ties, a heap of handkerchiefs, all discarded by the outgoing tenants because they could not be bothered to pack them.

That was only a week or two before I left, and most of America was still rich enough to be sublimely careless. In Wall Street an abyss like the Grand Canyon had opened before a multitude of frightened eyes, but from the Middle West and California confidence was slow to retreat; and when, in Orkney, I settled down to finish my American novel I felt no need to darken it with economic clouds that had not obscured the bright skies under which I began it. *Juan in America* is a historical novel, and describes a country and a society which were vanishing even as I left them.

I had seen something of the Southern States, and more open poverty there than I had expected. But poverty was not yet in rebellion against its prosperous neighbours. You could dance in Harlem without any sense of danger, and south of the Potomac you could speak of niggers without intending insult or provoking a riot. In South Carolina I had been told that black folk were niggers or 'nigras', and we, paler of face, were 'buckras': the words indicated a difference of complexion, but nothing more.

That, I imagine, was disingenuous, but certainly the black people called themselves and each other niggers without shame or self-consciousness. In Charleston small negroes used to approach, as one sat idly on a park bench, and for a penny or two would dance and sing little songs such as: 'If you want to bake a hoe-cake, to bake it good and done, just clap it on a nigger's heel and hold it to the sun.' And once, walking on a lonely road a mile or two from the town, I heard a simple, greatly moving exchange of song and emotion between a black girl working in a field on one side of the road, and a young man hoeing on the other. 'Oh, de blues ain't nothing,' he intoned in a robust and brazen voice, 'de blues ain't nothing' – and he waited for her reply. There was a little pause, and then it came: 'De blues ain't nothing,' she sang in a rich and ringing contralto, 'de blues ain't nothing' – and she repeated her statement – 'but a bad nigger girl', she sang, 'on a good nigger's mind.'

Were I to pretend that a quality of innocence lingered, as a characteristic or dominant quality, in South Carolina in 1929, I should be guilty of gross sentimentality. But I am not guilty of sentimentality when I say that in comparison with the temper of succeeding decades there was then a quality remarkably like a remnant of innocence, not only in South Carolina, but throughout the union of all forty-eight states. Only in minds that retained a vestige of innocence could the Eighteenth Amendment have been hatched, and only by such minds was it grafted on a constitution intended to be practical; and only a comparable innocence could have supposed that crime might be encouraged, enriched, almost enfranchised – to satisfy a natural appetite that had suddenly been made illegal – without crime corrupting the society that permitted its growth. And innocence of that sort – vestigial or a stubborn remnant – was what I saw beneath the fabulous wealth of the United States, and it was that which let me write, as I did, *Juan in America*. I wrote it open-eyed, with delight and a total acceptance of what I saw, with little animadversion on the scenes I described except, perhaps, after I had watched, in Detroit, the helpless agent of an insensate government destroying good whisky on the quays. About that I felt very deeply, as was right and proper.

The old man sat on a barrel. With a brittle *tap!* another bottle was broken. Whisky ran down his bare arms, down his oilskin trousers, down a broad gutter to the stream. The smell of whisky rose like incense. At his side was a mound of sacks, ripped open, their contents displayed: bottles lying snug, with handsome labels, and wrapt – some of them – in pink tissue paper. *Tap-tap!* Half a gallon more trickled down to the river. Enough to make a whole family happy and keep it happy for hours. Enough to drive away the spectres of hate, and poverty, and pain, and futility, and failure. Enough to give a man the sensations of adventure and passion and power. Enough to compensate him – briefly perhaps, but with sufficient truth, if all is indeed illusion – for never having seen the Himalayas, or lived like Haroun al-Raschid, or heard the Jupiter Symphony, or known freedom. Enough to comfort timidity, humanise arrogance, amend the selfish, and vindicate faith that the world abused.

For a moment the old man looked up from his toil. He had a bitter, shamefaced, and tortured look. So Ixion might for a moment raise his eyes to meet the horrified gaze of men. So regicides, conscious of their sin, might look. With such a face would the Wandering Jew peer in at lighted windows and find no home on earth. *Tap, tap, tap!* The old man broke more bottles, crouching over his work like an old man in hell. Beside him was the dirty warehouse, and behind him the icy sullen stream, and over his head a hostile sky.

Juan was published early in 1931, and presents an accurate picture of North America in its brief heyday of remedial crime and sentimental well-being: 'We have seen the American people create a new heaven and a new earth,' wrote Calvin Coolidge, and the bootleggers did their best to substantiate his words. Then, in naked hurry, he scuttled from his throne and left to Herbert Hoover a legacy of seeming wealth that soon burst like a bubble whose iridescence had falsely promised enduring elasticity. But *Juan* reflects the country in which Coolidge lived and believed, and deserves a place, now, on a library shelf beside Mark Twain's *Life on the Mississippi*. In the acceleration of time it is almost as far behind us, and quite as true.

I realised, well before I had finished it, that it was a novel of some importance, and no sooner had I written the last chapter than I fell ill with one of those nervous complaints that are a constant hazard of my trade. For many years indeed – until the war of 1939 released me from an arduous and unhealthy occupation – I was recurrently subject to a disabling resurgence of my duodenal ulcer, or an excruciating dermatitis. For about eight or nine years I never finished a novel without being halted in the middle of it by a protesting belly and the remedial starvation that followed; and the fact that I realised the nervous or psychological origin of my pain did nothing to prevent it.

In 1930, however, my convalescence was expedited by good news. *Juan* was chosen by the Book Society, then young and influential, as a forthcoming Book of the Month, and the admirable manager of my bank in Aberdeen, where my account was reduced to the price of two or three bottles of whisky, immediately guaranteed an overdraft which I ran up, without complaint, to several hundred pounds. My publisher, moreover, was deeply impressed by the commercial importance of the young author whom he had taken into his stable, and hurriedly sent me a telegram to ask when it would be convenient for us to meet in Edinburgh.

I, greatly flattered, replied 'At any time convenient to you'; and when I went to Edinburgh, and met Jonathan Cape, he scarcely gave me time to finish my first drink before he presented me with a newly drawn contract, pledging my next three novels to him, and – as he commanded a waiter to bring me more whisky – required me to sign it. I, in the innocence that still surrounded me – sometimes a benignant light, but sometimes a blinding fog – gladly obeyed him; and not till some years later did I realise the mistake I had made.

Jonathan was a horse-dealer, a cattle-trader, of whom I became oddly fond, even after my realisation that he had taken advantage of my unforgivable ignorance. He was assured of a very substantial sale for the new novel, and the contract I signed was for an initial 10 per cent royalty, a long-delayed progress to 15 per cent: payment, that is, no greater than I had received for my first book. But I signed the wretched contract, well pleased, and dear horse-faced Jonathan went back to London, better pleased than I.

I gained much, however, by my unprofitable deal with him because it brought me the brief friendship of a very remarkable, dedicated man, his literary adviser – that, I think was his title – Edward Garnett. Never have I known anyone more whole-heartedly convinced of the almost sacred importance of well-chosen, well-appointed words, and his long association, his great friendship, with Joseph Conrad endued him, for me, with an apostolic magic which neither Rome nor Canterbury could better; for Conrad, by that time, had ousted Kipling from the primacy of my regard. Yet I rejected the advice that Jonathan Cape and Edward Garnett both gave me.

Jonathan, the horse-trader, wanted me to write *Juan in Italy*, *Juan in Spain*, *Juan in Germany*, because he saw profit in such a series. Edward Garnett shared his opinion, and to him I said, 'But the theme of seduction, that was useful to Byron, is obsolete. You can't seduce girls when girls are as willing to go to bed as you are, and even in *Juan in America* that knowledge had become something of an embarrassment.'

'But', said Garnett, 'the merit of *Juan* is that you wrote about America, not about seduction, and if you take him to Spain and Italy and Germany, you will write about them, and not about the commonplace – very much the same wherever you go – of tackling a girl on a Spanish, Italian, or German pillow. You've made a good start with a well-written, well-contrived set of adventures for a *picaro* of a sort who can go anywhere he chooses, and I think you should give him his head.'

Garnett's advice was good, and I now deplore the fact that I did not take it. I had some money in the bank, and more credit; I could have spent a year or eighteen months in Paris, another year or two in Madrid or Rome or Dresden, and there have expanded the saga of Juan that I had inherited, though with small approximation to legitimacy, from George Gordon, Lord Byron, who had attended – some years before I went there – the Grammar School of Aberdeen, and whose statue stood proudly but misleadingly at its gates; for he did not typify its style or ethos. I listened to Garnett, I listened to Cape; but I had exhausted my interest in Juan, and wanted to essay something quite different. So, to delay decision, I accepted an invitation from the *Daily Express* to present on its front page a set of articles about the pleasure and variety of life in London.

For that offer I was indebted, of course, to *Juan* and its immediate popularity. It was advertised widely – even on London buses – and I, more than a little shocked by so blatant a recommendation – I was thin after long illness, and in some ways curiously strait-laced – prayed heartily, 'Dear God, save me from the vulgarity of success!' Prayer, I have since recognised, is a dangerous exercise. Prayer may be answered, and in my case it was. God showed me favour, and spared me the vulgarity I feared. But in my old age, and even in my late middle age, I have deeply regretted his benignity. For several reasons, some of which were good, I have wanted the money that comes with success, and never got it. I seldom pray nowadays, because I am aware of the attendant perils.

In 1931 I was still avid of experience, and without hesitation stepped onto the front page of the *Express*. I was introduced, with some untruth, as a young writer who was at home in most of the capital cities of the world, but had never been in London. I had to suppress a memory of being taken, at a tender age, to see the Tower, and the embarrassing fact that I knew little of Europe beyond those dismal parts which had lately been channelled by trenches and festooned with barbed wire. I became a journalist again, and was paid £35 a week for three articles, each of about 1200 words: a salary on which I was able to live with all the comfort I required. I found, in New Cavendish Street, a furnished flat which could more accurately be described as over-furnished; for its owner was an actress, about to go off on a provincial tour, who believed that no home was complete without a superfluity of cushions and a mute family of very large dolls in exotic costume. A weekly rent of £3 10s was not excessive, and to a kindly woman who came in to make my bed and do a little dusting I paid a shilling or two a day. My salary may have been adjusted to the image contrived for me, of an itinerant peasant, but it let me dine out and establish a friendly connexion with a nearby wine-merchant. My name was cried up, and I began to meet more people than I had been accustomed to meeting. I met Lord Beaverbrook, who was most kind and friendly, though I disappointed him when I dined and slept at his house near Leatherhead.

He received me in his library, and for ten minutes I listened while he dictated letters to a typist. He showed a remarkable interest in the enquiries, for help or advice, to which he was replying, and when his typist was dismissed he was equally inquisitive about me and my antecedents. 'Your father, you tell me, was a sailor,' he said. 'Well, what do you mean by that? Was he a fisherman?' No, I said, not a fisherman, and Beaverbrook was plainly disappointed to find that I had been given a conventional education and could not claim that my manifest talent was a gift of God which had miraculously fetched me up from the lower depths. Tough on the surface, he was romantic at core, and more than once, at dinner, he talked about God as if a positive relationship existed between them.

In the kindliest way he took me up to my room, his arm about my shoulders, and at an angle of the stairs paused to ask, 'Do you like champagne?'

'Very much,' I said, 'but I prefer claret.'

'You like claret' — there was incredulity in his voice — 'better than champagne?'

I realised I had disappointed him again, and said hurriedly, 'I don't suppose I've ever drunk a really good champagne.'

'Well, mine's good, very good, and you'll like it.'

So I did, for the remarkable wine that first circulated was followed by the supernacular vintage of 1906. Beaverbrook, in his rasping voice, spoke sentimentally about his affection for the land of his forebears, who had gone to Canada from East or West Lothian and always remembered, with illogical affection, the land from which they had fled. The dinner-party was small and he, not unnaturally, dominated conversation. Then more visitors arrived, among them the monocled foreign correspondent, Ward Price, of distinguished appearance, and Randolph Churchill, aged twenty.

Ward Price remembered that on the staff of *The Times of India* there had formerly been a very gifted journalist, notorious for the irregularity of his life, called Lovat Fraser; and wanted to know if it was true that he had often been run to earth – when he should have been at his office desk – in one of the many brothels near Grant Road. Such were the stories still current, I said, when I worked in Bombay; and as often as not – if the stories were true – Lovat Fraser wrote his brilliant editorials in the brothel where he was found. But Grant Road, said someone – by then the ladies had retired – was a sort of human zoo where poor prostitutes were exhibited behind iron bars to the idle, gaping crowds who passed slowly to and fro. There were other, nearby establishments, I said, of a better sort, where there was no lack of comfort and a busy man, interrupted in his pleasure, could easily sit down and write a leading article. And what sort of girls, they asked, were to be found in those superior establishments?

Some of them, I said, were French-speaking Syrians and Lebanese, who often pretended to be French by birth. Occasionally you might find a very pretty little Kashmiri, the property of some brigandish Pathan, but most were Syrians, I thought. 'I've got to admit', I added, 'that I can't speak with much authority, but I remember a girl who said, "*Ça oui, il fait bon ici*, but to keep a brot'el where all is clean and in good taste, that costs much money, *et les clients n'attachent aucune importance à ce que nous disons là-dessus.*" She came from Beirut, she said, but both her parents had been born in France.'

'To me,' said someone, 'she sounds authentically French. Her concern with money – hasn't that got the proper accent?'

Then Randolph Churchill came and sat beside me, and I, crudely inquisitive, asked if he were grooming himself for politics. To which he, aged twenty, replied seriously, 'I think it would be more realistic to say that I *have* groomed myself. It's going to be politics, of course. Well, what else is there?'

What else, if you are born to such a heritage? But I had a larger choice, and again I chose to abandon what might have become a profitable career. My engagement with the *Daily Express* lasted for three weeks, I think, and then I sacked myself before a growing dissension – about what I wanted to write and what others said I ought to write – became embarrassing. I was, by then, reviewing novels for *The Listener*, and odd jobs came my way with the frequency invited by physical presence: if you live in New Cavendish Street you get more offers of employment than if you live in one of the remoter parts of Scotland. I could have settled down in London, and made a living there; but I was pinched and prodded by irrational desires.

I saw Edward Garnett again when he and I went to dine at Richmond with Sean O'Faolain and Eileen, his wife, who spoke with a softer Irish accent than Sean's. He too had been a Commonwealth Fellow in America, and one day in Boston, when I was sitting beside him in the shabby, clattering motor-car that he drove with reckless incompetence, we were abruptly halted by the harsh imperative of a policeman's whistle. We had driven across the traffic on a temporarily forbidden highway, and an enormous cop, with ponderous menace, came pacing slowly towards us.

'What's your name?' he asked through savage lips.

'Sean O'Faolain,' said Sean, and added to his accent a top-dressing I had never heard before.

'What's that you said?' asked the cop.

'Sean O'Faolain.'

'Where d'you come from?'

'Cork,' said Sean; but he pronounced it in a way that I cannot transliterate. It sounded like 'Caorrk', and as he spoke he smiled with a sort of shy complicity.

'Is it Caorrk, do you say?' asked the cop, repeating Sean's extraordinary pronunciation.

'It is,' said Sean.

'Then get the hell out of here before anyone sees what

you've done to the traffic,' said the cop; and fiercely blew his whistle again.

I had caught a glimpse of the Irish underground in America, and I became very fond of Sean, who later wrote some enchanting tales of the beauty, the waywardness, the insensate tragedy of his harassed country. Sean, in 1931, was foremost among the young men on whom Garnett was bestowing the avuncular benison of affection and good advice; and we dined, as I remember, with mutual kindliness and hilarity only occasionally modified by respect for the senior guest.

Then Garnett and I returned to London, and on one side of a third-class carriage he lay down and wrapped about him a voluminous coat — an Inverness cape perhaps? — that added magnitude to his ponderous figure; and began to speak of Yeats, of other Irish writers, and then of George Moore.

'A very odd, very interesting man,' he said, 'and, as a writer, even more interesting than as a man. For he was, of course, quite uneducated. He learnt to write, in the most extraordinary way, by associating with painters. And as he discovered how they went about their job — how they got their effects — he, in some inexplicable way, discovered how to get his effects in writing. Oh, a phenomenal man! He knew nothing about grammar, or even about spelling — he'd been brought up by his father's grooms — and yet he became a very good writer. But as a man — '

Our train stopped at Mortlake, and two small, elderly, and modest ladies — most modestly dressed and modest of demeanour — came into our carriage and inconspicuously sat down opposite the corner occupied by Garnett's feet. He, unaware of the intrusion and sprawling at full length, went on with his story: 'But as a man he really was an enigma. He wrote about women, and talked about them. Talked endlessly! About the penultimate moment, about the mating of a mutually growing affection that brought about the right and proper culmination of affection. But did it? In his own case, did it ever?'

The speed of the train was reduced, slowly we came into Barnes, and stopped. The two modest little women, alarmed by strange company, looked at each other in grave and growing doubt, but had not the force of decision to open a door and escape: in those suburban trains there was no corridor.

We gathered speed again, and Garnett, wrapped in dark seclusion but speaking in a voice that clearly showed his enjoyment of the tale he was telling, went on with it. 'No,' he said, 'despite all he wrote – and no one has a greater respect for what he wrote than I have – despite all that I'm pretty confident that George Moore, much as he talked about fornication, or the incipience of fornication, never did it. He approached it, and retreated from it. Fornication was always in his mind, but in his practice – where are we now? – in his practice he never got there!'

Grumbling to its next pause, the train came into Putney, and as soon as it stopped our terrified fellow-passengers – though bound for Waterloo – tip-toed in a great hurry to the door, and leapt down to the safety of the platform. The elder, in the position of honour, looked back for one panic-stricken moment at the encloaked satyr – so, quite certainly, she envisaged him – who still, unaware of her existence, lay in massive comfort, the very picture of *volupté* at ease on the narrow seat of a third-class carriage.

'No,' he said, as the train started again, 'he never did anything!' And then, when at Waterloo our ways parted, he asked me, 'Are you going to take Juan to France?'

'I can't make up my mind,' I said – but a week or two later I turned my back on both London and Paris, took train to the north, and presently found lodgings in St Andrews.

For some years I had been living far from Scotland in India, and then in America, and oddly enough – perhaps paradoxically – I had become more aware of Britain's knuckle-end than when I walked familiar streets in Aberdeen or roads, long known to me, in Orkney. I felt a growing interest in Scotland, and though I had, as yet, no political intention, nor any political ideas about its future, I had begun to accept an identification with it: or, to be more precise, with its northern parts, its farther highlands and islands.

I had been reading Yeats, and commentary or criticism on or of Ireland's literary renaissance. I had talked with Sean O'Faolain, and paid my first visit to Dublin: still demeaned by open poverty, but far more elegant than it is now. I had read, in some essay on or by Yeats or A.E., an injunction that they had found and obeyed in the works of Johann Gottfried von Herder: 'Study the superstitions and the sagas of the forefathers.'

That was wholly in accordance with my own ideas, for at an early age I had read, and been captured by, the saga of the Earls of Orkney, and thereafter gone on to some of the well-known Icelandic sagas; which were manifestly better than Conan Doyle, Rider Haggard or Stanley Weyman. At a later age I read them again, and gradually became aware of their deeper content. Now Orkney was the southernmost home of that pagan heroism which had changed the shape and temper of all northern Europe, and in its heroism – destructive though it had been of much that was valuable – I was beginning to discern a principle that had little reference to the common motive of profit. A hero on a foreign shore could enrich himself with what he found there; but also he could enrich his fame by what he did there. At work in Viking times – or so I thought – had been a superior motive that showed itself in a code of behaviour dominated, not primarily by a prospect of material gain, but by wish or determination idealistically conceived – by those who later won and deserved the saga-writers' regard – to complete an action in accordance with a pattern that was artistically satisfying.

No one – at the time of which I am writing – had thought of pillaging the Icelandic sagas for such a tale; but I, who knew several of them, and knew also the temper of Orkney speech, which in its habitual understatement often preserved the very tone of the sagas, felt myself entitled to confect a story which could borrow what it needed, and declare its originality by enclosing between its beginning and its end an account, in some detail, of a sea-voyage. None of the saga-writers had condescended to such a task. Seafaring, to the Vikings, was what office-life and office-work are to suburbia in our time, and did not call for description. But the manner of life aboard the longships of a thousand years ago was something wholly unknown to my age, and challenged imagination to recreate it. I wanted vehemently – but with a vehemence controlled for the occasion – to write a story about Orkney Vikings, fashioned in obedience to the historical motive I had discovered, and when I found that self-indulgence, of that sort, was recognised by von Herder as a kind of duty, I hesitated no longer. I took rooms in St Andrews, almost in sight of the old golf-course – bedroom, sitting-room, a shared bathroom – and sat down to write *The Men of Ness*.

That, I now realise, was the moment when I forfeited all claim to be recognised as a serious novelist. I am, of course, a serious writer: that is to say, I have always shown a proper respect for the language in which I write, a respect which is no longer general, nor even much applauded. But a true novelist is one who imposes his own character, his own way of thought and fashion of writing, on every page that leaves his table. The giants of my trade – few in the beginning were conscious artists – shaped and subdued their material to conform with their own temper and understanding. From Fielding to Flaubert they set their own mark on what they created. Dickens and Balzac patented worlds of their own; and so did Sterne and Smollett. Walter Scott and Tolstoy, as God before them, took clay and fashioned it in their own image; and Dostoievsky, like Lucifer, distorted creation and darkened it with evil. Since the death of the giants there have been many lesser men who, with smaller justification, have looked at some parcels of the world through eyes that measure only the capacity of their own retinas, and photo-graphed repeatedly all they have perceived through view-finders that never change direction. There has grown up, indeed, a belief in the virtue of the individual view-finder, however small its radius or limited its range. The writer –

in accordance with that belief – should assert his honesty by reporting only what he sees, though his vision may be limited by myopia or distorted by astigmatism. My own practice – which came into being largely by accident – has been more humble and realistic. To a very large extent I have allowed my subjects to determine the style and temper in which I have written of them.

I wrote *Juan in America* with the exuberance – an exuberance salted with a genial and quizzical satire – that I thought appropriate to my enormous scene. I wrote, a year or two later, the essay that emerged from my original, scholarly thesis on middle-class comedy in the Jacobean theatre; and *Ben Jonson and King James* was hotly coloured by my recollection of the verbal splendours that, in Elizabethan and early Jacobean times, gave to quotidian existence a baroque magnificence of speech. But when I wrote *The Men of Ness* I subdued and restricted my pleasure in words, I composed my story in a stark simplicity that banished all Latinisms from its sentences and relied almost entirely on a vocabulary that could, with some latitude, be called Anglo-Saxon.

I confected a good story. A good, dramatic story with a beginning, a middle and an end. A story peopled by strong and recognisable characters. But did I further, thereby, any claim I may have had to be recognised as a novelist?

Most certainly not. What I did do – at that time all unknowingly – was to revert to a fashion of writing characteristic of the great Scots *makars* of the sixteenth century. When Henryson wrote his fable of *The Two Mice* his mood and manner were very different from the tone he gave to *The Testament of Cresseid*; and Dunbar's *Ballad of Kind Kitty* bears little resemblance to *The Nativity of Christ* or *The Flyting of Dunbar and Kennedy*. They let their subject call the tune, and found words and a style suitable for the music. And to a large extent – in my smaller way – that is what I have often done.

My practice, indeed, may bear scrutiny and stand comparison of another sort. The sculptor has always been dependent on his material; and marble, softer stones, wood and clay have very largely determined the shape and nature of what emerges from them. The technique demanded by his material has been as influential as the sculptor himself in creating the idealised forms, surrendered to genius by Parian marble, and the emotional, racked-by-agony images made by German wood-carvers in the Middle Ages. I use neither wood nor clay, but preconceived ideas or stories, and, if the idea has been hard, so may be the writing that exposes it; if soft and malleable, so may be the comedy that illustrates it.

That is not, I hope, a statement too pompous or self-important for sympathy and understanding. All it implies is that I have written stories or novels of many different kinds, and my topic – my stone or wood or clay – has influenced my style of writing and chosen my words. If a novelist – a true novelist – is one who imposes himself on all he writes, then I am no novelist; for much of what I have written has imposed its character on me. I am something between a *makar* of the old Scottish sort and a sculptor who sensibly recognises the formative importance of his material. And that, I admit, prompts an interesting but disconcerting question: have I refused to impose my own character on what I write because, in fact, I have no character positive enough to impress itself on topics of every sort? Have I yielded to circumstance merely because I lack that sort of strength? I think that may be true. I may be a reed, responsive to the wind; not an oak, sublimely indifferent to it.

As a writer, moreover, I have been subject to a weakness which has betrayed many of my fellow-countrymen. I have not always been able to find, in writing, a total satisfaction of my natural appetites. From time to time I have felt a craving for more overt action, and, in the season of which I am writing, that craving was about to lead me into a calamitous experiment in a sort of action for which I had no natural gifts, but from which I emerged with the unscrupulous recompense reserved for writers. They can always write a novel – preferably a comic novel – about the misfortunes they suffer.

❧ Thirteen

I HAVE written elsewhere of a parliamentary by-election in East Fife at which I stood as a candidate for the Scottish Nationalist Party. That was in 1933, and I was resoundingly defeated. Later I wrote a novel, called *Magnus Merriman*, in which I described the circumstances of a fictitious by-election that had some resemblance to the real one, and my excuse for writing of it yet again is that I can now tell the truth about some minor details over which good manners – and a proper regard for the feelings of a man who became my friend – have previously imposed a decent reticence.

Allied to my sentimental identification with the northern parts of Scotland there was a notion of my own about the advantages of small nationalism. It originated, I think, in the United States, where I listened – especially in South Carolina – to many warmly expressed arguments in favour of the old, constitutional rights of individual states, then threatened by the growing central power of Washington. It seemed to me that a multitude of small, different nations would make a more interesting and agreeable world than a solidification into three or four major or super powers; and with a blind indifference to the Prussian goose-step of what, in America, was presently called 'the march of time', I joined the Scottish Nationalists who appeared to have ideas or beliefs congruent with mine.

As their candidate in East Fife, however, I did them no service. I quickly discovered that I had neither talent nor liking for electioneering; and my mind was depressed, my practice inhibited, as gradually I perceived that the Nationalists had no discernible policy. Their only remedy for the disabilities which Scotland suffered in consequence of its history and geography was separation from England; and a faith, without substance, that independence would beget a policy that was simultaneously necessary and benign. My own interests centred on Scotland's northern, farther parts, and there existed no plans for the amelioration of their difficulties. I still believed, moreover, in the vast importance, to us and the world, of the British Empire to whose creation Scotland had so lavishly contributed; and I was, I think, the only Nationalist who retained or proclaimed that belief. But the election provoked comedy, and I have no complaint about the energy I wasted on a misdirected party, or the money I vainly spent; for comedy is a better reward than energy and money usually earn.

There was an official candidate who called himself, I think, a Liberal-Unionist. There was another official nominee who stood in the Labour interest, but did not command the allegiance of right-wing members of the Labour Party. There was I, a Scottish Nationalist who as an Imperialist was in a lonely minority, and there was a candidate put forward by Lord Beaverbrook who, at that time, was in favour – as, indeed, I was – of a more energetic farming policy in Great Britain and increasing alliance with the Dominions. But the Beaverbrook candidate who was nominated was not – or so it was said – the candidate whom Beaverbrook wanted; and in the novel I subsequently wrote – a fictitious tale – I localised contemporary gossip and said that a Cockney voice, on the telephone, had maltreated a vowel, eliminated an aspirate, and secured the nomination of a relatively unknown Mr Emerson when he who was really wanted was the influential Mr Hammerson. It was firmly believed, in East Fife, that some such mistake had occurred, and 'Mr Emerson' soon showed that he was unlikely to win much support.

But Beaverbrook – no matter who was his candidate – was a formidable man, and the election acquired great warmth and liveliness when the Beaverbrook circus descended on St Andrews and found quarters in Rusack's

Hotel; where I had been living for some time. Congenial company enlivened my evenings, and among those who shared my corridor were Hector McNeil, later a Minister of State who became famous for bearding and brow-beating, at the United Nations, that fearsome Russian bully, Vyshinsky; and the legendary Lord Castlerosse. He, superbly fat, carrying a scarcely believable corpulence, was a man in whom wit was like an open tap. Irish rivers, glittering with fancy, ran through all his conversation, and wherever he sat – he needed the largest of chairs – there was a circumference of constant laughter.

He was, however, serious about his food, as I discovered one Sunday when he took me to lunch at the Royal and Ancient. On the rich menu of those days there was saddle of mutton. 'Five years or seven?' he asked. 'Ewe-mutton, seven years old – if it's properly hung – is the best you can get, but if a five-year saddle is all you can give us, well, we'll take that. And for a start . . .' He turned to me and asked, 'Will you take my advice?'

'But of course.'

'They have very good ham,' he said thoughtfully, and spoke to the steward, briefly but earnestly. Quickly we were presented with plates of thinly sliced, coral-pink ham, over each of which was poured, by the wine-waiter, a glass of vintage port. It was very good indeed. It would have been a superlative preliminary to a meal less solidly designed, but I lost favour with Castlerosse by failing to eat all my helping of ewe-mutton.

Then Beaverbrook himself arrived at Rusack's, and with him came an electric air. I was welcomed in the kindliest way, for at his first entrance he came towards me with a beaming, brimming smile – put his arm about my shoulders, as he had done before – and with grating geniality said 'Linklater! I was pretty sure we'd meet again. You've found your way into politics, have you? Well, you're on the wrong side, but you've discovered the greatest game of all. Yes, it's the greatest game there is!'

That was not what I had discovered, but within a day or

two Beaverbrook made evident his conception of the way it should be played. His candidate 'Mr Emerson' – as I may conveniently call him – had no hope of winning the election unless support for the Liberal-Unionist candidate could be drastically reduced. Now in East Fife there was an old and persistent loyalty to Asquithian Liberalism, and someone – perhaps Beaverbrook himself – thought it possible to undermine the Liberal-Unionist by offering yet another candidate, a pure-minded Independent Liberal.

David Keir, a young man of great promise never fulfilled – he later became my friend – was the innocent victim presented to the electors; and on the day of his nomination I said to a bevy of reporters, 'The electors of East Fife are now offered four candidates and one red herring.'

It was already evident that I was going to be bottom of the poll, but the other candidates were dull fellows, and I was the only one who ever gave sub-editors a quip that could be elevated to a headline; so reporters were usually my most numerous audience. In local opinion there was little doubt that David was indeed a red herring – or stalking horse: that may be more accurate – but David himself remained innocent and ignorant of his role, and campaigned with great energy and total integrity; and he and I shared the bottom places when the poll was declared.

On that dismal and tiresome occasion I stood and talked for a long time with David's appointed agent, who was Basil Murray, a son of the eminent Professor Gilbert Murray, a dedicated Liberal and the imaginative translator, into verse, of the tragic dramas of Euripides. But Basil did not resemble his high-minded father. In later years, indeed, it was widely believed that he supplied Evelyn Waugh with approximately one half of that deplorable character – so blackly sympathetic, so engagingly destructive – whom Evelyn called Basil Seal; the other half being supplied by Peter Rodd, whom I remember with gratitude as a polymath of unexampled virtuosity, and who, in his youth, is said to have deeply disturbed the undergraduates of Oxford; for his beauty, which Praxiteles would have admired, dislodged an ancient perversity – or so the story went – and substituted for it an improvement called *Rodomy*. However that may be, Basil Murray and he were probable contributaries to the fictitious character of Basil Seal; and to Murray I am much indebted.

While I waited to be told that I was bottom of the poll he produced an enormous silver flask and said, 'Drink some of this and you'll feel a lot better.' I expected the common flavour of pub whisky, and was marvellously uplifted when I tasted brandy of a sort that only a millionaire, or a vigneron of ancient lineage, could have offered. 'Take some more,' said Murray, 'it's a big flask, there's plenty for both of us, and all paid for.' – 'By whom?' I asked – 'Who do you think? Beaverbrook, of course, and bloody good it is. Go on, everything's been paid for. No expense spared, and nothing gained except this.'

A little while later, leaving St Andrews defeated and disgraced, I shared a first-class railway carriage, on the way to Edinburgh, with the young woman who was then – perhaps only briefly – Basil Murray's wife. She was a girl of great charm, vivacity and beauty. She too, I think, had been encouraged by Beaverbrook's good brandy. She had, as I remember, no interest at all in politics, and in the delight of such company I quickly lost all remembrance of my political humiliation.

It was early summer, I think, when I parted company with the Scottish Nationalists. At a meeting in Edinburgh I spoke, perhaps a little bitterly, about their failure to elaborate and declare a constructive policy, and said, injudiciously, 'You'll make nothing of this thing till you bring in the English to run it for you.' After that we had very little in the way of friendly association, but by then I was indifferent to politics, for I had become engaged to marry Marjorie MacIntyre.

I have told, on other pages, something of my rough wooing: her father Ian, sometime player of Rugby football capped for Scotland – sometime Member in the Conservative interest for West Edinburgh – challenged me to fight for her. Later I became one of his closest friends, and dearly loved my mother-in-law who, when I first met her, told me she so disliked my latest book that she had buried it in her rose-garden. Of my marriage I do not propose to say much. It has lasted, at this writing, about thirty-six years, which is thirty-four years more than I envisaged at the hour and day of our nuptials. How to explain its endurance I do not know, for we have quarrelled loudly and often, and today we still quarrel, though perhaps with less reverberation than the shouting which used to echo from our walls.

Our continued union may be a consequence of our infirm lack of imagination and initiative. It may, on the other hand, be due to reluctant admission of the fact – invisible to begin with, but gradually becoming evident – that marriage is an association that one accepts for better or for worse; and, unless one endures the bad days, one cannot rejoice in the good ones. Both Marjorie and I had been brought up by parents respectful of Christian values, and by accident of birth we were both members of the oppressed sect called Scottish Episcopalians; or, more commonly, *Piskies*. We were married on 1 June 1933 after I had had an animated discussion with the Rector of Old St Paul's, in Edinburgh, on the propriety of persuading the bride to promise obedience in return for the groom's generous offer to endow her with all his worldly goods. I convinced him that the authority of St Paul must be upheld, who said, 'Wives, submit yourselves unto your own husbands, as unto the Lord' – an injunction of which Marjorie has made nonsense ever since – and that her endowment with all my worldly goods entitled her to no more than an annual five per cent of my anticipated earnings.

We had, to begin with, nowhere to live, so we went to Italy. We rented, near Lerici, a small cottage and the service of a genial Italian family who lived beside it; and for several months were very cheerful there. We made a number of friends, of whom the most distinguished was Admiral Sir Reginald Bacon, and the most useful Lady Sybil Lubbock. I had read the Admiral's high-spirited defence of Jellicoe's strategy, of his tactics at Jutland, and he returned the compliment by borrowing from the shelves of our rented cottage a small book that I had lately written on the perennial topic of Mary, Queen of Scots. Two or three days later he brought it back and said, 'You've got a lot to learn about punctuation. Punctuation's like signalling: manual signalling, signalling by flag. It's got to follow a recognised practice, it's got to be clear and explicit. Well, yours doesn't, and isn't. So I've taken the liberty of repunctuating the first two or three pages of this book of yours, which otherwise I've enjoyed, though I don't agree with what you say.'

We drank a glass or two of local wine, the Admiral went off again with a firm, quarterdeck stride, and I – who had been prudent enough not to look at his treatment of my commas until he had gone – opened the book (which didn't belong to me) and saw that its early pages had been scarred by indignant correction. He had used – that was obvious – a carpenter's heavy pencil to obliterate my commas and semicolons, my colons and decisive full-stops, and superimposed on my sentences – as if replying to German gunfire at Jutland – a counter-bombardment of his own design.

'Well,' he said, when next we met – he could afford to give me whisky – 'what do you think of my system? An improvement on yours, isn't it?' And I – not weak-minded as an easy-going reader may suppose, no sycophant even to a knighted admiral, but lost in admiration, as I always have been, of the overwhelming confidence, the destroyer-captain's dashing assurance that used to characterise the Royal Navy – I answered, 'It's very interesting. Very interesting indeed.' It was, after all, not my book that he had defaced. So he gave me another whisky and soda, and we talked about the Dogger Bank and Admiral Sturdee's splendid victory near the Falkland Islands in December 1914. Marjorie, my wife, once said in my hearing – at one of those parties where it is difficult to hear anything – 'No, Eric is *not* a snob. Not an ordinary snob, that is. He's just a snob about admirals and generals.'

Far more important to us than the Admiral, however, was Lady Sybil Lubbock, who lived a few miles away in a marvellously situated, coast-nudging house called Gli Scafari with her third husband, Percy, who at that time received, as a sort of literary revenue, the punctual admiration of all the better-class critics: an admiration exacted by *Earlham, The Craft of Fiction, Shades of Eton,* and perhaps other books that I have forgotten. Marjorie found it easier than I did to establish a friendly relationship with Percy – I think, indeed, that he preferred women as friends – and in his garden at Gli Scafari, where he had achieved marvellous success in propagating alpine plants so minute that one had to go down upon one's knees to discover them – in that garden I found elements of boredom which seemed to me – in the coarseness of my judgment, the brutality of my taste – comparable to similar elements in his books. But Lady Sybil was pure enchantment of a sort I had never known before, nor have encountered since.

Irish by birth – her father was an impoverished earl, of great learning and recurrent wit – she had impediments of speech which decorated her conversation with a multiple lisp, and the staple of her conversation was so far removed from ordinary topics, or ordinary values, that rarely, since knowing her, have I had much difficulty in believing fairy-tales. But, like all the better characters in a fairy-tale, she was practical and helpful. About the time of Christmas, when it began to become obvious, she learnt that Marjorie was pregnant, and was immediately indignant when I told her that I had booked a room, for her lying-in, at a much respected nursing-home in Florence.

'What nonsense!' she said. 'The nursing-homes of Florence are all quite dreadful – staffed by nuns, who rejoice in suffering – and hardly anyone comes out alive. You must come to the Villino Medici, where Iris – my daughter Iris – refuses to live. But Iris is behaving foolishly, and if you'll come to the Villino, which is quite comfortable, with its own garden – and that's important, of course – then Iris, having seen that there's nothing wrong with the house, will come home again. Her baby was born there, but it didn't live, poor mite, and that's why she's taken a dislike to the place, which is quite absurd, of course.'

Here it seems necessary to say that Lady Sybil's daughter, the Marchesa Iris Origo, became known some years later as the author of *The Last Attachment*, perhaps the most informative and scholarly of all the books written about Byron and his involvement, not only with Teresa Guiccioli, but with Italian politics; and during the war that began in 1939 Iris proved her possession, not only of a learned and critical mind, a literary gift commensurate with her task, but also of a heroic temper about which – if my memory holds as far as that – I shall say something in a later chapter. Sybil, however, may have been speaking the simple truth of Iris's aversion to the *ambiance* of the Villino, and, if that is so, we were indebted to her as well as to her mother's generosity when we moved from Lerici to a more distinguished abode under the great garden-wall of the Villa Medici. That lovely house, of noble elegance, gave Fiesole a third tier – the grace of the Renaissance – to top a crown whose lower diadems were the Roman amphitheatre and the Etruscan wall.

'Quite comfortable,' said Lady Sybil of the Villino; but to us it seemed large, splendid and luxurious, with a garden bigger than a football-field under the long, towering wall – capped by forty great stone urns – which divided us from the greater garden of the Villa. But the division was penetrable. Sybil and Percy told me, one after the other, 'We've quite a lot of books in the house, and you must feel yourself absolutely free to come in whenever you want to, and take anything you like.' They had, indeed, a library which filled three large rooms, in each of which was a complete set of the works of Henry James: Sybil's three husbands, I gathered, had been united in their admiration, not only of her, but of him.

For much of our time in Fiesole Sybil was in poor health, and lay in bed. It seemed to me – but I may be unjust in this assessment – that Percy Lubbock preferred to keep her there. A woman so delightful – of such unpredictable Irish charm and waywardness – was undoubtedly difficult to live with; and it may be that Percy found her less difficult when she could be persuaded that she was ill. In Lerici we had heard, from local gossips, that she was a remarkably strong swimmer, and that Percy – frightened she might swim off some day to join a passing yacht – had persuaded her that she was delicate, and to preserve even a remnant of her health must spend five days a week upon her pillows. And in Fiesole she showed a sudden, astonishing convalescence when Percy, in obedience to a gloomy telegram, had to go back to England to attend the funeral of a brother, an uncle or some such near relation.

The following morning I went up to the Villa, to take back two or three books and borrow some more, and found Sybil brightly dressed, a gay little hat on her head, a parasol in her hand, and brightly she said to me, 'What a nice day it is! Would you like to take me for a little walk?'

The little walk, and the necessary return, covered two or three miles – all within the property she owned – and in one of our several conversations with peasants who lived and worked on the estate I heard a phrase which subsequently became of great value to me. She talked for a long time to two plump and genial, loudly laughing women, and after we left them, said: 'You remember the one called Maria? Well, in 1918, when the Italians were fighting the Austrians, but neither of them really wanted to fight, and in fact didn't do much fighting unless the Germans came down to watch them – rather like prefects, you know, when little boys don't want to play football because it's raining – well, on one of those occasions Maria's husband was reported missing, and poor dear Maria cried her heart out for week after week. But then that other woman – the slightly fatter woman, she's called Annunziata – she cured Maria by saying, "Oh, he'll turn up again! We all know him, and we all like him, but the fact is that your dearly beloved husband lacks the *dono di coraggio*, so instead of stupidly waiting to be killed, he has probably gone off and joined the Austrians. And when the war is over, he'll come home again." And so he did,' said

Sybil. 'He deserted, very sensibly, and saved his life, and he's still here. And a very good, honest, hard-working man he is.'

Ten years later I began, in Rome, to write my novel of war in Italy called *Private Angelo*; and to Angelo my hero – no anti-hero, but a true one – I ascribed the same deficiency: in a conventional judgment he lacked the *dono di coraggio*. The phrase, as I have since been told by many friends, is ungrammatical, and I have no doubt they are right; but peasants in Fiesole were not all well educated, and I preserved their choice of words as a footnote, so to speak, to my abiding gratitude to Lady Sybil Lubbock. I shall add that for two or three days we had our walks together, and Sybil under her parasol and sparkling little hats was the gayest of companions. But then Percy, having completed his family duties, his funereal exercise, returned to Fiesole, and the following day Sybil had a mysterious relapse, and was again confined to bed. Percy was a scholar and an influential writer, and it may be that Sybil was no more to hold or to bind than a will o' the wisp; but as a companion I much preferred her.

We made other friends in Florence, of whom the most notable were Norman Douglas and his publisher, Pino Orioli. To Norman – I was still, in those days, absurdly shy – I showed myself too openly respectful, which did not please him – he preferred amusing companions – and our tenuous friendship was sustained only by his curiously continued interest in his Scottish background. I knew, fairly well at that time, the neighbourhood of his ancestral acres and could give him local gossip and tell him about the planting of larch or spruce on nearby hills, the growth or decline of next-door properties. At home in all Europe, Norman Douglas remained stubbornly and sentimentally a Scot. I think, indeed, that he admitted no sentiment except for Scotland, small boys, and good food, good wine; and I was admitted to his table because I could talk about the landscape of his forebears. But one's approach to Pino Orioli was much easier. Pino was a rascal, and utterly delightful. I laughed with Pino, I drank too much with Pino, we became – as though we had been born in neighbouring villages – companions in a careless ease. And, far more remarkable than that, Pino and my mother-in-law became close-chuckling friends.

She had come out to attend Marjorie in her confinement, and after the baby was born I took Pino to inspect the child and meet Ida MacIntyre, who was a woman of urgent propriety, totally devout, constant in service to charity and her church. Now Pino was precisely her opposite. I doubt if he was ever seriously perturbed by the misfortune of those about him – misfortune is seldom far away in Italy – and even the most credulous never suspected him of piety. But he was sensitive and tactful, naturally kind, and he charmed my mother-in-law as clowns and elephants and piebald horses charm children at a circus. His stories, that he told with alternating simplicity and exuberance, were usually extravagant – sometimes wildly impossible and probably true – and she laughed at them, as the innocent and good can laugh, till she had to wipe the tears of laughter from her quivering cheeks. To Norman Douglas I gave admiration and respect, to Pino Orioli affection; and he, that rascal, looked after Norman's welfare – Norman had no gift of self-preservation – with a scrupulous care, and amused my mother-in-law in an atmosphere of innocence which, for a little while, enveloped both of them.

In Florence, too – the year was 1934 – I met some early victims of German or Nazi oppression, and was moved by indignation at what I heard from them to write an article, published in an English periodical of the time called *Life and Letters*, in which I spoke with a due and proper anger of the brutality already typical of German politics and German prisons. Now in recent years it has sometimes been said, or written, that we in Britain knew little or nothing of the repression and torment of German concentration camps until they became, during the course of war, so notorious that they could not be ignored. That, of course, is nonsense. I in Florence – a person without influence or importance –

learnt enough about Teutonic intolerance and Nazi brutality to write in condemnation of them; and, when I wrote, the German response was immediate.

Messrs Langen and Müller, the presumptive publishers of a German translation of *The Men of Ness*, informed Curtis Brown, at that time my literary agent, that the book had been banned, and indignantly declared – in an English translation of their letter which Curtis Brown politely sent me – 'It simply went against the grain to do a hand's turn for a book by this author after his attacks on the Germany of today. It would interest us very much to learn what Linklater himself thinks about having, through his quite unnecessary political excursions, caused us a loss of many thousands and repaid us so badly for our interest in his work.'

The Men of Ness might have been well received in Germany. By association with a prevalent idea it could have flattered the Teutonic pretension to Norse descent, to inheritance of pagan heroism; but I was a hostile critic of their practice and ideals, and the translation was publicly burnt. About a year later, when the sterility of Nazi thought had reduced, to the trickle of a dry summer, the native production of novels suitable for Germanic reading, I was again approached by a German publisher who thought it might be possible to sell, in translation, *Magnus Merriman*; but was so unwise as to formulate a condition I must accept. In return for his grace and favour I must agree to abstain from further criticism of the Nazi ethic and the Nazi régime. I replied with simple satisfaction: 'No! A year ago Germany banned me. Now I ban Germany.' The concluding article in our correspondence was posted on 9 December 1935, by the President of the Reichsschrifttumskammer, who referred to a letter of 20 September in which he had said 'there is no objection to the personality of the author, Eric Linklater'; he now reversed his opinion and coldly remarked 'this statement is no longer true'. In parting company with Germany I anticipated Neville Chamberlain by almost four years.

From Italy, too, I was attacked with some animosity when I disclosed my dislike of Fascism and its grosser practices; and, when I wrote of Russian Communism that it was an Oriental perversion aggravated by torments and a technique filched from Germanic practice, I was again abused by many who did not share my opinion. I was, however, scrupulously fair in my comparison of the abominations of Communist rule with the unprincipled ferocity of Hitler and his ruffians.

I wrote a light-hearted, most genial novel, called *Ripeness is All*, the mainspring of which was my exuberant delight in becoming a father. I doted – as every young or youngish father must – on my first child, and I was enraptured by the miraculous evidence of growth – physical growth, growth of recognition, emergence of a personality – in my daughter Sally. To be a father and watch one's daughter growing into being, into consciousness – to know the joy of being welcomed by an open, hooting mouth, and eyes alight with knowledge, by hands outstretched – what can match the pleasure of that? I was in love with my infant daughter – in love with my own condition of being a father – and I concocted an exuberant little novel about the joys of parenthood, enforced or natural, that a rich old man's eccentric will had imposed on a heterogeneous set of his potential beneficiaries. But in the temper of the time I could not avoid some comment on the politics of those years, and with a curious anticipation of what has now, I believe, become a recognised extension of traditional art forms, I invented concrete poetry.

One of my minor characters was a young man who wished to be a poet, and to be recognised as a poet, and in pursuance of his wish created a diagrammatic style of poetry-writing, of which I need give only one example. It substantiates my claim to have invented a sort of poetry that was unlikely, I thought, to become popular; and illustrates the perturbation aroused in many people, who had previously thought that Russian Communism represented the uttermost degradation of human practice, by the emergence in

Germany of a terrorism that threatened to eclipse even the dreadfulness of Soviet rule:

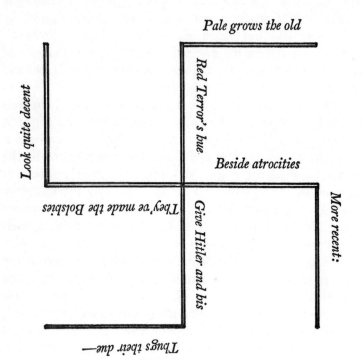

🦁 Fourteen

A COMPETITION in cruelty, a contest of horrors – that is no unfair description of much that has characterised and befouled our century. But humanity – dextrous and slippery humanity – survived the degradations and avoided the deepest morasses of a dark epoch, and left a comment on our times in its open preference for stories of escape: after the war of 1939 and the uneasy, hungry peace of 1945 the most popular books – the most popular by far – were tales of escape from the brutalities and confinement of prisoner-of-war camps. The heroes of the post-war years were the agile, ingenious and determined men who found freedom, against all the odds, from the confinement of odious camps that could be regarded as symbols of a confinement common to, and resented by, an angry and resentful generation.

A few years later the tales of escape were succeeded, in popularity, by stories about animals: beautiful, brilliantly accomplished animals – lions and otters were the favourites – which, though vulnerable on all sides and constantly menaced by the greed and aggression of human-kind, had escaped, by evolutionary good luck, the physical, moral and social problems that bewilder or torture humanity. Readers, who had identified with escaping prisoners, identified ten years later with lions and otters which had avoided, not confinement, but the predicaments of human society; and in a fictional release found passing comfort. Escape or evasion became the most benign and coveted of all adventures.

In many ways my life has been lucky, and luck never played me a better turn than when I married Marjorie who, before our marriage, had spent a couple of summers in

Orkney, in a house her father rented, and acquired an affection for the islands which was ready to go hand-in-hand with my own addiction to their harsh and brilliant, inscrutable and friendly charm. We, by many years, anticipated a mood and motive of escape, and decided to live there. Escape, of course, was not our motive — our motive was the pleasure we anticipated from life in a remote, island community — but escape gave us a large reward. We escaped several problems and every sort of social competition by retiring to Orkney, where competition of any sort was virtually unknown. We were never faced with the astringent difficulty of keeping up with the Joneses, for there were no Joneses in the archipelago. We followed our inclinations, and by self-indulgence uncovered a very happy and remarkable freedom.

We were enabled to do so by my mother's generosity. She had bought and enlarged a little cottage that stood close to the house my father had built, and that house she gave to me. I added to it, and contemplated further addition. What had been the sitting-room of the original building became a central hall in the larger construction, and from it a re-modelled staircase ran straight to the upper storey. 'Man,' said my clerk-of-works, 'thoo'll find that a great convenience as the years go by. A staircase like that, wi'oot bends and corners, is a wonderful advantage when there's a coffin to be carried doon.'

We had many agreeable visitors, but none required a coffin for departure, and at a time when my average earnings came to little more than £1500 a year we lived more richly, more comfortably, than we do now. I used to shoot, and with an old friend from the Grammar School of Aberdeen rented several hundred acres of wild moorland for a modest sum, to give our guests in August grouse for dinner, with lobster to precede the grouse: in Stromness, that delightful little town, I could buy a pair of live lobsters for half-a-crown, and the fisherman would say, 'Would thoo like a few partans, to make a sauce? Tak' what thoo want, boy, there's no charge for crabs.' And Merkister, my house, stood on a small slope above the Harray Loch, which abounded in the best brown trout to be found in Britain. Our visitors, when we were young, were fed on luxuries that cost us almost nothing. And the greatest of our luxuries was that we had servants whom we liked, and who appeared to like us.

Within my expanded house there was a lavatory that opened off the hall, and in summer, when the kitchen windows were usually wide open, one could sit in the lavatory, with its upper window down, and listen to the exuberant conversation of the three maids who served us with genial efficiency. There was a cook, a housemaid, and a nursemaid: they were uncommonly pretty girls, and they lived lives of adventure and emotional extravagance – in theory or wishful thinking rather than reality – that reduced our existence to humdrum insignificance. What tales, what jokes, what wild, pretended confessions, and, above all, what squalls of soprano laughter came out from the kitchen window to be captured through the window of the lavatory where I sat in admiration and envy of those lovely girls! Never since then have we been so richly attended. Never since then have we enjoyed the luxury of a populous and loudly laughing kitchen.

We were very closely involved in the life about us. We took part in amateur theatricals, and dangerously played mixed hockey on steeply sloping fields obscured by a thickening twilight, for games were not played until farm-work was finished, and cows at milking-time were often temperamental. We attended weddings and funerals, and ploughing matches and sheep-dog trials. At hay-time and harvest I helped my neighbours, and found pleasure in forking hay to the top of a tall cart-load, in binding and stooking great golden sheaves of oats. Marjorie sang at concerts organised by the Women's Rural Institute, and played her 'cello in the Kirkwall Orchestra. On a legendary occasion there was a duet for 'cellos, and when at last it came to an end a vulgar woman in the front row said to her neighbour, 'Weel, thank God there was no' a smell wi' it!' But that was before our time. We helped to celebrate the

8ooth anniversary of the founding of St Magnus Cathedral with a splendid pageant, and dutifully pursued the archaeologists who yearly came to open yet another neolithic tomb. I spoke at farmers' dinners, and sailed my boat in local regattas. If we had, in fact, escaped the great world, it was only to become happily imprisoned in a very small one.

In that small world my mother occupied a niche of some distinction. She had an extraordinarily retentive memory, and in a community where good gossip was highly valued, that was a fundamental advantage. To it she added her own delight in gossip, a genuine interest in her neighbours, and a budget of stories about her childhood at sea. To our Orkney neighbours they were as fascinating as, in my childhood, they had been to me. 'You should write a book!' said our simple neighbours; and, to my consternation, that is what my mother did.

She gave me, one day, a rather untidy parcel and said, 'I want you to punctuate this. I've never really understood how punctuation works, or ought to work, but I'm sure you know all about it. And I suppose it should be divided into chapters? I just wrote it out as I remembered, and one thing led to another.'

I began my task without pleasure, for her typing was impressionistic and at first glance her manuscript was shapeless and beyond my power to give it shape. But soon I became aware of design in her story: by luck or instinct she had found a good starting-place, and from that beginning her narrative proceeded, with remarkable confidence, to an assured and timely conclusion. I changed nothing in her story, I added nothing to it. I split and parted and rejoined it. I scattered commas and cemented it with semi-colons, and when Jonathan Cape published it, as *A Child Under Sail*, it was warmly welcomed. It was, indeed, a remarkable story that she told. Much had been written about the vanished world of the great clippers that drove through untenanted seas for a cargo of Australian wool — or with tea came storming home from Canton — and now, perhaps for the first time, such voyaging was recorded from a domestic point of view. As a growing child my mother had been more interested in food than in navigation, and though her story was brightened by memories of Java, or darkened by the great seas of Cape Horn, it was dominated throughout by the immediacy with which small events were seen and shown against the enormous background of the Roaring Forties and a turning globe that would stop, for a little while, at Calcutta or Portland in Oregon.

I shall not blame my mother for all that is unstable in my own character, but I think she was partly responsible for my reluctance to settle down, sensibly and securely, in the comfort I had created. Our life in Orkney gave me pleasure – as much pleasure as I wanted – but not nearly enough satisfaction. It was absurd, I thought, to live in a globular world without going round it. I had, moreover, an idea for a novel which needed a Chinese background, and between Orkney and China lay the warm, brown, humming mass of India, of which I had seen so little when I worked there. Perhaps it was my duty to look at India again?

I returned to the clamorous world from which I pretended to have escaped, and with a ticket to Bombay in my pocket boarded a ship bound for sight-seeing, globe-trotting, and the Chinese background that was so urgently needed for another novel. Marjorie was happily pregnant again, and agreed that our temporary separation would be justified by a book that might pay for the larger nursery we should have to furnish. It occurs to me, now, that one of the major reasons for the long continuance of our marriage is that it has often been relieved by my absence abroad. That absence makes the heart grow fonder is not necessarily true, but that recurrent absence relieves the inevitable stress and strain of marriage can hardly be doubted.

I put to sea in the autumn of 1935, when those austere and splendid ships of the P. & O. Steam Navigation Company still served an imperial purpose and ferried, like gleaming and immaculate buses across the ocean, the officers and servants of the *raj* to their duties in India. That was the year when Mussolini, swollen by monstrous ambition, was sending his armies to invade Abyssinia, and in the Suez Canal we were auditors and participants in a moment of history that glossed his outrageous policy with the bawdy objectivity of that supreme commentator on history, the British soldier.

Somewhere in the Canal we tied up to allow the northward passage of one of our troopships, homeward bound from India. Also tied up was an Italian trooper, outward bound for Ethiopian adventure, and as the two ships approached – each crowded with soldiers – there was a hurricane of cat-calls and counter cheers, of Britannic mockery and Roman or romantic patriotism. Then, in the Italian ship, a tall, vociferous, indignant man mounted to the broad top of a railing, unfastened his trousers, unlimbered a penis of impressive size, and directed towards the British trooper an arc of glittering, contemptuous urine. For a moment there was total silence. Our well-disciplined, innately respectable soldiers were deeply shocked by the indecency of such Mediterranean exhibitionism. But one of them quickly recovered his wits, and remembering a common belief of those days, that the Abyssinians mutilated the dead bodies of their enemies in a very offensive way, shouted across the narrow water in a voice as excessive as the Italian's virile member, 'That's all right, mate! Make the most of it while you 'ave it. You won't 'ave it long!'

Our voyage continued in the happily complacent assurance that our soldiers' cheerful humour was, and always would be, an adequate protection for the fantastical empire that we ruled only by confidence; and blissful indeed was our crossing of the sun-dazzled, azure sea between Aden and the hot west coast of India. Of my sight-seeing, globe-trotting weeks in Rajputana, northern India, and Assam I have already written, and *Juan in China* – the novel that was the justifying product of my journey – records an impression of the tormented country which already was showing signs, not yet desperate, of the chaos and loss of control which would eventually open a way for the Communist horde and the deadly impact of Chairman Mao.

156

When my novel was published, it excited adverse criticism. It was written, some said, in heartless ill-taste: it mocked the tribulations of an ancient people who were passionately seeking a *modus vivendi* that would release them from immemorial tyrannies and a static culture that prohibited their advance towards, their enlargement in, the modern world which was the goal of their most enlightened leaders. So far from being heartless, however, the novel disclosed my immediate response to the beauty, grace, gaiety and dignity of the people of China; it harshly denounced the vulgarity of Japanese aggression; and when it mocked the futility of Chinese leadership – the faction that was more destructive than invasion – its mockery was justified by the witless dissension that had crippled the most populous of empires.

I can, moreover, claim to have anticipated one of the stranger, more improbable elements in the political life of China today, or yesterday: the control of thought, the instigation of opinion, exercised by the aphorisms and precepts assembled in Chairman Mao's little red phylactery. Juan went to China because he had fallen in love with a beautiful, high-spirited, rather dotty girl called Kuo Kuo, who was prepared to fight for the realisation of a patriotic dream. It was her belief that a master-plan for China's salvation had been evolved by Lo Yu, a bandit-general who had retired to a mountain fastness to cultivate his soul and learn wisdom. He had inscribed his plan on a scroll inserted into a length of lacquered bamboo, and the action of the novel largely depends on her dangerous search for that phylactery. When at last she finds it, however, she is disappointed, for the way to salvation is sign-posted only by *Precepts for the Individual and Good Counsel for Government*.

Now in the Little Red Book of Chairman Mao there are such adages and sentiments as:

What we need is an enthusiastic but calm state of mind and intense, but orderly, work.

Don't wait until problems pile up and cause a lot of trouble before trying to solve them.

Such advice is sound and practical, but lacking, perhaps, in imagination. It should be compared with some of the precepts of General Lo Yu, the arcane sage of *Juan in China*:

The rivalry of honourable men is the source of evil and discomfort. But if you do not exalt virtue, there will be no incentive to rivalry.

Do not discuss their unhappiness with the people. When they become dissatisfied with their life, they are also dissatisfied with their government.

Chairman Mao has written:

Whenever problems arise, call a meeting, place the problems on the table for discussion, take some decisions and the problems will be solved. If problems exist and are not placed on a table, they will remain unsolved for a long time and even drag on for years.

In playing the piano all ten fingers are in motion; it won't do to move some fingers only and not others. But if all ten fingers press down at once, there is no melody.

Our fundamental task is to adjust the use of labour in an organised way and to encourage women to do farm work.

It's very sensible and down-to-earth, of course; but I still prefer the near Taoist insight of Lo Yu, who wrote:

If the government does nothing, the people will have no cause to defy it. But for every new law there is a new transgression.

A house without windows is bound to be uncomfortable. A nation without weaknesses is intolerable.

If you admire virtue, do not seek to acquire it for yourself, for then you will lose sight of it. Be content to admire it in others.

I am, of course, prejudiced in favour of Lo Yu, and I do not expect everyone to share my preference. But I am not, I think, unduly arrogant or improperly self-satisfied when I say that his apophthegms are more interesting than those of Chairman Mao; and there is no disputing the fact that he anticipated Mao and his method by many years; for *Juan in China* was published in 1937.

When I left China I sailed from Shanghai to Japan – crossed the Pacific in a roaring gale and the United States in a tempest of rain that flooded several of them – and returned to Scotland in good time to assist at the birth of my second daughter. Then, like most of my contemporaries, I became increasingly frightened by darkening skies, the threat of another major war, and my conscience was lacerated – as were many others – because, in the Spanish prelude to war, I could not see an issue so clearly defined as to command my service on the better side. There was a better side but, as Franco's cause was sullied by his German and Italian allies, so was the apparently constitutional cause stained and confused by Russian aid. Writing, however, was my practice and my trade – perhaps my vocation – and I found the comfort prescribed and designated for people of my sort by writing with passionate intensity a denunciation of war that I called *The Impregnable Women*.

I filched a good plot from Aristophanes, but mismanaged my story because I let emotion involve me too closely in it. In the muddled thought, the indecision and shilly-shallying of our government and those it governed I saw the possibility, not only of war, but of a war declared against the wrong enemy. That such a war had to be stopped was obvious, and the way to stop it, I pretended, was that chosen – in Aristophanes' invention – by Lysistrata. But I made the mistake of describing the new war in terms of the Kaiser's war – it was the same war though we were on the other side – and with sufficient realism I wrote of the heroism and horror of war in a high, resounding style. That entailed description of the counter-war, which the women waged, in a style of mock heroics; and though the women's war was successful, my novel was a failure because my cure for evil was less convincing than the evil I had evoked.

I should have opposed to war a down-to-earth, bawdy ridicule. I should have let bawdy nature be the conqueror, and peace the reward of those who preferred four bare legs in bed to the profitless cavorting of honour and probity and such-like tattered concepts. But I was too serious for that. I looked at war with realistic eyes, and tried to defeat it by a farcical extension of war. And there was my mistake. I should have purged myself of emotion, pushed realism out of the window, and relied on rough and dirty mockery. I might, in that way, have written a better story, but it would, of course, have been equally vain: it would not have altered history. The Book Society, which made *The Impregnable Women* its Book of the Month, was no wiser than I, but we had some excuse for error. A little while ago I reread the novel, and found in it both good intention and some good descriptive writing; but I still deplore a weakness of mind that would not let me separate intelligence from emotion.

Most of us, however, are dominated by time and the temper of our times, and my passionate protest against the threat of war's recurrence turned a sudden somersault when Nazi Germany marched into Czecho-Slovakia and we in Britain – and they in France – made no effective protest. War became doorstep nearer, and now its imminent menace was manifestly our fault because we had failed in honesty and honour. There is little doubt, now, that if we and France had made common cause with Czecho-Slovakia, and with instant indignation – despite our lack of anti-aircraft guns – had forbidden aggression, then Germany's truculence would have shrivelled and retreated. But we were over-cautious, we thought caution wise, and congratulated ourselves on a destructive prudence. 1938 was one of the shabbiest years of our history, and I, because I was a writer and had no need to re-arm – my ink-pot was full – made war, in my own fashion, against the betrayal that had diminished us. I found my new story in a more infamous betrayal, and called it *Judas*. It made no great impact on this country, but in 1946 or 1947 a French translation, published in Brussels, had a *succès d'estime* and sold several thousand copies.

I am writing autobiography, not history, and though *Judas* may be regarded as a footnote to history – for it reflected an indignation that was wide-spread though not general – it has, for me, a private and more persistent interest because it shows, quite decisively, a habit of my writing of which I spoke when I contrasted *The Men of Ness* with *Ben Jonson and King James*. I said then that I let my

5 *Marjorie MacIntyre, 1933*

6 *In Dalecarlia, Sweden*
7 *Merkister, Orkney*

topic determine my style, almost as a sculptor lets his material – marble or wood or clay – dictate the manner of his work; and *Judas* is as different from *The Impregnable Women* as is my Viking novel from my Jacobean essay.

Judas retells the events of Holy Week, and its style is almost as stript and bare as *The Men of Ness*. I told the story in modern terms, as if the betrayal of Jesus were a contemporary tragedy, and I was aware that no attempt to heighten or decorate it could be tolerated. In writing of war it was permissible to insufflate or blow up the story with an emotion proper to it; but insufflation could not intrude on the events of Holy Week. The story spoke for itself, and I added nothing to it except manipulation. I say this without any attempt to pretend that my practice is right – 'There are nine and sixty ways of constructing tribal lays' – or preferable to the habit of writers who impose their own personalities on every page. I advance no theory, but merely declare – as to a Customs officer – the provenance of some articles in my luggage.

For several years I was very much a man of my own time, though perhaps, as a writer, neither typical of the age nor observant of its fashions. I admitted fear, I rebounded in indignation – a reversal of temper that many experienced – and presently I went to a tailor in Edinburgh and was measured for two suits of khaki.

A letter from the War Office – slovenly typing over half a dozen worn-out carbons – requested confirmation of my address, and I was reminded, to my surprise, that my name was still on the lists of the Territorial Army Reserve of Officers. The Lord Lieutenant of Orkney was Alfred Baikie, a man of minute stature and easy, genial authority, and he, a little while later, asked me to go and see him. He had been commanded, he said, to raise companies or batteries of Anti-Aircraft Artillery, Coastal Artillery, and Sappers: 'And I think you should come in and help us. The Ack-Ack battery is over-subscribed, but I can give you a choice between Sappers and the heavy Gunners.'

'I know nothing about either,' I said.

'No more does anyone else,' said the Lord Lieutenant, 'but we've got to try and do what we can, haven't we?'

'I've always hated loud noises,' I said.

'In that case,' said the Lord Lieutenant, 'you had better be a Sapper. I'll send your name in, and I hope you'll be able to recruit your own company.'

❧ Fifteen

I shut the door of my office with a soldierly bang, and stood for a moment, rather importantly, glancing up and down the street.

Two women passed on the opposite pavement, 'Look,' said one of them, 'there's an officer.'

'It's no' a real officer,' said the other scornfully. 'It's only Eric Linklater.'

That was in Kirkwall, towards the end of August 1939, when a khaki uniform was still a rare spectacle. I had just received an order, however, which was soon to make it commonplace, for we had begun to mobilise. As darkness fell on the previous evening the northern sky had caught fire from the long fierce flames of the Aurora Borealis, that climbed to the zenith and suffused it with the red glow, as it seemed, of distant fires. Few of us, who watched that polar blaze, did not feel the shiver of an ancient superstition.

We were, of course, ludicrously unprepared for war. By a late decision – reluctantly accepted, I think – the Admiralty had agreed that Scapa Flow must be the Royal Navy's principal anchorage, and to defend the Flow there were, in the beginning, only a few hundred local Territorials who had had little time to train, and were meagrely armed. On the island of Hoy there were eight anti-aircraft guns, a few old six-inch guns overlooked the southern and western gateways to the Flow, and my Fortress Company had searchlights, a couple of Lewis guns, and its rifles.

The Flow itself was imperfectly closed by a couple of booms that did not quite cover the entrances – there were gaps at either end – and by some sunken ships that were supposed to block the eastern channels. Within that permeable wall, however, there lay, from time to time, the great ships of the Fleet: *Nelson*, *Rodney*, *Repulse*, the aircraft-carrier *Ark Royal*, the battle-cruisers *Hood* and *Renown*, lesser cruisers such as *Aurora*, *Sheffield*, *Southampton*, *Glasgow*, and, among others of their sort, the beautiful and formidable destroyers of the Tribal Class. The Navy was drilled, armed, and ready for action, but for a long time we had no other ponderable defence.

It was on 24 or 25 August that we, Gunners and Sappers, mobilised and occupied our war-stations on the small island of Flotta, at the southern entrance to the Flow, and beside Stromness on the shore of Hoy Sound. Flotta, when we first went there, was an innocent and gentle island where some of the farmers still ploughed behind tall, slow-moving oxen, and golden plover, in calm untroubled flocks, wheeled low above the fields. Within a year or two, however, it was to change its appearance completely, and become crowded with soldiers, a platform for anti-aircraft guns, a windy foundation for untidy villages of Nissen huts, a perilous anchorage for barrage balloons.

In the beginning reinforcements came slowly and erratically, and among the first was a man who made a very odd appearance. The sun was sparkling on Hoxa Sound, laying bright shadows on the harsh rock-face of South Ronaldsay, and I was standing idly by the guns, admiring the view, when over the brow of the cliff, not far away, there came into sight a person who wore a soft black hat, a large butterfly collar, a black coat and waistcoat, and striped trousers. I went to meet him, and learnt that he was a retired naval officer, summoned so hurriedly from his home that he had had no time to change into uniform. At the foot of the cliff his boat's crew were unloading a steel safe and heavy boxes full of code-books: they had rowed against the tide from Lyness in Hoy, and failed to find a proper landing-place in Flotta.

The oddly dressed officer in the homburg hat had come to establish a Port War Signal Station, in command of which there presently arrived a retired captain who in his last employment had been naval attaché to the British Embassy in Washington. With him came three watch-keeping lieutenants of the R.N.V.R., two of whom were Irish – a high proportion, considering the loud neutrality of Eire. A day or two after making their acquaintance I met, in Stromness, a Gunner from the school at Shoeburyness. He had arrived by air, and with him he brought a pair of shot-guns in a handsome leather case, and a black Labrador retriever bitch. So amiable and inoffensive was our earliest preparation for war.

My own officers were three local schoolmasters, all sound and dependable; a farmer of prodigious shoulder-breadth, who had sometime served with the Hudson Bay Company; a debonair young man who had so far not considered life very seriously, but later was to do so in Burma; and an architect so passionately averse to every aspect of military life that neither he nor anyone else could discover a reason, other than sheer friendliness, for his having joined the Territorial Army. We knew all our sappers by name, many of them by their Christian names, and some of them found it hard to abandon use of our Christian names when the formalities of orderly room or parade ground made such familiarity improper. We were decently accommodated in wooden huts, and our food, abominable to begin with, was much improved when a Gunner subaltern, a publican in private life – and a sergeant in the Scots Guards in the first war – consented to be messing officer.

By 3 September we had settled down to an undemanding routine, and though on that day we listened to Neville Chamberlain's gentle, unhappy declaration of a state of war it made little difference to us. Our problems were mainly domestic, and most of them we solved. The army, in the beginning, provided neither underclothes nor gum-boots, and in a northern climate both were needed. We bought boots out of the profits of a canteen that we ran without authority, and organised a simple laundry-service by which, on Friday, dirty socks and underwear were posted to wives and mothers, who washed, darned and returned them on Tuesday. Of my two sergeant instructors one was by nature an accountant, and him I retained as my unofficial paymaster: I knew enough about the unhappiness that could be caused by inattention to pay and allowances to be determined that my book-keeping should be impeccable; and as I could not trust myself to do sums I made Sergeant Davies do them for me.

We were, indeed, very fortunate. We had time to set our house in order, in a domestic way, before we encountered, as a passing blow, anything of the violence of war. That came suddenly, in the very early morning of 14 October, when Lieutenant Prien, commanding U.47, found his way into Scapa Flow through Kirk Sound, a narrow channel between the East Mainland and an islet called Lamb Holm. The channel, foul with reefs and shoals, was one of those thought to have been closed by block-ships. But Prien was a consummate seaman, and at high water he took his submarine through on the surface – it was a clear moonless night – and shortly after one o'clock, having submerged, torpedoed the battleship *Royal Oak*. The ship rolled over and capsized thirteen minutes later, drowning between eight and nine hundred officers and men; and Prien escaped from the Flow on a falling tide.

Oil from the sunken ship spread far across the Flow, evil colours in it gleaming dully when the sun rose, seagulls with matted feathers choking in it – as in the darkness sailors of the *Royal Oak*, trying to swim ashore, had choked – and pebble beaches receiving it as a brown treacherous film. Gloom and dismay spread like the oil, for no one knew what had caused the disaster, but there were those who remembered strange fatalities of the earlier war, in which the battleships *Natal* and *Vanguard* had been sunk by saboteurs; and sabotage carries a worse fear than U-boats. If the *Royal Oak* was also a victim of treachery – 'Oh, hell!' said one of our Irish watch-keeping lieutenants, 'I can't see how a submarine could get in to do it, but I hope to God it *was* a submarine.'

All day in breezy water the small ships of the Navy

searched for an intruder. One of them got a fine echo from a submarine hull that was disappointingly identified as the wreck of a U-boat sunk off the east side of Flotta in the ultimate paragraph of the last war; the skipper of a drifter claimed that he hit a submerged vessel of which, unfortunately, no other proof could be found; and about noon on Sunday – a sunlit day of pale bright colours – there was intense excitement when it was observed that the boom across Hoxa Sound was dragging, and several of its floats were under water. Destroyers and smaller craft gathered about it, and from the overlooking cliff one watched with a hunting eagerness that almost clotted the blood. But slowly the floats came up again, and anticipation faded into bitter disappointment. There was no U-boat there, the enemy had escaped.

The following day I went to Lyness to attend the funeral of a score of sailors whose bodies had been recovered. The survivors who attended wore an impromptu costume of dungarees, white mufflers, and canvas shoes. Many were bare-headed. They stood on one side of a long wet grave that had recently been pumped dry – the pump was still there – but at the lower end water was seeping in again. There were four coffins in it, of deal covered with black cloth, and fifteen or sixteen bodies in canvas. From a distance the survivors looked calm enough and well disciplined, though one of them collapsed when the volleys were fired, but later I passed them on the road, and saw how white and bloodless they were. The bone showed through their cheeks, they had seen death at close quarters, and not liked the look of it. Most of them were very young.

A little while later I went aboard the *Iron Duke*, Jellicoe's old flagship at Jutland, now diminished in status to a floating, well-armed office that lay close to the shore between Flotta and Lyness; and with a friendly paymaster discussed an exchange of guest nights. But there were to be no more guest nights in the *Iron Duke*, for the next day she was straddled by a pair of bombs, and pushed ashore to prevent her sinking.

Tuesday, 17 October was a laggard day of summer, the air warm, with white clouds floating plumply in a pellucid sky. I was talking about a new opening-bearing for a searchlight with Alastair Steele, a Gunner who was to be lost with Singapore, when we heard gunfire and saw, high up, brown puff-balls of smoke fading quickly into white. Ahead of them was an aeroplane with a long thin body, rather like a dragonfly, and from the eastward, from cloud above South Ronaldsay, came three others of the same sort, and the gunfire grew heavier.

Let the date be noted: it was October 1939. Air attack, later on, became a commonplace in many parts of Britain, but then it was a startling novelty, and for a moment or two I felt a slightly choking excitement. It was, for the most part, quite a simple excitement, but there was some admixture of fear.

We hurried from the cliff to higher ground to see what was happening, and watched one of the raiders go down in a long dive – not steeply, like a stooping hawk, but on a slant like a hen-harrier going downhill – towards Lyness in a flurry of machine-gun fire and a puff-ball hail of shells. It disappeared from sight, then rose again, climbing steeply till it met the gust of a shell-burst. It wavered in the blast and, heeling as if to turn and dive, came round and put its nose down. An opening parachute appeared beside it. A thin funnel of smoke, growing longer and longer, came from the tail of the plane, and it went down in a straight line. Our Orkney gunners, in their first action, had scored their first hit.

On the high ground beside Steele and myself were half a hundred of our Territorial soldiers, and when they saw the German raider dropping a few of them began to cheer. But quickly the cheering was muted, to be succeeded by a more restrained approval. With a rather solemn demeanour they stood and clapped their hands. It was a curious sound to hear against the roaring blether of shell-fire, but they had chosen what seemed to them an appropriate and dignified way of showing their pleasure. They were solid men, appreciative of good shooting, but not bloodthirsty.

Another plane was wounded by a destroyer's guns, and then one of the watch-keeping lieutenants came hurriedly and asked me to put a guard over the local post-office to prevent the civil telephone from being used. With that passion for an impossible secrecy so inseparable from war, he said, 'Don't tell anyone, but they've got *Iron Duke*. She's sinking.'

I told Alastair Steele the news, and drove with him to that part of Flotta which overlooked the *Iron Duke's* anchorage. The poor old battleship was leaning down in a tired and tragic list, her port rail close to the water, and the whole breadth of her deck showing. No one could be seen aboard, and her crew and the many administrative officers who lived in her had presumably been ordered to abandon ship. She was being hauled and nosed ashore, a tug ahead of her, and a clutch of drifters under her stern and port quarter like piglings crowding their mother for milk. We saw her pushed safely aground, went back to lunch, and before lunch was over there was another raid warning.

In successive flights fifteen or sixteen aeroplanes flew high above us – too high to be hit by gunfire, and there were no fighter planes in Orkney – and for nearly two hours unsuccessfully aimed their bombs at the ships lying in a ragged periphery round our little island. The morning raid, being short and dramatic, had been popular, but no one liked the afternoon attack. It lasted too long, though it was surprising indeed, when the All Clear was signalled, to learn its actual duration. A good deal of anxiety and rather feverish interest appeared to have been compressed into a solid, indigestible lump of time. The emotional minutes had been fewer but thicker than those of the clock-face.

On the day after the double raid a single reconnaissance-plane came from Germany and flew for a long time above the Flow. But now the Flow was deserted. Having discovered, at some expense, that the enemy could strike it in its anchorage both from the air and through our poor surface-defences, the Fleet had abandoned Scapa, and for the rest of the winter found shelter from battle and patrol in Loch Ewe on the Atlantic coast. That was the winter when Britain and the war got a bad name abroad for insincerity, because, from their frozen lines in northern France, our army and the French made no attack. But in Orkney, all through those cold and stormy months, the islands encircling the Flow were being fortified with batteries of light and heavy guns, with soldiers of many arms of the service, and with passionate labour. In the north there was evidence in plenty of our ponderous and grave intention.

It was, I think, a few days after the beaching of the *Iron Duke* that I was summoned, with other local commanders, to a conference at Headquarters, Orkney and Shetland Defences, in Stromness. Our general, sometime a Horse Gunner in India, was vigorous, swiftly moving, with a thin, bony, claret-coloured face, lively blue eyes, a meagre sward of ginger hair, and a patch of ginger bristles on a long upper lip. His temper could flare fierce as a blow-lamp — there was much occasion for it — and it consumed in its fire many of the obstructions that our ignorance created; but in his private habit — when in friendly company he unbuttoned — Ginger Kemp was a man of immense geniality who gathered affection, not fear.

We had been summoned to discuss what could best be done to meet an attempted landing on our shores. We had been subject to sea-borne attack and attack from the air, and the Fleet had been driven from an anchorage we could not defend: it was not unreasonable to suppose that the Germans would follow up success by trying to put small parties of soldiers ashore to destroy such military installations as we had. We listened to explanation of the general plan for defence, and then, each in turn, we were asked what local and particular instructions we had given to the soldiers in our own commands. I, responsible for a stony segment of the island of Flotta in which it was impossible to dig trenches, replied meekly, 'Don't shoot till you see the whites of their eyes.'

'Don't be a damned fool!' exclaimed our fiery general. 'This is no time for joking, this is a serious occasion.'

'I have, sir, two Lewis guns, each with two drums of

ammunition, and only ten rounds to a rifle. I thought it would be advisable to conserve ammunition.'

'Get him more ammunition, and get it quickly,' said General Kemp, and his A. and Q. – the long-suffering colonel who had to find non-existent supplies, unavailable equipment – was given no chance to reply, for the General was questioning others, still hopeful of hearing a sensible reply. But after that conference we were untroubled by scarcity, for the Fleet would be homeless until the Flow was fortified, and what the Fleet needed had to be found somewhere.

My own command was multiplied. Emplacements had to be made for thirteen or fourteen more pairs of searchlights, foundations dug for the heavy diesel-engines that gave them power, and accommodation provided for thirteen or fourteen new subalterns, each with a team of ten or a dozen men. I spent much of my time at sea, in drifters commandeered from the fishing ports of the Moray Firth – occasionally in an old steam-trawler – as I went from island to island to inspect and report on progress, and learn something of my unknown officers. They were all young men of great good-will, eager to do their best in dull and comfortless surroundings, but few of them had any notion of how to look after the men who depended on them. Warmth and cleanliness in their huts – dry clothes when they came in wet from a cold watch – decent cooking, adequate rations, but no waste – spare socks and regular foot-inspection – a reasonable leniency in the censorship of letters – a readiness to listen to complaints, but little sympathy for those who complained too often: these were some of the things that a subaltern had to think about, as well as his weapons and equipment, and their proper maintenance; and only one of my new officers had a natural aptitude for his unceasing tasks. He, in the absurd but common phrase of those years, was 'a roaring pansy', and a very good officer indeed.

❧ Sixteen

IN 1940 I rebuilt a condemned house, lost command of my Fortress Company, revealed my conspicuous ineptitude as a Sapper, and launched a weekly paper, *The Orkney Blast*, which, I think, was the first of the Service newspapers to make an appearance. 1940 was a year of gross and calamitous disruption, and we in Orkney shared, on the small scale of our local activity, the falling-apart which characterised that alarming period. The homely structure of our Territorial Army – or that part of it committed to Coast Defence – was reorganised, on paper, and on more paper patched up and organised again; torn apart, or threatened with dislocation, then given yet another system of command and division of responsibilities. It would be infinitely boring to describe in detail the uncertainties that perplexed us, the changing policies that bewildered us, and I have no intention of cataloguing the commands and counter-commands I received. It is relevant, however, to say that the Territorial Army had been built on the strength of local association, and when that association was broken – however good the reasons for its rupture – there was widespread anger, and commanding officers had an uncomfortable task in explaining, to soldiers who had enlisted under clearly defined conditions, that those conditions were no longer valid but their zeal in the service must be undiminished, their loyalty unimpaired. 'Ce n'est pas magnifique', we said, 'mais c'est la guerre'.

It is with great pleasure that I remember an occasion when I obeyed an order which had no relation at all to any known chain of command. In the expansion of our forces there was need for a new headquarters, and in Stromness a house, condemned as unfit for habitation, had been acquired. Could I reinforce, refurbish it, and make it safe and suitable for a couple of senior officers and a small clerical staff? But of course, I replied. Then do so immediately, I was told, and from their several stations I brought in a few carefully chosen men – a plumber, a mason, a joiner, a painter, a couple of sturdy labourers – and assuming an authority which was clearly necessary, though I asked no one to define it, I obtained the materials they wanted, and within a week or two the house was not merely as good as new, but better than it had ever been before. A few awkward bills came in, but it is easier to get authority for payment after work has been done than to seek authority in anticipation for work to be done.

The immediate result of my labour was unexpected, however, for in the principal room two lieutenant-colonels and one major – all of them bright red in colour and bald enough to dazzle the ceiling with reflected sunlight – sat jealously round a table too small for them. The elder colonel, a Territorial Gunner of stubborn disposition, had been superseded by a younger man, but refused to recognise his successor; and his successor was disinclined to admit his predecessor's existence. I, as the architect of our new building, had an obvious right to a place at the table, but to maintain our rights, real or pretended, regular attendance was necessary; and there were mornings when one or other of us had nothing better to do than write letters to long-forgotten cousins or aunts in Manitoba and Kuala Lumpur. By the beginning of May we were alternating between manic determination and a depressive inability to write anything at all; but then the situation in France deteriorated, and I got orders to prepare the house for defence.

A consignment of Mills bombs arrived, several dozen in wooden boxes each containing twelve. I took them out to our little back-garden – there was a lawn rather bigger than a billiards table – and opening one of the boxes examined, with gingerly care, the once-familiar corrugated grenades it held.

There was the detachable lever, there the split safety-pin and the ring by which you pulled it away. I had better see, I thought, if the detonators fitted. A little copper detonator filled with fulminate of mercury – 'The warmth of a warm hand is enough to explode it,' we used to be told – and a short length of pliable safety fuze: that was the igniter system, and what could be simpler? But the safety fuze wasn't pliable; it split and cracked open when I squeezed the detonator in. I tried another and another – half a dozen of them – and the same thing happened. Then I went in and told the colonels that the bombs weren't safe to handle. 'Possibly sabotage,' I said darkly. The bombs – so far as I know – remained in the garden for the duration of the war, and the following morning I sat in undisputed occupation of the good front-room which had been so uncomfortably overcrowded.

The German invasion of Norway again brought bombs to Orkney, and created a mood of taut expectancy. From the beginning of the year Scapa Flow and its circumference of islands had been under regular surveillance, but air-raid warnings signalled only the arrival of one or two Heinkels on reconnaissance until 16 March, when eight aircraft flew in just before dark and dropped about a hundred high-explosive and incendiary bombs on shipping in the Flow and two aerodromes. It was an evening of mist, thickening into twilight, that defeated the searchlights, and though the raiders came under fire from about thirty heavy and many light anti-aircraft guns they left no burnt-out carcasses, no positive evidence of loss. Nor did they score a hit on any military target, but wrecked some cottages at the Bridge of Waith where a man was killed – the first civilian casualty in Britain – and four people were wounded.

Then, on 2 April, a raid of about the same strength met resistance of an unexpected sort. The raiders, following the path taken by their predecessors, and arriving at about the same time of day, flew into a three-dimensional barrage. That almost solid defence, which filled a segment of the sky with exploding shells, was the brain-child of George Tuck,

General Kemp's G.S.O.I.,* who in plotting the altitude and density of the barrage had been helped by the shrewd and imaginative Commander of an Anti-Aircraft Regiment. A practice-barrage had already been fired, that persuaded naval observers it would be effective, but from the high authority of Anti-Aircraft Command brought stern reproof for the unauthorised expenditure of valuable ammunition. Authority was quick to acknowledge its mistake, however, and for their success, costly though it was, the General and his ingenious G.I. were warmly congratulated both by the Admiralty and the A.O.C.-in-C.†

A few days later a larger raid, that did no damage, was driven off, but the Luftwaffe was still busily interested in the Flow and its defences. The last raid, of any consequence, came in on 16 April, when it was estimated that more than sixty enemy aircraft were in the sky. There was ample warning of their coming, they were engaged by our own fighters, and in the three-dimensional barrage that met them some 1400 rounds were fired by Orkney's fixed defences and a vast number by the many ships at anchor in the Flow.

There were French and Polish ships as well as the familiar vessels of the Royal Navy, and our friendly visitors poured into the sky a many-coloured hail that broke about the invaders in coruscating showers of lethal brilliance. The attack lasted for more than two hours, and lost or wounded Heinkels were heard above the darkened islands for a good deal longer. With excitement and admiration I watched the battle from a little hill above Stromness, and when it was over I drove home: Stromness, by then, was over-full of khaki uniforms, and I was billeted in my own house. As soon as I reached it I heard above me the uncertain engines of an invisible but low-flying plane, and with sensations that alternated between a recognition of necessity and a suspicion of play-acting I patrolled, for perhaps half an hour, the moor behind my house with a loaded revolver in my hand and a nagging doubt in my mind: if the lost Heinkel crashed –

* General Staff Officer, Grade 1.
† Air Officer Commanding-in-Chief.

sometimes it sounded very near – should I advertise my advance with a couple of shots, or should I loudly declare that mercy was my motive and I was coming to the help of a probably wounded crew? Fortunately it was a question I had not to answer, for the unseen enemy, whose engines were now stuttering badly, flew off into the east.

That was the final threat, of any magnitude or serious intent, to Orkney's defences, and I think it appropriate to say how fortunate we were, in those islands, to have had sent us, at the start of the war, a few officers of outstanding professional capacity and a temper, widely differing one from the other, but united in a natural independence of mind that let them abide by their own judgment and pay little attention, if attention was ill deserved, to the many directives issued from above.

There was Admiral Binney; there was Ginger Kemp, sometime a Horse Gunner in India; there was George Tuck, a Sapper and therefore, by military definition, an intellectual. When Kemp and Tuck arrived, in September 1939, they had no staff to smooth their way; they had no help at all except what we, willing but untaught Territorials, could offer; and the Royal Navy, the protection of whose northern base was their prime purpose, had, to begin with, no use for them. In the innocence of that year the Navy was assured of its own ability to protect itself against both U-boats and hostile aircraft. The Navy was wrong, of course – how often its judgment has been at fault, and its victories have derided its lack of judgment! – and very soon A.C.O.S.* and fiercely frowning Kemp were on the friendliest of terms. Kemp, Tuck and a saturnine Colonel Jones, their Ack and Quack,† were the pioneers who had to prospect before they could begin to create the defensive system which, by the spring of 1940, had so clearly demonstrated its efficiency that the Luftwaffe, thereafter, made only desultory approaches, and the Germans, from the Norwegian coast that lay not much more than two hundred miles away, made no

* Admiral Commanding Orkney and Shetland.
† A.Q.M.G. (Assistant Quartermaster-General).

attempt to launch sea-borne raids which, if effective, might have altered the balance of Naval strategy.

The French ships, which contributed the fiercer hues of the many-coloured barrage in April, had come to carry and escort a brigade of Chasseurs Alpins who were to assist a British assault on Namsos, while two British brigades attempted a landing at Andalsnes. The British expedition was botched from the start, but my present task – I repeat what I have already said – is not the writing of history, but the recording of some small events which I remember for the pleasure or pain that tangentially related me to history. Before our ships sailed to Andalsnes I met, aboard one of them, an old friend who was very dear to me.

While the news from Norway was still confused – but taking on a darker complexion – a signal came from a hospital ship, newly arrived in Scapa Flow, that peremptorily commanded me to go aboard. Much perplexed, I persuaded the skipper of a drifter to give me a passage, and when we came alongside I recognised, among the officers looking down from high above us, the mocking face – so strangely unhandsome but dear to all who knew him – of Osborne Mavor, the Glasgow doctor who in the theatre made himself improbably famous as the dramatist, James Bridie. He was, at that time, in his early fifties, but he had got himself re-commissioned in the R.A.M.C., and he wore a khaki tunic so comfortably shabby that it was obviously a relic of the first war, in which he had served in the deserts of Mesopotamia and on the romantic venture into Persia, and across the Caspian to Baku, that General Dunsterville commanded. He had already made a voyage to the eastern Mediterranean, and he was now on his way to Andalsnes.

Neither as man nor dramatist has Bridie ever been adequately described or sufficiently explained. In a very intelligent study, of him and his work, Winifred Bannister* labelled him, in obvious despair, an enigma; and it is true, I think, to say he was *sui generis*. In a short introduction to that study I wrote:

* James Bridie and his Theatre (1955).

It seems to me that Bridie, as a man, was as good as any man need be, and better than most can hope to be: sheer goodness of character – an intertwining of charity, courage, a wayward and passionate sincerity, a benign and stubborn instinct for creation – is a major strand in the riddle, and, perhaps to make it more difficult, goodness is tightly knotted with a brilliant cord of indomitable gaiety. Gaiety is not a major factor in the intellectual mood of our time, and it may seem an improbable constituent in a man who had suffered much from the malady of shyness, and whose charity precluded neither violent prejudice nor a classical suspicion that man, the 'droll wee slug wi' the shifty e'e', was infected by an incurable complaint. But gaiety lies in almost every convolution of the Bridie riddle: it ruled much of his conversation, it danced in his argument, it shines through the texture of his prose, and it compelled him – James Bridie, who was no reformer, but a man with a fine talent for idleness – to undertake a vast and laborious reform of the city of Glasgow, and endow it with the permanent gaiety of an indigenous theatre.

He could, perhaps, be called a romantic Calvinist who disguised himself in Harlequin's motley. He was an extravagant man, and lost reputation by reckless joking; but hilarity and high seriousness lived together, in his capacious mind, like Siamese twins. In a brisk, agile comedy called *Mr Bolfry* he raised the Devil and exposed his natural alliance with a pious country minister, the Reverend Mr McCrimmon: both are aware that the very pulse of life is its divine purpose. In another play, *The Sleeping Clergyman*, he committed himself to the flat-footed assertion that 'to make for righteousness is a biological necessity'. As a student in Glasgow he had played the lead in a long-remembered harlequinade, and later he was said to have been to the University what Queen Victoria was to the Victorians; it was also said, with less truth, that throughout his life he remained a Glasgow undergraduate.

He loved argument as Izaak Walton loved angling – or Petrarch his Laura – and argument is the staple of his plays. But he lived with one foot in the old world of the Border ballads, and for him there lingered in a life of action the obstinate smell of poetry. So off he went to Andalsnes, where his ship was bombed, took aboard a cargo of wounded men and was bombed again, but came safely home. It was then decreed, by anonymous authority, that James Bridie at the age of fifty-two was entitled only to duller employment, and Bridie, quickly bored, returned to the theatre and the controversy he there provoked. Glasgow, his own town, never appreciated him at his proper, adult worth, and when a long, painful illness extinguished his native gaiety 'he for a little tried to live without it, liked it not, and died'. It was more than a pleasure – it was great comfort – to meet him on the broad expanse of Scapa Flow when the outcome of our contest was still undecided.

There were many, much younger than Bridie, who had died before the survivors of that hurriedly conceived, ill-managed venture into Norway began to return from Namsos and Andalsnes and Narvik, and in Orkney there was considerable embarrassment when their ships arrived. There were some, unruly or depressed by their experiences, who were not allowed to leave their ships, and others, though permitted to land, were as straitly confined as if they were in prison: husbands and sons were forbidden to write or telephone to their anxious wives and wondering fathers, and Orkney lay under a fog of silence created by canonical reverence for 'security'.

For some months we continued to expect sea-borne raids from Norway, and from time to time a general order was issued that reiterated a policy of total resistance to any hostile attempt to land upon our shores. The garrison was again reinforced, and by Christmas we had, I think, about 12,000 combatant troops in the islands, and in the following year that number was enlarged. By the end of August, however, it was fairly clear that the Germans' interest in Orkney was diminishing, and on Christmas Day it was a wholly unexpected pleasure to see some of our opponents at close quarters.

In the stress and uncertainties of summer it had been decided to evacuate a number of women and children, and despite my protests and hers – hers were louder than mine – Marjorie, my two small daughters, and my mother were among those deported. Then, by some carelessness or failure of reason, a few newly arriving officers were allowed to import their wives and families; and one of them – a Sapper with the euphonious name of Paul Postlethwaite – became a welcome tenant in my empty house. At Christmas he and his wife kindly invited me to share their turkey and plum-pudding, but scarcely had we sat down when we were roused by gunfire to the west, and from my doorstep we saw a German bomber, one of the sort called Ju.88, in obvious difficulties a few miles away. Jumping into a motor-car, Paul and I drove with all possible speed – my motor-car was small and far from new – into the parish of Sandwick where the bomber was reluctantly descending; and on our way there we were rewarded by the splendid sight of an elderly woman – thick-set, darkly clad, between fifty and sixty years of age – marching in great haste across a sloping field towards the scene of action she anticipated, and for which she was prepared: slanted across her left shoulder, she carried a twelve-bore shotgun.

Neither she nor we, however, were needed to subdue the four occupants of the disabled Ju.88. A local company of the Home Guard was at exercise near the field where the Germans landed, and, quickly arriving, prevented them from blowing up their machine. Paul and I – he was a regular Sapper and knew what to look for – removed some little packages of gelignite and, remembering it was Christmas Day, offered our cigarettes to the disconsolate quartet, one of whom had been wounded by fire from the fighters that brought them down. 'There is no need to give cigarettes to him,' said the white-faced flight-lieutenant commanding the aircraft. 'He is not, like us, an officer.' To the wounded man who was not an officer I gave my packet of Gold Flake, and with a rebuke that seemed called-for, but in my gentlest voice, said to the flight-lieutenant, 'I think, when you are talking to me, you should stand at attention.' To my great surprise he, and the two others who held commissioned rank, responded with a disciplined alacrity that I had seldom seen in my own Territorial Company.

Long before that, however, I had had to accept my decreasing authority in the Orkney garrison. Reorganisation, of a sort finally approved, became effective, and Gunners took over responsibility for the searchlight stations I had lovingly established. I had become redundant at a time when I longed to be usefully employed.

As my command dwindled and approached total dissolution I was allowed to seek other employment, but found no one anxious for my services. At one time, indeed, an offer seemed imminent from M.I.5, but I laughed at the wrong time – I made an inappropriate joke – and that prospect faded. Then I was sent to the School of Military Engineering at Ripon in the hope that I could absorb sufficient instruction to make me eligible, with reduction in rank, for a field company; and that was an opportunity I gladly accepted, though its consequence was lamentable.

The School of Military Engineering had removed to Ripon from its old foundation in Woolwich, and brought with it some of the dignity and formalities of its former home. Once a week, on guest nights, the long tables reflected a gracious light from ornate silver, and young officers grew impatient as they watched the slow procession, in noble decanters, of vintage port and wood port, of sherry and madeira: eager to go out and frolic with the girls who waited for them, they had no sympathy with a ritual that I, sitting among their seniors, gravely enjoyed. The madeira – warmly recommended by an elderly major with whom I became friendly – was excellent, and I relished the amiable, rather ponderous conversation that accompanied it. Then, on a Sunday morning after church, we gathered about the Commandant and his lady, exchanged polite nothings and harmless comment, and with some married officer – well cared for by a loudly confident, brisk wife – drank a glass or two of sherry. All that sort of activity or inactivity – a way of life that survived from the year before yesteryear and calmly ignored the rude circumstance of war – I watched as if it were a play comfortably at ease after a long run; but too many lectures and field exercises were like rehearsals in a language I could not understand for a play that required aptitudes I did not possess.

Three or four years later – in Italy, I think – I met a young man who had been a fellow-student at Ripon. 'I remember', he said, 'an occasion when we were sitting at our desks, wrestling with a quite impossible calculation, and you broke the silence – we were all grateful to you – by loudly exclaiming, "I don't mind digging holes and putting out barbed wire, but at my time of life I'm damned if I'm going to do sums!"'

As well as my inability to do sums, I had to admit larger incapacities. As others may be witless, so am I 'handless': I have no gift for using tools, and machinery – like a horse under a nervous rider – refuses me obedience. I remember a night exercise in which we were supposed to demolish a railway bridge, and all my little parcels of imitation gelignite fell off because I am almost night-blind, and I could not balance myself on a nearly invisible girder and simultaneously tie parcels in the proper places. Even more humiliating was a water-borne exercise, because from infancy I had been at home in small boats, but the boat I had to steer – a sort of tea-tray with inflated sides and an outboard motor – would only go round in circles.

Everyone was helpful and sympathetic, but I returned to Orkney with the inescapable sad knowledge that I had revealed, as a Sapper, my total ineptitude.

In Orkney, however, I won a short reprieve. General Kemp and George Tuck, his G.S.O.I., had decided that the troops of their scattered garrison needed a newspaper. After the Germans' defeat in the air battles of 1940, and their failure to launch sea-borne raids against Orkney and Shetland, it had become fairly clear that an alternative enemy – which also had to be taken seriously – was boredom. The soldiers must be given information, entertainment and a continuing reminder that they, and their work and amusements, were important enough to be written and read about. George Tuck was sympathetic, highly intelligent – inevitably he became a general – and had the sensible habit of delegating duties and authority.

'You', he told me, 'have at the moment very little else to do, so you can busy yourself with plans to produce and edit a weekly paper. We can't keep you here as editor – you wouldn't want that, anyway – but it's up to you to get it going and then hand it over to someone you think suitable: you'll have to look for him. But your first job, I suppose, will be to find newsprint, which is rationed nowadays. Do you think that will be difficult?'

With the General's authority to amplify my voice I went to Edinburgh, where Scottish Command was sympathetic, and our supply of newsprint was assured. There were two weekly papers published in Orkney, whose machinery was made available at a modest charge. Distribution was arranged, local commanders were interviewed and pledged support. Advertisers were wooed, contributors cajoled, and a dummy was printed: four pages, full newspaper-size, price twopence. There had been some debate about a suitable name, but I thought *The Orkney Blast* appropriate, and Captain Heath, the Camouflage Officer, designed a pretty title-piece in which a mermaid in partial uniform – she wore a cap – saluted a genial Sergeant Neptune who with one hand drove a pair of sea-horses, and in the other held a tankard of beer. Heath also drew strip-cartoons of which the heroine was Audrey Allbust, newly recruited to the A.T.S.

For the first number General Kemp wrote not only a message to the troops, but a short, hilarious thriller called 'The Crime of Lord Hoy'. Storer Clouston, Orkney's distinguished historian, contributed a long article on St Magnus Cathedral; the Provost of Stromness wrote entertainingly of bird life in the islands; there was a story about Nel Tarleton, sometime Featherweight Champion of the Empire, who had lately spent a few weeks in Orkney; Audrey Allbust made a promising appearance; and I wrote the first of a dozen columns in imitation of Beachcomber – but a Beachcomber whose interest was confined to Orkney.

Most important of my tasks, as founder, was my search for an editor. I made up and edited the first number, published on 17 January 1941, and then handed over responsibility to Private Meyer. My legacy to him was eleven pseudo- or *ersatz* Beachcomber columns – no more than that – but within a couple of weeks he was writing his own Agony Column under the name of Geremy, and the paper had acquired a settled form and an almost professional look that promised the long life it was to enjoy. Geremy remained in the editorial chair throughout its life, and when at last peace was declared he decided to remain in Orkney. For some twenty years – more, perhaps – the local paper, the *Orcadian*, has been edited with high competence by him in partnership with *ci-devant* Lieutenant Hewison, R.E., who in 1939 was the youngest of my subalterns and survived his adventure in Burma.

I had more success in establishing a newspaper than in demolishing railway bridges, but that was my last contribution to *la vie militaire* in Orkney.

✣ Seventeen

I was rescued from unemployment – or employment in some pedestrian office, as a Railway Transport Officer, perhaps – by a telephone call, late at night, from the War Office, where Walter Elliot had lately been appointed Director of Public Relations. Walter was an old friend, from their University days in Glasgow, of James Bridie whom I had last seen aboard a hospital ship in Scapa Flow; and for several years I had known him, casually indeed, but closely enough to have acquired both affection and admiration for him. In the first war he had served gallantly and won a Military Cross and Bar as Medical Officer to the Scots Greys; but he was an intellectual with an untimely sense of humour, and his promising political career – at one time he had been Secretary of State for Scotland – had been halted, according to popular belief, by his habit of interrupting Cabinet meetings with jokes too apposite for his colleagues' liking, or too erudite for their comprehension.

His voice came faint and distant from Whitehall. 'I hear you've lost your job and are likely to be unemployed,' he said. 'Would you consider coming to work for me?'

'There's nothing I'd like better.'

'Well, that's settled. I want you to go to Iceland immediately.'

'How immediately?'

'Can you leave Orkney within forty-eight hours?'

'Yes, I think so.'

'Then report to N.O.I.C. at Invergordon on Wednesday morning – he'll have your instructions – and there'll be a flying-boat waiting.'

'Thank you, sir.'

'Good luck, and I'll see you in London when you've done your job. It may take some time.'

There was no difficulty in leaving Orkney. I had nothing more to do, and to General Kemp and George Tuck I said good-bye with unfeigned gratitude for their long kindness. I crossed the Pentland Firth, took train to Invergordon, and a few hours later boarded a Sunderland flying-boat and flew to Sullom Voe in Shetland. We could go no farther till the weather cleared, for the North Atlantic was a howling wilderness of gale-driven clouds. But in Sullom Voe, where the Royal Air Force had established a stormy base, I had time to read and meditate my instructions.

I was to compose, for publication by the Stationary Office, a pamphlet in which I would describe – with unfailing accuracy but in a manner designed for popular reading – the peculiar conditions of garrison service in our northern outposts: Iceland, the Faeroes, Shetland and Orkney. It would also be useful, said my new master, if I could find time and opportunity to write confidential reports on the political temper of Iceland and the Faeroes, about which contradictory accounts had been received, but I should not be in a hurry to leave Iceland. I might find it possible – if the ice melted early in the Denmark Strait – to go as far as Greenland.

Walter Elliot was not merely an intellectual burdened by a sense of humour; he was also a romantic. He had heard that the Americans were installing meteorological stations in Greenland, and it was possible – just possible – that their interest in meteorology coincided with some obscure strategic purpose. If I could find out what sort of people the alleged meteorologists were, deduction might be possible. Americans, moreover, were notoriously the most hospitable of people, and from Greenland they would certainly fly me back to Boston, New York or the Navy Yard at Norfolk, Virginia. There was already a small trickle of air traffic across the Atlantic, and I could probably fly back in a bomber. The only part of the programme for which I felt a positive and immediate dislike was flying the Atlantic in a bomber; but I need not have worried.

In January 1941 the weather at Sullom Voe was cold and brutal, but the company was warm, and when the gale moderated there was great pleasure in returning to our Sunderland. Those heavily armed, ponderous seaplanes had been built like ships, and there was a sense of space and freedom – even of luxury – in being able to climb from the lower deck to the upper, and there stand with one's head in the crystal cover of the astral-hatch to watch, with the intimacy of an almost physical contact, the approaching architecture of the ever-changing sky. Nor was material comfort lacking: in the flying-ship there was a useful galley, and in honour of my fellow-passenger, a general, a three-course luncheon was served. In those Spartan days – when rationing had already begun to bite, and flying-machines were less familiar than they are now – there was marvellous satisfaction in eating a steak-and-kidney pie fifteen hundred feet above the heaving, white-hooded Atlantic in latitude 62° north.

Darker than the driving clouds showed, on our starboard side, the tall, iron-black crest of Syderö, southernmost of the Faeroe isles. Nothing after that, for a long time, but the furrows of the sea that a westerly gale was ploughing. Then, high in the sky, a streak of snow and under it a beach, level and vast and black. That was Iceland: lava flats and the snowy crest of invisible mountains. Ingolf Arnarson's first view of the empty land to which he sailed from Norway, in 874, may not have differed greatly from our landfall.

We turned west along the land, and saw a lonely house or two. The sky cleared, and the ribs of the mountains shone. Glaciers without movement came pouring down, and waterfalls stood frozen and amazed. On a yellowish plain more houses appeared – one every twenty miles or so – and Hekla rose in the distance, the snow on its shoulders like a fleece in the sun. We climbed to 5000 feet to cross a range of cindery hills, and discovered a bewildering panorama of blanched volcanoes, of intrusive fjords and league-long pools in the plain. We came gently down – here the air was calm – and motored towards Reykjavik over a dappled sea. We had been seven hours in the air.

An island bigger than Ireland, almost roadless, depending from the Arctic Circle, where summer is without night and winter monstrously dark. An island which is a desert table-land, two thousand feet high and sprouting to six or seven thousand, surrounded by a narrow fringe of river-cut plains where life is possible. An island of active volcanoes and perpetual snow: Vatnajökull is a glacier bigger than Corsica, but to mitigate the ice the land is perforated by springs from which boiling water spurts. That was the country of which our soldiers, valiant in their innocence, took possession in May 1940. To their surprise and perturbation they were not welcomed by the inhabitants.

The Icelanders are a stiff and stubborn people, ruggedly independent. They were deeply offended by the invasion of foreign troops, and few of them could be reconciled to the fact that our occupation of their island was dictated by strategic necessity: if the Germans had established bases in Iceland and the Faeroes, advantage in the battle of the Atlantic would have swung disastrously to their side. The Germans had to be kept out, and there was only one way of doing that: we had to arrive first. Many Icelanders, however, would have preferred a German garrison to ours. For some years the Germans had flattered them by taking an intelligent interest in all manner of things from Icelandic literature to the younger people's eagerness to learn, from German instructors, skiing and gliding. Some of the older people were graduates of German universities, and the Nazis had been trying to maintain an academic connexion by offering higher education at a low cost. But we had never paid much attention to Iceland. A few rich Englishmen had fished Icelandic rivers, but none of them knew anything about the Laxdale Saga or the poems of Egil Skallagrimsson. England, said the Icelanders, counts for little in the modern world; England is effete. But for German efficiency they had a superstitious regard.

Slowly their hostility retreated, and grudging tolerance replaced it. For that improvement our soldiers were responsible. Many were Yorkshire Territorials whose common sense and sturdy geniality quickly recommended them, especially in the smaller places and outlying districts where an official policy of frosty indifference to their presence could hardly be maintained. Within a few months it was widely admitted that the foreign troops were behaving extremely well. The Icelanders were honest about that, and with the emphasis typical of their speech would say, 'The conduct of your soldiers has been unbelievably correct.' There were motherly women, indeed, who approved of their daughters going to a dance with the soldiers: 'An Englishman will bring her home again, but her own boy-friend gets drunk, and she has to take him home.' And, of course, the garrison brought a lot of money into the country. We bought local produce – mutton and milk and fish – and paid good wages for labour. Amicable relations were firmly established, but the occupation never evoked enthusiasm.

The soldiers, for their part, endured the discomforts of an Icelandic winter with extraordinary good humour, and showed a chameleon's adaptability in their acceptance of the roaring gales, the frozen deserts, and the distant isolation of a land so utterly unlike anything they had ever known in Huddersfield or Bradford. Not all was desert, of course, nor gales constant. Reykjavik had the comfort of its hot springs, there were flowers in shop windows; but most of the north lay blanketed in snow.

I took ship, after some weeks in the south, for a roughly tossing voyage to Seydisfjördur on the east, and thence to Husavik on the north coast; and at Seydisfjördur the snow was so deep that the lanes which led from one hut to another were as deep and narrow as trenches in the first war: two young officers claimed to have skied across the camp. Here – because there was no communication except by sea, and often the sea was unfriendly – the company in residence lived almost entirely on basic rations and its own resources, and occasionally suffered the sort of misfortune which people in towns have never known. Each of the huts was lighted by a couple of paraffin lamps, and if someone was so careless as to break their chimneys the hut lay in darkness till the next ship came.

They had the pleasure, however – when the days lengthened – of training for arctic or mountain warfare. Someone, indeed, had thought it possible to extend their range of movement by sending, from the north-west of Canada, sledges and dog-teams: husky dogs of the sort that opened the Yukon to prospectors and were, as every schoolboy knew, fiercely untameable. But the huskies had never met English soldiers before, and the soldiers had forgotten they were untameable. Within a week or two – it was cold in the north – the huskies were sleeping with the soldiers, and being so privileged would no longer condescend to work for their living. The soldiers would harness them to their sledges, and utter the strange words of command they had been taught; but the huskies, hearing those friendly voices, came back on their traces to fawn upon their masters and make slobbery, ingratiating noises. Operation Husky was a failure.

It was, I think, at Husavik on the north coast that I met an officer who had served, for two consecutive terms, in the Somali Camel Corps and was, he told me, one of the few possessors of a senior certificate of proficiency in the languages of Somaliland. His presence in Iceland was obviously due to clerical error, or the geographical ignorance of someone in the War Office, but he had not complained of his posting; he had always wanted to learn to ski, and he liked Husavik. Both there and in Akureyri I found many who thought themselves lucky to be so well situated. The north, they said, was vastly preferable to the south of Iceland, and much more bracing. Down in Reykjavik or Hofnafjördur, they said, it was very muggy. You might as well be in England. But up here – 'Well, in summer this is going to be a positive sun-trap.'

I returned to Reykjavik by sea, through the Denmark Strait and down the west coast; over against Greenland, I was told, the ice lay far out, it would be late in the year before it melted. I thought of the romantic mission that Walter Elliot had suggested, and the prospect of accomplishing it receded. But I still had work to do – there were other camps I wanted to visit, or exercises to watch – and a few more weeks passed quickly away. Then I found some friends in the Naval base at Hvalfjord, and by them I was told that the Greenland ice might not melt before July. I could find no excuse for staying as long as that, and having sent my master a discreet signal, I requested permission to leave.

Then, while I waited for a ship, I became involved, at ground level, in an aerial drama that moved me greatly. Spring had come suddenly to the south, the air was mild, the frozen earth was melting. I found someone whose duty would take him to a camp near Thingvellir, and who had time to go a little farther, to Great Geysir. It was a laborious journey, for at intervals we had to get out and dig, where the road was dissolving beneath us, but a few miles from Geysir we came into unexpectedly rewarding company. A vastly scattered flock of pink-footed geese were flying in the same direction. They were tired after their long ocean journey, and flew slowly, a few feet above the ground, so that we had two or three pairs level with our right-hand window, a pair or two close beside us on the other side, and twice we had to stop while a courting pair, on the road ahead, made conversation and lightly, joyfully, caressed each other. It was an extraordinary sensation to be on such close terms with those noble birds, those gallant voyagers. They had come home across a desolate, enormous sea, and found sanctuary in an arctic wilderness. There were hundreds of them, weary but unafraid. They tolerated our presence, and it was curiously gratifying – absurdly but certainly gratifying – to be accepted by them.

Then, as if to announce our pleasure with a steamy flourish, Great Geysir spouted. He had been encouraged, it is true, by a large lump of yellow soap, but the emission was spectacular. All about him were little muttering puddles, circlets of hot mud that puffed and bubbled, or weakly piddled, and did no more. They were like a dull, resentful crowd, brooding their grievances but lacking the spirit, the power to speak and act, that would exalt their discontent and give it form and expression. But then, as their sudden champion, Great Geysir spoke for all. His ejaculation rose straight and high, with a hissing roar, and a mantle of steam enclosed him. The sky receded – or so it seemed – as if appalled by earth's explosive anger, and though the demonstration lasted only a few seconds we were cogently reminded of the power that lies beneath us. H-bombs, the mushroom release of the forces of fission and fusion, are trivial weapons in comparison with the subterranean arsenal that our wandering globe so snugly carries.

8 *Eric Linklater in 1944, from a drawing by Michael Ayrton*

9 *Pitcalzean House, Easter Ross*
10 *The Pitcalzean Highlanders*

❧ Eighteen

I LEFT Reykjavik a few days later, in fine weather but with a somewhat uneasy mind. Two small ships had been torpedoed, the night before, within fifty miles of land, and there was a rumour that the *Bismarck* was out and about in northern waters. We did not wholly believe that, because rumours in Iceland came gushing from the earth as numerous as hot springs; but we had not quite enough faith in scepticism to reject it altogether.

Our ship, a vessel of some fifteen hundred tons, had once traded quietly between London and Glasgow, but now was serving as a convoy rescue-ship. We would join a convoy somewhere to the south of Iceland, and if any ship in it was torpedoed, bombed, or struck a mine, we should hurry to the scene and pick up survivors. There was a surgeon on board, and a sick-bay. Rope-ladders were coiled in readiness to be thrown over the side, and a couple of rafts, triced to the rigging, could be let go in a few seconds.

It was a Thursday, about midday, when we went aboard, and our escort was already waiting. Two little ships, about a hundred and sixty feet long, that had been built for catching whales in the chill neighbourhood of South Georgia, were to look after us on the first part of the voyage, and for rather more than twenty-four hours they led us into a desolate sea that, hour by hour, grew more deeply ridged and colder. The wind in the funnel-stays made a melancholy harping, and fulmars glided rail-high or skimmed the crumbling edges of the waves. There was no other sign of life.

We were in ballast, very light on the water, and rolled heavily. But our escorts, smaller and with gun-platforms to make a heavy top-hamper, rolled fantastically, so that while he on the starboard was showing all his deck he to port would be exposing half his bottom. Then, late on Friday afternoon, after an hour or two of searching here and there — now plunging head to the waves, now rolling deeply, now lurching before a following sea — we discovered, far away on the port bow, something that looked like a small town. There was smoke, and a tiny row of dark excrescences that might have been the chimneys of a village street. Slowly we came nearer, and the chimneys became funnels, the houses were revealed as the upper parts of a merchant fleet. There were thirty ships in the convoy, and they were heading a little south of east.

Our leading escort, after a conversation with Aldis lamp, handed us over to a destroyer. He turned again for Reykjavik and as he headed north, facing the sea, his flaring bows threw curtain after curtain of spray bridge-high across him.

We took station in the convoy. It was sailing on a broad front, in eight columns, with a destroyer patrolling ahead, a destroyer astern, and corvettes like outriders on either flank. It was very pleasant to be in company, and as we examined our company more closely, and found it good, the sensation became exhilarating.

The thirty ships were of many different shapes, and of different nationalities, but all were alike in being deeply laden. Their holds were stuffed to the limit with war-gear for Britain, and many had cargo lashed upon their decks. Ahead and to starboard we could see a sturdy freighter that carried, in full view, half a dozen American fighter-planes. On the other side, on a strange-looking vessel that sprouted derricks on either flank, were two submarine-chasers, American mosquito-craft. And tankers, low in the water, were full as eggs with fuel for our ships, our bombers and our tanks. It was a goodly convoy, and as slowly we perceived the richness of it we felt, as the most urgent desire of our hearts, a straining wish — it grew to be a prayer — that all might come safely home.

Darkness in those latitudes was short, and in the very

early morning the ships again were visible. We grew familiar with them, and searched the several columns to make sure that all were there. The weather was improving, and we ran mostly before a following sea, though every little while the course was altered, and the wind would come now on one quarter, now on the other.

Suddenly one of the destroyers swung to the west and put on full speed. A couple of broad fountains showed where she had dropped a pair of depth charges, and presently we heard the *crunch-crunch* of their explosion. The convoy, which had been heading due east, turned sharply with a blowing of steam-whistles to the south-east, and a corvette joined the destroyer in a circling hunt. There was an enemy in the deep.

But their quarry escaped. Their quarry was cunning and may have hidden himself below the convoy, where, in the passage of many ships and the thresh of many screws, the listening ears of the destroyer would find it hard to distinguish the particular note of a submarine. In the afternoon the steel hull of our ship again echoed the shake and the *crunch-crunch-crunch* of depth charges. Again, in interlacing circles, destroyer and corvette went hunting their elusive prey. Two flying-boats appeared from nowhere, as it seemed, and joined them in the search.

A little while before darkness came, one of the smaller ships fell to the rear and stopped. From her funnel blew a billowy unceasing cloud of steam. Her engines had failed her.

An hour or so earlier a Swedish tanker had had similar trouble, and fallen behind. The convoy reduced speed to seven knots till she had made repairs, and caught us again. To see her in distress, and threatened with desertion – for the convoy must go on – had filled us with anxiety, and our feeling of relief when she rejoined us was streaked with elation and sprinkled with joy. But now this little freighter was in more serious trouble and night was very near. She grew smaller on the horizon, and dusk enshrouded her. To be left in that Atlantic loneliness, with an enemy, it was likely, fathoms deep but waiting to surface at the cruel and proper moment, was a fate one shrank from contemplating.

Then, most gladly, we saw a corvette turn back. The convoy went on, but the corvette would stand by the troubled merchantman. Some young lieutenant in his first command, with a crew half-trained – landsmen six months ago – would patrol the darkening sea, and watch with straining eyes, listen with ears alert, for an ocean-beast to break covert and attack. We went to bed more cheerfully – but kept our trousers on.

Sunday morning came with sunshine and a calm sea. We looked immediately for the freighter, and there it was, in its old position in the second column from the left. It had made its repairs under the watchful eyes of the corvette, and rejoined us at dawn. The sun shone more brightly, and all the ships put on a gayer look. Black hull and buff topsides were handsome against a sparkling sea, and an olive-green Norwegian tanker – at which we had grumbled yesterday, because when changing course it nearly ran us down – was now, to clearer sight, a gallant picture. We were very close to the ship that carried aeroplanes on her deck, and their sleek painted bodies looked swift and beautiful.

The war at sea was punctuated by formal battle only at long intervals, but war at sea was continuous, and I had been watching a fragment of its daily routine. Few people, except those engaged in it, ever knew much of that dreary, deadly contest with unseen enemies – a contest that demanded ceaseless watch and never relaxed its assault on nerves and imagination – but it was, I think, the only continuing exercise of the second war which could be compared with the protracted brutality of trench-warfare a generation earlier. The crews of the little ships – frigates and small corvettes – which escorted Atlantic convoys suffered, not only the strain of constant danger, but constant discomfort of the most violent sort. Rolled to starboard, rolled to larboard – swept by breaking seas – in the winter months they were never dry, and their crews ate from plates that slewed in their hands as if they were picnicking on the edge of an earthquake. If I, suffering for my sins, were given a choice of punishment, I think I would prefer a month in the Salient to a month aboard a Flower class corvette on Atlantic convoy duty.

On our voyage from Iceland we were fortunate. Our escorting destroyers were two of those ungainly, factory-funnelled vessels that we had acquired from America in exchange for some West Indian bases, and before we saw land there was another *crunch-crunch* – a deep-sea shudder that shook our responsive hull – which detached, from its memory of long idleness in the Philadelphia Navy Yard, one of our American purchases for urgent investigation. A corvette followed her four tall funnels, and their hunting was serious and prolonged. The convoy went on, and we lost sight of them. That night we made good progress, and before noon on the following day we could see, through a drifting haze, a grey shape of land. An hour or two later there was land on either side: Scotland on the one hand, Ireland on the other. Our thirty ships, deep laden, had brought their cargoes in, and pointing the other way – pointing westwards – we saw another fleet. Unlike our gravid flock they rode high in the water, They were outward bound and empty, seeking more provision for our hungry larder.

I retired, for a few days, to an overcrowded cottage near Melrose. One of those slightly insane edicts, characteristic of wartime, had banished from Orkney the wives and families of serving officers, and Marjorie was living in exile under the Eildon Hills; with her were her sister Ida – whose husband, a Royal Marine, was at sea – and my mother. I had no orders but to wait for instruction to join another ship, which would take me to the Faeroes, but I was not exempt from domestic duty. 'I think', said Marjorie – when I had been at home for three or four days – 'you should take the children for a walk.'

'It's going to rain,' I said.

'Nonsense! The sky's clearing, it's going to be a lovely afternoon, and they need exercise. Ida had a difficult time with them this morning, when we were at church. They were very fractious.'

They were self-willed little girls – Sally aged about seven, Kristin a couple of years younger – and far from complaisant when we set out, across country, towards the Eildon Hills: they had always had an innate dislike of what parents called 'exercise' and they regarded as punishment. But for a mile or two, exhilarated by sunshine and green grass, they skipped and ran, and appeared to be enjoying themselves. Then, however, the sun was veiled, dark clouds emerged from beyond the hills. There was a drizzle of rain which became a downpour, and the children began to cry. I lifted them across a fence and said, 'We'll go down to the road – it's quite close – and we're not much more than a mile from home.' – 'A mile!' they exclaimed.

By the time we reached the road they were crying angrily, and on a Sunday afternoon there were a good many other people, walking for pleasure but surprised by the rain, and now hurrying home under the umbrellas with which they had thoughtfully furnished themselves. Most of them looked with sympathy at my blubbering children, and many, with disapproval, at me. I had been to church, I was very well dressed in my better suit of khaki – Sam Browne belt and strap darkly gleaming – and I carried a little swagger cane. From the frowning faces of the passers-by it was obvious that they suspected me of having used it to beat my wretched daughters. What other reason had they for crying?

I grew almost as unhappy as Sally and Kristin who, with lungs like a piper's, maintained with unabating vigour their bellowing complaint against the weather. 'Listen,' I exclaimed in desperation. 'Listen to me! I'm going to tell you a story about two little girls I know – '

'Who are they?'

'That's what I'm going to tell you. They're extremely naughty little girls, but that's not their fault. They're naughty because of something that happened on the moon.'

'On the *moon*?'

'That's what I said, and the very first thing they did . . .'

I caught their attention, they stopped crying, and with invention spurred by sheer necessity I began my story. I spoke in a very loud voice, to subdue an occasional whimper, and by the time we reached home they had forgotten their discomfort and were listening intently.

Marjorie came to the door and exclaimed, 'They're soaked to the skin! Oh, poor little Kristin! My poor dear Sally!' They began to cry again, and indignantly she demanded, 'Why did you take them so far? And why on earth didn't you carry an umbrella?'

'I don't carry an umbrella when I'm in uniform,' I said.

'Well, you ought to,' she answered, and hurried the children away to undress them. I gave myself a whisky and soda, and thoughtfully sat down to write. A story – the beginning of a story – which had persuaded two wet and angry little girls to stop crying might have some virtue in it, and it would be a pity to forget what embarrassment had so urgently compelled me to invent. I wrote three or four pages – odd notes, a possible outline of the story – and refilled my glass. My sister-in-law came into the room, and asked what I was doing. 'Keeping the wolf from the door,' I said.

My reply bore the accent of truth, for the story I had begun was eventually published as *The Wind on the Moon*. I wrote it, at long intervals, during the next two or three years, and it came out in 1944. It was successful far beyond my expectation, and still brings me a little comfort. Those dear children, bellowing their anger.... How grateful I was!

I enjoyed a few more days in that overcrowded cottage, then sadly said good-bye, and with lively anticipation boarded a ship for the Faeroes.

Old sailors called them 'the Faraways', and their remoteness is matched by their strange appearance. To the visiting eye, approaching from the sea, they are a geographical menace. Among overfalls and the anger of the tide their tall peaks rise from an iron-grey sea to iron-grey clouds that conceal their upper parts, and the slope of the land is so precipitous that nothing, one feels, can grow on it, and no man subsist. But on shore the view improves, it becomes cheerful in the stir of human endeavour, and with the colours of early summer it shows a surprising gaiety.

At Torshavn the quay was crowded, and in little boats like miniatures of Viking longships there were red-capped fishermen coming ashore, many of whom had added to their catch of ling and haddock a feathery bundle of razorbills, puffins and guillemots. The great cliffs of the islands carry a population almost as numerous as that of the seas beneath them, and birds give the Faeroese more food than their fields. I went ashore, to be greeted by an officer of the Lovat Scouts, and immediately it became apparent that I was in a land far more friendly than Iceland. The Faeroese are philoprogenitive, and we were surrounded by eager, inquisitive children; but as we walked away the officer who had come to meet me was halted, every few yards, by a loudly genial citizen of Torshavn who had some scrap of local gossip to share. 'They seem to have adopted you,' I said. 'And some of us', he answered, 'are in danger of becoming more Faeroese than the Faeroese.'

The people of the Faeroes are, in habit and temper, fully as independent as the Icelanders, their instinct for freedom is as native as their appetite for *skerpikjot* – which is wind-dried mutton with the consistency of toffee – and thirty years ago they exceeded the Icelanders in enterprise. But they, unlike their farther neighbours, had immediately welcomed our small occupation force, and for that there appeared to be several reasons. They are instinctively a friendly, hospitable people. They were, at that time, hurt and angered by Denmark's immediate surrender to the irresistible force of German invasion: Denmark had had no option – Denmark was to show its spirit in later years – but Denmark was their parent land and they were offended by their parent's admission of impotence. And – for a third reason – the War Office had made an inspired decision when it dismounted the Lovat Scouts and scattered them through the islands as garrison troops.

The Scouts were Highlanders – a whole squadron was Gaelic speaking – and they settled down among the Faeroese like cousins who had come to visit their relations. They adapted themselves, without apparent difficulty, to the loneliness of service on the smaller, farther islands. They accepted, without complaint, the wildest tossing of the seas – the high-pitched turbulence of the tidal stream that ran past Big Demon and Little Demon – as they went to and fro in a little drifter that had escaped the German occupation of Norway. They maintained, to a remarkable degree, a smart appearance, a well-drilled bearing. And to their ceaseless duty of patrolling hill-high paths and hidden fjords they brought a tireless ability to walk great distances with easy speed.

I went out with one of their patrols – they were festooned with arms and ammunition, blankets and rations and cook-ing-pots, while I carried nothing but a long Highland walking-stick – and to me, panting uphill, they talked with animation, out of inexhaustible lungs, and philosophised about the differences between the Faeroe language and their own, about Faeroe food, farming, fishing and housekeeping, about the purpose and progress of the war, as easily as if we were standing, arms propped on the bar, in a Stornoway pub. There was another day when I watched, from a com-manding height, a squadron advancing against a defended locality, and the familiar exercise acquired uncommon interest from the art of those who led it: in civil life they had been stalkers, and they made such good use of the ground – moving at speed under invisible contours – that they looked like the foremost rivulets of an advancing flood, flowing into channels designed by nature for them.

Among their pipers were two or three of exceptional virtuosity from South Uist, where piping is a serious art, and I remember a still grey evening, with the sea murmurous on a hidden beach, when one of them played that great pibroch, 'The Lament for the Children', with such explicit phrasing and poignant expression that it sounded like a universal threnody for youth, condemned to death in war or dis-illusion in peace. About four years later, when the war in Italy was newly over, I went to look for the grave of a young man who had been killed, and whose parents I knew; I found it, and not far away, in hilly land, were the graves of six or seven Lovat Scouts; and in my mind, like a distant echo, I heard again the McCrimmon pibroch.

In the Faeroes, however, they were lucky and escaped the fatalities of war. Occasionally it rattled a window-frame, and one morning, wakened by the staccato hammering of a machine-gun, I looked out and saw, hurrying away, a big seaplane that had stooped in wanton brutality to assault a small open fishing-boat. But the Faeroese were not easily perturbed, and never daunted. They were lively and imaginative, they had been bred to hardihood and lived on what they took from the towering cliffs of their western sea-face, or the tempestuous seas that surrounded them. They filled their larders with the puffins and guillemots that they snared on the dizzy heights of seemingly inaccessible ledges, they fished as far as Greenland in the old wooden boats they had bought from the south of England sixty years before. Their houses were neat and prim, their little towns were roofed with waving grass – not now, of course: nowadays all is modern, bright and prosperous – but their turf roofs grew flowers in summer as if to proclaim their native gaiety. And when the Icelanders, after some of their trawlers had been sunk by German bombers, refused to sell their fish in Britain, the Faeroese took over a dangerous traffic, and despite some loss of life continued to carry Iceland cod and haddock to Aberdeen.

A few days before I left Torshavn I said to the Colonel of the Scouts, 'Can't you put it in orders that every single man – and married men who aren't happy in their marriage – must take a Faeroese girl home with him? A big influx of Faeroe blood is just what Scotland needs.' But Army Council Instructions made no provision for the exercise of such benign authority, and the opportunity was lost. I had, by then, done all I had been told to do, and reluctantly I enquired when I could expect a passage south, and what sort of vessel might give me passage. I failed to get a positive answer, for communication with Britain, though not entirely haphazard, depended on circumstances. But then the fortune of war came to my help, and I was included in a salvage operation.

A tanker, deep in the water with a great cargo of petrol, had been attacked by a German bomber about a hundred and twenty miles west of the Faeroes. A bomb struck the vessel amidships, on the starboard side, and blew away the bridge. Piercing one or more of the tanks, it set the escaping petrol on fire, and, as if in a furnace, all the upper part of the ship was burnt to utter ruin. Nineteen of the crew were killed, but sixteen managed to get away. The ship was abandoned in a cloud of flame and filthy smoke. And then, without exploding the other tanks, the fire mysteriously went out, and the ship, still deeply laden, remained afloat.

Two rescue-tugs were sent to bring her in. They found her wallowing in the Atlantic swell, her port rail level with the sea, and her rudder jammed. They boarded her and made fast their cables, but because her helm was hard over, and could not be freed, she would not tow in the ordinary fashion. They had to shift their cables and tow her, slowly and clumsily, stern-first. They brought her to Torshavn and anchored her under the shelving side of Nolsö, the island that lies like a breakwater eastward of the port. It is a peaceful island, and its little village – it used to be said – was more backward than most of the Faeroese hamlets. Its inhabitants bred ducks in large numbers, and played a game like croquet.

But the arrival of the tanker disturbed their peace. Soon after its coming a German plane flew out of a cloudy dawn, machine-gunned a lonely hill, and apparently noted the position of the rescued hulk. Two days later a Condor flew along the sound and dropped four bombs around the tanker.

In the meantime the crews of the rescue-tugs had been hard at work. They got the ship's rudder straightened, and succeeded in trimming her by pumping out a flooded tank on the one side, by sealing and filling a damaged tank on the other. The ship now rode on nearly an even keel, but still, for some obscure reason, was quite unmanageable. An attempt was made to tow her, but she behaved with so contrary a motion that she had to be brought back to her anchorage under Nolsö.

Then the naval authorities sent Tom Mackenzie to the Faeroes: Mackenzie who raised from Scapa Flow the German fleet that scuttled itself after the first war; who knew all there was to be known about salvage, and was diagnostician in excelsis, bone-setter in chief, and miraculous healer to all marine wreckage. Mackenzie spent a day aboard the tanker, and by evening announced that she was ready to sail. I had known him, in a casual way, for several years, and when we met in Torshavn he asked me to go with him. I packed in a hurry and joined him aboard an armed trawler.

The weather had been fine, and the glass was high, but about eight o'clock a strong breeze sprang up, and the tugboat skippers were reluctant to put to sea. Mackenzie pointed to the hills, from which the clouds were lifting as though sucked away by the westering sun, and to the upper sky. There was no carry in the sky, he said, and the wind was local. They would up-anchor and go.

His judgment was right, and the sea beyond Nolsö grew calm again. But suddenly the tanker made a wild sheer to port, and while the tugs were valiantly straining to the south, she was pulling viciously to the east. A tidal stream, running from the islands, had got under her, and for an hour or two her progress was wayward as an ox on a rope. But before nightfall she had settled down and was towing steadily, though still with an obstinate nose to the east.

We were five ships altogether. There were the two tugs, snub-nosed and sturdy, with the yellowish hulk behind them, and on either flank a trawler for escort. Very early in the morning, when a grey light was shouldering off the meagre dark, we were joined by an aeroplane, a Hudson of Coastal Command, and for hour after hour it circled widely above, watching the sky and the sea for enemies. About eleven o'clock it was relieved by another of the same sort, which continued the guard.

The day was fine, with a calm sea, and there was no

interruption to our progress till mid-afternoon, when suddenly one of the tows parted. We had been making good speed – nearly seven knots – and we were about half-way to Orkney. It was exasperating to be brought to a halt, and to see our prize, so vulnerable, lie still upon the water.

Aldis lamps began to speak, from tug to trawler, from trawler to the aeroplane. 'Tug has parted its tow,' we informed the Hudson. 'Bit of a bugger,' replied the Hudson philosophically, and continued its spiral guard. 'How long will it take you to get your tow aboard?' we asked the tug. 'One hour to haul it in,' he answered.

The tow-rope was eighteen inches in circumference, as thick as a man's thigh, and to haul its great length from the sea was a tedious job. We steamed up and down, and passing close to the tanker saw that the wire hawser by which the rope was made fast had parted near the fair-lead. The nose of the tanker, always worrying to work away to port, had slowly fretted through it. To pass the time we went alongside the tanker, and I boarded her with Tom Mackenzie.

Never was a more desolate sight than that rusty tanker. Her bridge had disappeared, all of it but some steel decking, bent like a bow, and some twisted stanchions, and this remnant drooped miserably overside. There was a great ragged hole in her deck, surrounded by thick petals of torn steel, and from here the fire, gushing like an oil well, had clothed the whole ship in flame. All her stern part, the after-bridge and the accommodation under it, had been burnt to a shell. The long cat-walk, from bridge to after-bridge, had been contorted by the heat, and sprung apart. Her main deck was buckled, and nowhere did an inch of paint remain. Her naked hull had covered itself with rust. And in little heaps of débris on her deck – little rubbish heaps of red dust – were hard fragments of bone. Swallowed in the furnace of escaping oil, many of her crew had been burnt to death.

But the bulk of her cargo remained. There were nearly eight thousand tons of petrol in her holds, and the ship herself might be repaired, or at the worst broken up to make valuable scrap. She had escaped fire and a Condor – and the glass was still high.

Two hours went by, a long hundred of slowly dragging minutes. Then the tug, having made fast a new cable, began to pay out his tow. He rang his engines to half-speed ahead, and the rope straightened. Too fast, too fast, we thought, as the rope lifted and like a sea-serpent leapt from the water. Too fast, he'll break it! There was thirty-five hundred horse-power in the tug-boat's engines, and a huge dead weight behind.

But he slowed in time, and gradually the tanker began to move, and the two tugs, side by side like carriage horses, went steadily on. A little white wave showed at the tanker's stem, and quite suddenly we were all happy again.

Just before dusk, on the port bow, a rocky shape grew visible on the horizon. 'Foula,' said the captain of the trawler. 'The edge of beyond.'

At four o'clock on the following morning I returned to the bridge. It was not dark, but not yet light enough to see very far. But quickly the sky cleared, and far away on the one side was the tall broken back of Fair Isle, and on the other, barely visible above the sea, like a pencil lying on a shadowy table, the flat island of North Ronaldsay. By breakfast time we were in Orkney waters, and a little later, with fighter-planes above and the guns of a shore battery ahead, our escort duty was done.

Commodore Tom Mackenzie and the tugs had saved another ship from Germany and the engulfing sea.

❧ Nineteen

Walter Elliot, himself both gallant and generous, had the faculty of being moved to admiration by gallantry in others. It was he who decided that some attempt must be made to record – for the praise of their contemporaries – the courage and military virtues of the Riflemen who, by their defence of Calais in May 1940, had done so much to make possible the evacuation of our defeated army from Dunkirk. And to me he gave the task of sieving what evidence was available – of gathering material, a patch here and a patch there – to make a story as authentic, as close to the truth, as was possible when most of the witnesses were either dead or prisoners of war.

I had written a pamphlet called *The Northern Garrisons* – seventy-two pages, published by the Stationery Office at 6*d* – and my next job was going to be more difficult, though by a printer's measure it would be only half as long.

'On the 22nd and 23rd May, 1940, a small British force was disembarked in Calais. Its purpose was to keep the port open and establish lines of communication with Dunkirk. A rather sinister attention was by then focused on Dunkirk; though few people had yet thought of it as the gate whose opening or closing would mean life or death to our continental Army.' So I began a story which mounted in tension, was obscured by the traditional fog of war, but was dominated by a stubborn purpose that dissipated the fog and let the fortitude of a dedicated garrison show as clearly as the light on Pharos in Egyptian darkness. Within four days the battle was over, but those four days were of vital importance:

Between Calais and Dunkirk the French were given time to flood and hold the Gravelines water-lines, and this was a decisive operation in the successful rearguard action that permitted the evacuation of more than three hundred thousand French and British soldiers. The scythe-like sweep of the German divisions stopped, with a jerk, at Calais. The tip of the scythe had met a stone.

The little garrison, commanded by Brigadier Claude Nicholson, consisted of about three thousand men of the 60th Rifles, the Rifle Brigade, Queen Victoria's Rifles, a Tank regiment, and some Gunners. I got much material from a Major Williams, M.C., who had been taken prisoner and promptly escaped, and from Rifleman Hosington, D.C.M., who had escaped from forced labour in Poland and found freedom by way of an underground railway that ran – as if it had been plotted by John Buchan – to the Danube and the Black Sea. In those days the strangest stories demanded belief; dull stories roused a suspicion that they who told them had something to conceal. It may have been Williams who told me of having seen a corporal of Queen Victoria's Rifles – sent to buy wine because the water-mains had been cut – who, on Friday the twenty-fourth when most of the town was burning, punctiliously enquired the price of half a dozen bottles, and politely paid.

Both Williams and Hosington remembered, not only shell-fire and the lapsing noise of the sea, but the insistent song of nightingales. The nightingales, not long arrived from Africa, were in full song and throughout the battle were as melodious by night as the guns were harsh by day. Another Rifleman survived to complain that on Saturday, when Calais was a small inferno, he was stopped by a Military Policeman as he ran down a ruined street with a message. 'Name and number?' asked the Red Cap, and booked him for being improperly dressed, in that he was not carrying a respirator.

My account of the defence of Calais was no more than an interim report, but even a fragment of the story was worth the telling. The Stationery Office published at 4d. a large edition which was immediately sold out. The pamphlet, I have been told, is now a collector's item, and any copies that survive may be worth twenty-five shillings or more. None, alas, of my larger works has appreciated to that extent.

Almost immediately I then began to sew another patchwork quilt: the story of the Highland Division, the 51st, of which the greater part went into involuntary retirement after being surrounded – its ammunition spent – at the little port of St Valéry-en-Caux. In May the division was skirmishing in the valley of the Saar, in front of the Maginot Line. It traversed France and came within sight of the sea. It fought before Abbeville, and on the Bresle. Then, caught in the rout of France, two of its brigades, or what was left of them, were trapped on a morning of rain and the miscarriage of their plans, and forced to surrender. To Scotland the news came like another Flodden. Scotland is a small country, and in its northern half there was hardly a household that had not at least a cousin in one of the Highland regiments. The disaster, for a little while, seemed almost overwhelming, because, to begin with, nothing was known of what happened to the 51st except the apparent shame of its surrender, and the capture of nearly six thousand men.

To all Scotland the 51st had been a source of pride. In the first war it had earned an esteem that came close to veneration, and when war was renewed there were few who did not expect it to certify its reputation with victories that would match its triumph at Beaumont Hamel. No one – except, perhaps, in nightmare – had dreamt of its defeat, and many refused to believe that it had been ordered to surrender. Victor Fortune, the Divisional Commander, was an outstanding soldier and a man of great gallantry: his friends indignantly repudiated the very thought of his issuing such an order.

Some years earlier I had met General Sir Arthur Wauchope, who as High Commissioner of Palestine and Trans-Jordan had been a benefactor of both Jews and Arabs, and as sometime Colonel of the Black Watch was a revered, historic figure. He wrote me a long letter in which he warmly argued that there should be no public assertion that the order had been given until Victor Fortune – then a prisoner of war – could tell his own story and give his own reasons for whatever action he had taken. If I committed myself to outright statement I would only rouse fruitless and bitter controversy, said Wauchope.

I went to those northern parts of Scotland, where the 51st was being re-formed, with the knowledge that, like Agag, I must walk delicately; but I was comforted when my hosts assured me – almost in Agag's words – that the bitterness of death was past. In the fact of surrender there had been no cause for shame. The Divisional artillery had fired its last rounds, there was chaos in St Valéry where refugees, and French troops who had already surrendered, crowded the narrow streets. The Navy was unable to enter the port – there was no possibility of evacuation – and the broken perimeter of hungry, exhausted infantry, who had had no proper rest since early May – now it was June – had only their small arms, empty bandoliers, and some puny two-inch mortars with which to oppose the overwhelming weight of Rommel's Panzer division. In that tattered perimeter, it is true, there were men who wept when they heard the order to surrender; but in a military sense they were no longer of value, they had spent their strength; they were merely human beings whose lives could be saved, and Victor Fortune saved them.

The Commander of the new or renewed division that was being formed in Scotland was that redoubtable enthusiast, Douglas Wimberley, later famous on the roof of Africa as Tartan Tam. His headquarters were at Aberlour in Banffshire, his brigades were centred on Dingwall, Elgin and Banchory. I, who went to investigate and learn, was immediately impressed as an extra-mural lecturer. Of what I talked about I have no memory at all, but the very fact of being accepted, as one of the team, made my task easier, and familiarity released a great deal of gossip, good or bad, that otherwise I might have missed.

There was much written evidence to be read, a large amount of detailed and authentic intelligence was on tap – of plans and performance, of movement and intention, of co-operation and failure of co-operation with the French – and pre-eminent among my informants was Major Thomas Rennie who, after being captured at St Valéry, escaped with nonchalant dexterity. He and another evader acquired bicycles, rode most of the way to Marseilles, and after crossing the Pyrenees were flown home from Lisbon. Rennie later commanded the 3rd Division – the first to land in France on D-day – and then returned, in command, to the 51st, and was killed almost in the hour of final victory. He was a man whose strength of character and soldierly virtues lay as deeply concealed, by an apparently simple good humour, as seeds in a melon, and he had a donnish reputation for absent-mindedness, that may have been cultivated. There was a story, for example, of his rebuke to a driver for taking the wrong road. They sat side by side in a jeep, and the jeep moved steadily forward. The cross-roads ahead of them was under fire, and again the General said, 'I told you this was the wrong road!' – 'Yes, sir,' said the Jock who sat beside him. 'But it's you that's driving, sir.'

I found no sign of absent-mindedness in him on a day when, for eight solid hours, I sat with a notebook, asking prepared questions, and wrote what he told me. He had a memory that was extraordinarily exact, and a gift of exposition that was clear and precise. At that period of my life I was much engaged in the exercise of question-and-answer – throwing questions like a trout-fly, hopeful of a rising fish – and I never had a witness to equal Thomas Rennie.

Before I had finished *The Highland Division* – longer than the others, it cost 9*d* – Walter Elliot was dangling before me a prospect of enviable employment. For some years to come there would be no major action in northern Europe, but in Africa Wavell had fought two successful campaigns, and in the Western Desert the Eighth Army was forming for new enterprise. The 4th and 5th Indian Divisions had already shown their remarkable quality, and much was to be expected from them in the future. But Britain – dull-witted, insular Britain – knew all too little about the Indian Army, and who better to repair its ignorance than Major Linklater, useless as a Sapper but *au courant* about the differences between Sikhs and Dogras, Mahrattas and Punjabi Mussulmans? Would I like to go on attachment, or be posted to the Indian Army?

'But of course,' I said. 'Either one or the other – I'll leave that to you. I'll finish the Highland story by the end of the week, and then I'll have to get some inoculations, I suppose –'

'We'll have to get final approval from India first. There's no difficulty at this end – I've seen to that – and I don't think there'll be any objection from the other. But we've got to make certain, of course.'

On 28 August I received a signal, 'Secretary of State India sympathetic proposal', and I was vaccinated, inoculated, pricked against plague and cholera – but not against disappointment, and disappointment followed hard in another signal that harshly cancelled the first. On no account would the Indian Army accept an observer nominated by the War Office, we were now told. The Indian Army could find observers of its own, and would appoint as many as might be thought desirable when circumstances were propitious.

I knew the man responsible for that decision. He had been a journalist in Bombay, as I had been; with the advent of war he had acquired a position of some authority in the Government of India; and from Delhi I had heard that he was on friendly terms with a young lady close to the accursed power which stands on privilege, as Belloc defined it. He had, no doubt, his own nominee for the job I wanted, but I thought him a rascal then, and until he died I bore him a grudge. I shall not reveal his name, for his father was an estimable man.

Walter Elliot was only briefly cast down by failure. He had a lively and inventive mind, and a few days later he was talking about the enormous growth of air traffic. 'Modern surgery', he said – by way of a beginning – 'owes everything to the first war. It was an operating-theatre where every sort of experiment could be tried – where, ten times a day, experiment was necessary if life was going to be saved – and where no one could be blamed for the failure of experiment. Well, in that sort of freedom surgery made advances that we wouldn't have seen in fifty years of peace, and nowadays, in precisely the same way, air power and travel by air are going ahead. There'll be failure, of course, but no one will be blamed for it, and no one's going to count the cost of experiment because in wartime accountancy is always an early casualty. Now, then, it might be possible – it would certainly be interesting – for you to do detailed exploration of the new strategic air-routes already in use, and describe where they go and what they do, and that sort of thing. We'd have to consider security, of course, but I'll look into that.'

He thought for a little while, and went on: 'There's quite a lot of things you could do. I was talking about surgery a moment ago, and the other day I heard of something quite new in the early treatment of wounds. What they're proposing to do – or already doing it, perhaps – is to form small teams which follow up a battle and attend to the wounded on the field. None of that old tedious business of being carried back to an R.A.P. – dying on the way, as often as not – and waiting your turn till *rigor mortis* sets in. No, that's finished, and the new surgical units give morphia and plasma on the spot: sitting under the lee of a tank, perhaps. Now you were a medical once, and I expect we could get permission for you to go out with one of those units, and describe what they're doing at the very moment they're doing it. That ought to be interesting, don't you think?'

I suppressed a shiver of fear, and thought that if Walter Elliot continued as Director of Public Relations – and my master – one of two things would certainly happen: either I would see war in all its variety, or Marjorie would be left a young widow with a chance to better herself. But Walter was too big a man to be confined for long in a room at the War Office; he found other fields on which to pasture his imagination, and was succeeded by Major-General Lawson, a Territorial soldier with an impressive record of service in the first war, who, a year or two later, became Lord Burnham and inherited the *Daily Telegraph*.

Before demitting office, however, Walter did me a last service, for which I was, and am, most grateful. I said to him one day, 'You have never asked me to write propaganda.'

'Your job with me', he answered, 'has been to provide information. Information not otherwise available. That's not propaganda unless you firmly believe that *magna est veritas et praevalebit.*'

'Would I be allowed', I asked, 'to write something – as a private person – which could be described as propaganda?'

'What have you got in mind?'

'Something about war aims.'

'Are you going to ask the Old Man what *he*'s got in mind? He'll only tell you to mind your own business.'

'I don't think I'd do any harm,' I said.

'Well, have a try, and let me see your ideas.'

'Here they are,' I said, and gave him a sheaf of cleanly typed pages.

At this time of writing, towards the end of 1969, we in Britain have been living in peace for nearly a quarter of a century. It has been, admittedly, a scratched and tormented peace, but peace it must be called because, as a nation, we have not been at war. There are many, therefore, who may have forgotten – what many others have never known – that war is intrinsically different from peace in that it easily gives birth to optimism.

One hopes that someday it will come to an end, and irrationally one believes that effort will be rewarded and the years to come will be better than years gone by. War is not unlike pregnancy – a pregnancy that may be the consequence of rape – and pregnancy is often accompanied by an unexpected sense of euphory. In Britain, after the collapse of France had isolated us – when the army which had escaped from Dunkirk was chaotically unprepared for major war, when London was burning under bombardment from the air, and the Royal Air Force was fighting a hazardous battle – there existed a sense of euphory which was illogically robust, and for a little while optimism crowed with defiant confidence. That was the mood – carried forward into 1941 –

in which I wrote *The Cornerstones*: a conversation-piece, pleasantly sited in the Elysian Fields, in which Abraham Lincoln, Lenin, Confucius and a fighter pilot of the Royal Air Force argued about humanity, their own countries, and the possibility of building peace on a four-fold alliance.

Today, of course, the very notion seems absurd, and even in 1941 it was difficult to make it plausible. Since the German attack in June, Russia had engaged our sympathy and increasingly earned admiration by the stubbornness of its defence; but that did not automatically create approval of Lenin, his revolutionary theories, and his hard, professional, revolutionary practice. I remembered, however, that during his exile in Siberia he had amused himself by wild-fowling and training a Gordon setter: affection for a dog, and an addiction to the early-morning discomfort of duck-shooting should recommend him to the English, I thought, and disingenuously I made much of them. Then I spoke of similarities between Russian aspiration and American achievement: though the Daughters of the American Revolution would disagree – as Lincoln pointed out – comparison could be made of Soviet history and the history of the United States, of their suddenly created national fervour and their devotion to modern technology.

England and China, on the other hand, might recognise a bond in their common insularity and uncompromising faith in a natural superiority that, for a very long time, had absolved them from unnecessary attention to their neighbours. In the Confucian ethic principles had taken precedence over statutory laws, and that was comparable with England's traditional belief that there was no need for a formal constitution if equity and common sense were respected. Confucius talked too much – they all talked too much – but in the Elysian Fields there was nothing else for them to do, and there could be no complaint against their conclusion that peace was a desirable state for mankind, and that strength to establish a rule of law would be essential for the maintenance of peace.

Walter Elliot read my Elysian report, and gratified me

by his partial approval of it. 'But', he said, 'you've left out an essential factor. Perhaps *the* essential factor. Wisdom and goodwill aren't enough. You present three wise men — each wise in his own way — and one young man who's ingenuous and stuffed with goodwill. Well, that may be a reasonable balance, but you need something more, don't you? There's got to be an executive arm, and what's the executive arm today?'

I retired with my uncompleted conversation, and added another character. The wise men leave the scene, and Arden, the newly dead fighter-pilot, remains. But he is not alone. A soldier in ragged khaki has been sleeping under a bush, and he too has an appointment elsewhere. 'It's all right, sir, I'm just going,' he says. 'I've got to get back.'

'Back where?' asks Arden.

'The usual place. Up the line again.'

He is a soldier who has fought in many campaigns from Hellenic times to the last battles of 1918. He has lately been in Greece again, and recognised a familiar landscape — 'A man doesn't forget Thermopylae' — and now his little holiday is finished.

'They can't win the war without me,' he says, 'and they'll make a poor thing of the peace without me, in spite of all their good intentions. And now I've got to go.'

'You shan't go till you have told me who you are,' says Arden. 'What's your name?'

'Courage,' says the soldier.

❧ Twenty

'Surplus to requirement' is, I think, the phrase that described my position in the War Office under new management. I was treated with great forbearance – with generosity, indeed – but General Lawson was a newspaper man who did not believe that Fleet Street required my assistance. By him I was given no such tasks as Walter Elliot had been eager to find, but though he made little use of me he kept me on his establishment, and for that I was deeply indebted to him; for eventually his tolerance allowed me to spend, without supervision, almost a year in Italy. Until then, however, I cannot remember, in sequence, all that I did to justify my uniform, my pay or even my existence; and it was, I think, after a year or so of dullish employment that I told a newly arrived American officer, 'You'll have to ask someone else about active service. I have spent the war in the Savile Club.'

For a long time, indeed, I slept under its hospitable roof, enjoyed good company, and twice a day walked to Whitehall Court where I had been allotted a handsome room that overlooked the river. I wish I could remember what kept me busy there, but all that remain in memory are excursions to Edinburgh, Falmouth, Aberystwyth – and where else?

Under Scottish Command there was experiment in the selection of officers by psychological divination, and the testing of junior officers, by similar methods, for their capacity to hold higher rank. My orders were to observe and report on what was being done, and much of what I saw was sound and reasonable, and less revolutionary than I had expected. The unanticipated pleasure I found was the presence, among those being vetted for promotion, of Evelyn Waugh. I knew him only slightly, but we had dined together, in amicable circumstances that became hilarious before evening expired; and in Edinburgh, where he had few friends, we renewed and reinforced a tenuous acquaintance.

In the uniform of a Royal Marine Evelyn had a taut soldierly appearance. Of no great height, but squarely, economically built, he moved – in those days – smartly but stiffly, and his red face had a well-chiselled firmness. A colonel of the old-fashioned sort, at first sight of him, would undoubtedly have said, 'That's the sort of chap we want' – though he might have changed his mind if he had stayed till Evelyn began to talk. For his temper was critical, his judgment could be harsh, and his habit of speech – which never departed from propriety – was incisive as a scalpel. He had, too, a fondness for simple joking which often dissipated the severity, or pretended severity, of his criticism.

He rang me up one day, and said I must dine with him because he had something to tell me. His wife was there – a gentle balance to his simmering indignation – and Evelyn had made admirable provision for a dinner that would justify portentous news: there was a decanter of sherry, another of claret, and in the background a decanter of port. We gossiped until the table was cleared and the port set down, and then, abruptly, Evelyn said, 'I spent this afternoon talking to a psychiatrist.'

'Did you satisfy him?'

'I don't know. He was an ignorant fellow – quite obviously ignorant – and when I started to interrogate him –'

'You interrogated *him*?'

'Indeed I did.'

'I doubt if anyone else has done that. Most of them are too frightened. There's a witch doctor sitting at the other side of the table, and all they're thinking of is escape.'

'He'd been asking me a lot of questions,' said Evelyn, 'and I thought it my turn to question him. So I said to him, "The whole purpose of this examination, I suppose, is to find out whether I've sufficient strength of character to stand the shock of battle?"

' "Yes," he said. "In a general, unscientific way that does describe it."

' "Then why", I asked him, "have you made no reference – no reference at all – to the most important of the influences or agencies that form a man's character?"

' "What do you mean?" he asked.

' "Religion," I told him.'

'Was he disconcerted?'

'He had no answer, so I went away. But you – you're reporting what goes on here – well, what can you do to prevent the whole process being stultified by men who are totally uneducated and basically ignorant?'

In comparison with Evelyn I was a moral weakling, I could offer no hope of reforming psychiatry and its practitioners. Evelyn grew angry with me, and but for Mrs Waugh and the decanter of port might have grown angrier still. But they mollified him, and we parted on amiable terms. He had had short but savage experience of battle in Crete, where according to report he had behaved with imperturbable self-assurance; but of that he would say nothing. 'I wasn't much interested, because I'm not a soldier, you see. To tell you the truth, I'm an old-fashioned Oxford aesthete.'

A few months later a story about him was given wide circulation: a story which, if not precisely true, was *ben trovato*. He became aide-de-camp to a general, with whom, on appointment, he dined. He drank too much – or so it was said – and, talking too much, talked indiscreetly. On the following morning the general complained of his behaviour, and accused him of having been drunk. Captain Waugh made no attempt to exculpate himself, but merely said, 'I don't feel inclined, sir, to interrupt the habit of a lifetime, merely to suit your temporary convenience.' In 1944, when I met him again in Rome, he was seriously ill, but his spirit was no more diminished by physical weakness than it had been by a general.

My next excursion, to Falmouth, was due to the suddenly

vocal dissatisfaction, with their terms of service, of soldiers who had been attached to the Merchant Navy. Ships that had been armed with machine-guns, of one sort or another, required soldiers to handle them, and it seemed that some soldiers enjoyed better conditions than others. I had already had a little experience in Scotland of what was agreeably called 'trouble shooting', and I found no great difficulty in uncovering the source of the machine-gunners' displeasure. Some, of course, were more subject to danger and discomfort than others, and of that they complained, but without bitterness. What had deeply upset them was that some had excellent rations while others fed very poorly; and there was inequality, not in their basic pay, but in their allowances. Our other topics were discipline and leave, but I had little more to do than take note of what they told me – check facts and figures, for different groups seldom told the same tale – and visit a few ships to look at galleys, accommodation and the sort of protection provided for gunners on the wings of a bridge; after which I made some simple, sensible recommendations.

I realised, however, that if I returned too quickly to London I might be suspected of having scamped my work, so to give it a semblance of respectable deliberation I took a little holiday on the Helford river, and presently heard that a slow convoy was mustering to proceed up Channel. I thought it would give verisimilitude to my report if I added a short description of a voyage protected, to some degree, by the gunners whose difficulties I had been investigating, and I got a berth aboard a small and extremely dirty coaster. Under a blazing sun and over a sea of oily calm we had a leisurely voyage – four or five knots was our average speed – and our only excitement came when a corvette dropped a couple of depth charges, turned and stopped, and put out a boat: to look for survivors, we thought. But her purpose was merely domestic, as we saw when the boat's crew began to gather in a great draught of fishes, stunned by the explosion, that lay like a silver patch on the smooth sea.

I slept in a hot and odorous iron cupboard, that opened

off the deck and intruded on the engine-room, and when I came ashore I bore evidence of what I had suffered. The bed-bug moves along a straight line, and if he changes direction finds another straight to follow. A pair of them had found my neck attractive, and above the collar of my shirt had left evidence of their browsing on two red paths which closely resembled a corporal's stripes. In that war – it is a humiliating confession – I received no other wound.

For some time little had happened to sustain enthusiasm for the war, and a high regard for security had concealed from popular knowledge all, or nearly all, the small regimental actions which, by the high spirit of those engaged, could have stirred imagination and done something to gratify that hunger for action which civilians showed so much more greedily than soldiers. Very belatedly I was given the task of disinterring, not forgotten tales, but tales which had never been told, and now had lost much of their savour. My search, after some initial enquiry, took me, strangely enough, to the hinterland of Aberystwyth.

Shelter had there been found for pictures removed for safety from the National Gallery; and in some confusion of values – as if they were of equal value with Caxton's Chaucer and *Morte d'Arthur* or the Gutenberg Bible – a large number of battalion war-diaries were given similar protection against German bombers. Pile after pile of them I shredded and read, and in the rain, when evening darkness fell, retired to Aberystwyth to dine and sleep in a Welsh mess of the dreariest sort. Several of its members were puffy-faced survivors of the first war, who lived in a hazy, alcoholic dream of Arras, Bapaume and Cambrai; others were disconsolate young men who had found employment of some dim, stationary sort; and the Colonel was an elderly, vivacious elf who, whenever he had guests – and he was very hospitable – would entertain them with a graphic tale of a severe abdominal operation he had suffered: the conclusion to it being, 'And when the surgeon opened my lower bowel, so appalling was the stench that even the theatre sister fainted!'

In the war-diaries, however, I found several stories of

memorable quality – stories which might have been read with avid attention if they had not been buried until their impact had been blunted – and then I travelled to and fro to find survivors who could upholster bare, factual bones with living memories. By far the most difficult of my tasks was an attempt to re-create a very gallant enterprise by the Essex Regiment, which, towards the end of November 1941, had led a sortie from beleaguered Tobruk to capture a rugged eminence called Ed Duda. I went to Colchester where, in the depot battalion of the regiment, were ten or a dozen men – more, I think – who had been wounded in the battle, and were healed of their wounds. On three blackboards I drew diagrams, to recall to them the three phases of the battle, and to a silent audience I said, 'Now you went out, "D" company leading, and when you came to the lower slopes of Ed Duda you jumped out of your trucks, bayonets fixed, and ran forward under fairly heavy fire from the west and north-west. From here, that is.' And I pointed to the first of my diagrams.

'Now, Sergeant, what did you yourself *see* when you looked towards the north-west?'

'Ar,' said the Sergeant thoughtfully.

'There wasn't much cover, but the ground was cut by small *wadis*, and some of the German guns weren't far off. Well, what did you do?'

There was a long pause – ample time for thought – and now with lingering enunciation the Sergeant said, 'Aar!'

'All right, Sergeant, we'll come back to you presently. Now you, Corporal: what do you remember of that first phase?'

Slowly the Corporal shook his head, and refused all comment. I began to smell defeat, and to recognise, I think, their reason for defeating me. It was *their* battle, and they had no intention of sharing it with a stranger. In their own minds, I was sure, they remembered every detail of it – they admitted, grudgingly, that my diagrams were approximately true to fact – but their private memories they kept under lock and key for their own pleasure.

It was an exasperating experience, for these stolid men had fought with dash and daring, but now, like surly watchdogs, would allow no foreigners within their doors. After two or three hours of vain interrogation I left them in despair, and their officers, giving me gin and a frugal lunch, said they had never expected I would get much out of them. 'After they came home,' I was told, 'a lot of reporters came down and talked to them, and got nothing at all.' But before I left I had a little conversation with a subaltern who came out to help me find my driver, and he said, 'There's a cousin of mine, still in hospital in Hastings with what they used to call shell-shock – they call it something else nowadays, but it's the same thing, I suppose – and he's pretty intelligent. He'd have been out of hospital long ago if the doctors weren't so bloody intent on finding traumas, and that sort of game. Well, he might tell you something.'

On the following morning I went to Hastings – or was it Eastbourne? – and, after tactful enquiry, declared I was Lieutenant So-and-so's uncle, and would like to see him. I found him suffering acutely from boredom – no symptoms, so far as I could see, of shell-shock – and when I asked him if he would like to dine with me that evening he replied, 'If you're my uncle it's your duty to take me out – and they can't refuse permission because they know perfectly well that there's nothing wrong with me.' We dined together, very cheerfully, and from him I got the story that the stolid men of Colchester had refused to divulge.

There was no reticence, there were no inhibitions, in Colonel Ian Stewart of the Argyll and Sutherland Highlanders. In Malaya, before the Japs launched their devastating attack, he had had time – he had had the energy and imagination – to train his battalion for jungle warfare, and only the Argylls had been able to oppose the Japs with tactics similar to their own: in the jungle no one could hold a defensive position, but to those who knew it the jungle offered roundabout routes of attack. The Argylls covered the long retreat to Singapore, their two surviving pipers played the last troops across the Causeway, and Ian Stewart was sent to India to teach others what he had learnt and practised. But when I first met him he was commanding a battle school at Barnard Castle in County Durham.

We walked together through a little wood, and in the most illuminating way he began to tell me about the importance of rapid movement in jungle fighting. Then a rifle bullet hit a puddle of water a few feet in front of us, another cut a twig above our heads. I pretended indifference, but as the *ping* and *plump* and *whew* of rifle fire continued I said, a little nervously, 'If that chap is trying to hit us, he's not a very good shot, is he?' — 'He's a first-class shot,' said Stewart. 'It's only the best of them who do this sort of thing. It's part of the training, we do almost everything under fire. You get accustomed to being shot over, and psychologically that's invaluable.'

It was widely believed that Ian Stewart's knowledge of jungle warfare was quite unrivalled; and there were many who said that he had not received the recognition to which he was entitled. It was possible, I thought, that he had given unwitting offence — senior officers are easily offended — by exposing distinguished visitors to a hail of bullets while he expounded his theories and experience. He was a Highlander who lived with the enthusiasm of a Highland charge.

Towards the end of the year I met another notable enthusiast — my old friend Compton Mackenzie — when we were requested, by someone in the Ministry of Information, to celebrate St Andrew's Day with speeches in the Regal Cinema in Edinburgh. The barrage that began the battle of Alamein had darkened an Egyptian moon five weeks before, and I was allowed to name the regiments which were fighting in the Highland Division: that was a privilege almost without precedent — it defied the sacred rules of security, it derided the orthodox reverence for secrecy — and my revelations were received with startled applause. But a spring-tide of acclamation awaited Monty Mackenzie.

He could be a formidable orator when the proper mood was matched by the right occasion, and on that evening his thought took wings, his voice found its full range, and the audience responded with grateful fervour. His performance – an inspired performance – was enhanced, moreover, by dramatic movement. He stood behind a line of blazing footlights, and after a sentence or two he began marching to and fro, his kilt swinging proudly, and the noble voice that flung such spirited words across a dazzling wall was magnified by the impetus of his steps. It was not, however, a deliberate trick or device to amplify effect. Movement, as he later admitted, was a physical necessity. Such was the heat of the footlights – and such the absence of protection under his kilt – that he could not bear the pain of standing still.

He was living, at that time, on the island of Barra, which dangles like a medal under the chain of the Outer Hebrides, and his daily life was a miracle of sustained effort. He was writing his major work, *The Four Winds of Love*, that novel of enormous length and unflagging vitality; he was inventing one or other of those hilarious Highland tales, *The Monarch of the Glen* or *Whisky Galore*; he kept up a huge, miscellaneous correspondence; and from his bed – to which sciatica recurrently confined him – he commanded a company of the Home Guard with an enterprise of which higher authority did not always approve. There were those – some thirty or forty years ago – who used to pretend that he was too flamboyant to be a serious writer; my own complaint would be that he is too industrious to permit a proper assessment of his work. He offers a table fully spread, and in the kitchen there is still a constant busyness.

Earlier in the year, in London, I had become friendly with a young man whose reputation was to rest on one book only, and on his early death. Richard Hillary when I first met him was scarred by fire and plastic surgery – the grafted tissue of his new eyelids was not yet perfectly at home – and his hands, crumpled in the flames of a burning Spitfire, were still half-open fists. He had written his story, of life and sudden death, and called it *The Last Enemy*. Much of it pulsated with the agony he had endured in hospital; flying over the Channel, in the Battle of Britain, he had been shot down, burning like a torch, and was then patched up for life again by devoted nurses and the skill of that superlative surgeon, Sir Archibald McIndoe.

Richard had few inhibitions, and he made no attempt to conceal what he had suffered; he unfolded a tale that carried pain in every sentence, and, more haltingly – with manifest effort – recorded his gradual renunciation of the hard-shelled egotism which had been his built-on-the-premises ivory tower. It was a tale that started in Oxford – where his primary task was stroking the Trinity boat to the head of the river – and proceeded to a happily cynical account of early training in the Royal Air Force. It evoked, with masterly precision, the summer fighting high above the Channel, and towards the end described his 'conversion' to the unlovely but compelling cause of humanity. Formal religion played no part in his enlightenment; but the intensity of feeling in his account of a drastic change shows his awareness of the profound importance of that change.

There was no solemnity, however, in his everyday demeanour. Gaiety, irreverence, a habit of mockery, an avid pleasure in life – all these had survived the torture of his mind and body. He had been boldly handsome before his Spitfire went down in flames, and gradually the eyelids and the upper lip, that McIndoe had stitched for him, lost their artificial look, and his face grew whole again. Women were warmly attracted to him, and I – flattered by the easy friendship of someone half my age – felt for him an affection that his death threw into darkest mourning.

He was determined to fly again. His crumpled hands were growing stronger, and in the newly awakened generosity of his mind there was a nagging feeling that he – in comparison with his friends who had died – had 'given so little' to a cause which he now identified as humanity's cause against the powers of evil. Since leaving hospital he had flown single-engined fighters – without permission, I think – but Fighter Command rebuffed him when he applied for training in night-fighters, and fellow-officers tried brusquely to dissuade him. So did other of his friends, of whom I was one.

There was a posthumous edition of *The Last Enemy* to which I wrote a foreword, and a little while ago I looked for it to see what I had said to explain our failure to keep him alive. 'I wanted', I wrote, 'to keep him out of the sky, and make him earth-bound. And then, one evening, I was frightened that I might succeed, and said no more. . . . In his character – in his mind, his spirit, his personality – there was a quality like something with a sharpened edge and a fine surface, and I was suddenly frightened that my argument would dull the edge and tarnish the surface. And that is the sober truth of it.' I think now that my fear was groundless, and nothing I could have said would have blunted his decision. Fighter Command gave way, and he was allowed to go to the training station at Charter Hall in Berwickshire.

Between the pages of *The Last Enemy* I found a forgotten letter that Richard had written to me, soon after his arrival there. He was very unhappy, and as usual made no attempt to hide his feelings. 'This place, a veritable wilderness,' he wrote, 'has very nearly broken me in two days, and last night I crawled back to my freezing little hut and wept like a child.' He complained of a 'complete lack of human contact', for by the end of 1942 the Royal Air Force was different in many ways from the light-hearted squadrons he had known; and to prepare him for loneliness, or reconcile him to it, 'my high-flying life in London has not helped, nor listening to the sensible arguments of people like yourself. I know I was mad to return, and yet I know I was right.'

There are, in his letter, eight pages of pencilled doubt and reiterated decision. He had read *The Mint* – T. E. Lawrence's unhappy testament – and in Charter Hall the first book that he picked up was Lawrence's *Letters*, edited by David Garnett. 'It was largely reading *The Mint* that decided me to return,' he wrote, and quoted Garnett on Lawrence: ' "Since the period at Uxbridge had been a time of great suffering, one wonders whether his will had not become greater than his intelligence." ' – 'Is this true?' he asked. But *The Mint* was not wholly to blame; nor 'largely', indeed. The life he had been leading in London was artificial, and he wanted 'to get back into communion with the simple type of pilot'. Different though the new men were, he was, it seems, quickly accepted by them: 'They think me a droll fellow, possibly able to get them off some bullshit.'

He complains again of the discomforts of Charter Hall, but then: 'Excuse me babbling on like this. It sounds as though I'm wanting to quit. Last night that was true, but now it's going to be all right.' For a page or two he talks of the prospect of leave – and again of books – and concludes, 'Must pop into bed now, my hands are freezing.'

He died in the very early morning of 8 January, while circling a flashing beacon. It was a routine drill, and though the sky was cloudy and sleet was falling the weather was not unduly severe. But the Blenheim he was flying – a machine said to have been heavy in hand – was apparently too much for the crippled strength of hands that were apt to freeze; he was seen to be losing height; and when the Blenheim crashed he and his observer were both killed.

Something in his friends died also.

✺ Twenty-One

The Cornerstones – with its additional character god-fathered by Walter Elliot – was published in December 1941, and twice broadcast early in 1942. It was directed, with sympathy and uncommon skill, by Val Gielgud; as were other conversation-pieces that I wrote in the periods of idleness – or unemployment – that became more frequent after Walter ceased to be my master. He had given me a certain independence, and I continued to exercise it. General Lawson tolerated my freedom, and I was never asked to submit a manuscript for approval. Gielgud and I were allowed to issue propaganda of our own device.

The Raft was broadcast in August 1942, *Socrates Asks Why* in October. The former was propaganda unashamed and only slightly adorned. On the raft, floating in mid-Atlantic, were six survivors of a torpedoed ship, all 'in the borderland between life and death'. Said one, 'I believe in the people of this kingdom.' Said another, 'Such a faith has not been – shall we say obvious? – in the young men of your generation.' To which the first replied, 'Faith began to come when we were put to the proof.' Return of faith and its justification: there was the text of a discourse that, in wartime Britain, was unlikely to give offence. But *Socrates Asks Why* shows a very different temper.

I returned to my *mise-en-scène* in the Elysian Fields, and assembled a distinguished cast: Socrates, Abraham Lincoln, Voltaire and Dr Johnson. An Elysian television set – with a range exceeding that of earthly models – lets them see what is happening in the world, and a commentator's description of America's prodigious expenditure, of men and money, offends Voltaire, who complains: 'I begin to feel doubtful about the impartiality of our Commentator. I incline more and more to the belief that it was he who instigated this doleful war. There is in his voice a deepening note of gratification when he tells us how big it is. He reminds me of a theatrical producer who has put upon the stage the most extravagant spectacle of all time, and hopes by advertising its enormous cost to excuse its lack of taste.'

'But surely', says Lincoln, 'he is justified in combing the dictionary for every superlative he can find. If we are to realise even a fraction of this war's significance, we must strain our minds to the very limit of comprehension. . . . There must be, in this new chaos, twenty, thirty, forty million men in arms.'

'Why?' asks Socrates. 'What are they fighting for?'

To preserve 'the American way of life' is not a cause that he finds wholly satisfying, and Britain's engagement also puzzles him. Britain, he reminds them, was not attacked by Germany, but went to war on behalf of Poland, though a year earlier it had refused to fight for Czecho-Slovakia. Was the reason for Britain's participation, he asks, 'a particular and decisive admiration for Poland's way of life?'

'Which, in the general estimation of Britain,' says Voltaire, 'must have been superior to the Czecho-Slovak way of life.'

Dr Johnson rebukes him — 'Sir, you are sophisticating' — and speaks judiciously in favour of a balance of power: 'A balance, sir, is a very useful instrument. On the counter of a shop it guarantees honesty in trade, and in the hand of Justice it is the symbol of equity.'

It appears, however, that our traditional respect for balanced power is shared neither by the United States nor by our own younger generation, and Lincoln speaks of the fighter-pilot Arden — a character introduced in *The Corner-stones* — whose hope is to see a rule of international law enforced and guaranteed by the major powers.

But a four-fold rule of law is not, of course, the declared aim and objective of the allied nations. 'And if', says

Socrates, 'it is merely an expression of hope on the part of some well-meaning people who, for all I know, have little influence in the world, then it seems likely that their aspirations will succumb to nature, and fail. That being so, all this fighting is a waste, not only of time and effort, but also of soldiers' lives.'

That conversation was broadcast in the autumn of 1942, in the heat and middle of the war; and today, I feel, it can be accepted as proof that our rulers in Britain – no matter what faults they had – believed in freedom of speech, and gave remarkable latitude to the B.B.C.

In the Elysian Fields, moreover, scepticism was not restricted to intellectuals. I introduced two soldiers from an Elysian Transit Camp, one of them a sergeant in the American Marine Corps, killed on Wake Island in the Pacific; the other a piper of the Argyll and Sutherland Highlanders who had died in the Malayan jungle. They, under interrogation, boldly declared they had died because the governments they served were ignorant, stupid and devoid of imagination.

But both their countries, as Socrates points out, are democracies; and 'since they are democracies, your Governments do not merely represent the people, but *are* the people. They are a concentration of the popular mind. And if, as you seem to think, they have been guilty of criminal negligence, there must be some grave fault, not merely in your ministers, but in your whole population.'

Had they, in fact, been fighting for countries, unworthy of them, whose rulers deserved no confidence?

The soldiers grow angry. They cannot carry the argument so far, and have no need to. The simple voice of conscience answers for them, in the piper's words: 'We ken what's right and we ken what's wrong, and there's a difference between them that nothing can hide.'

But their simplicity does not satisfy Socrates, who says: 'The Allied nations, being in agreement about whom they are fighting against, will probably win the war. But unless they are in equal agreement about the cause they are fighting for they will not be able to make a good and fruitful peace. And I ask you yet again: does a positive cause exist?'

That was the question which the B.B.C., Val Gielgud and I dared to ask when, from Alamein, the Eighth Army, after much tribulation, was at last advancing with a prospect of victory before it; and I am still astonished that we were allowed to ask it.

'A bit near the knuckle,' someone commented, but I got no other reprimand, and I was soon at work on other things. It was early in 1943, I think, that I fell a victim to one of those strange embranglements that may be native to *la vie militaire*. I was caught in a web from which there seemed no escape – hauled out of it to flounder in a smaller, more occluding mesh – and extricated from that to be returned to the earlier nexus.

It was decided – by whom I do not know – that the people of Britain knew far too little about the Army in which so many of them were serving, and I was given the job of describing its component parts, exposing its problems, and explaining its many functions. It was, I complained, an impossible task, for much of the Army was still adapting a traditional drill to meet new demands – learning to handle weapons of which only prototypes had been issued – armoured regiments were changing their shape and constitution as often as Proteus – and if ever I caught up with the latest designs and the last intentions I should be charged with betraying official secrets. But my objections were overruled, and setting off to learn what I could from what I was allowed to see I became a transient guest in twenty different battalion or regimental messes.

Then, in haste, I was recalled to the War Office, and told that I had no status there, and had lately been working under false pretensions. I had, it appeared, been 'attached' but not 'posted'. I was not wedded to Whitehall, but, since my period of attachment had expired, living in sin. To regularise my position I must return, for an unspecified period, to my darent corps, while the War Office published the banns which eventually might allow us legitimate cohabitation.

'And my present job?' I enquired. – 'It can wait,' I was told. 'You'll go on with it as soon as we've made you respectable.'

For some inscrutable reason I went first to Halifax, where I lodged with a local NAAFI manager who, when cigarettes were not easily obtained, supplied me with as many as I wanted. The organisation to which I had been sent – I forget what it was called – issued a training programme which included, in a host of activities, a lecture on the history of the British Empire, a visit to the municipal slaughter-house, and unarmed combat. I avoided all parades, and every afternoon went to a local cinema. Then I got orders to report to the School of Military Engineering at Ripon – the scene of old humiliation – and there I was given command of a company in the Depot Battalion, and acquired some useful experience.

The nucleus of my company was about a hundred and fifty men, most of them old soldiers, who were employed about the camp; but men arriving for instructional courses were attached to it, and sometimes it numbered four or five hundred. There was so much 'crime' – crime in the Army sense, that is – that I instituted a daily confessional, at six o'clock, to which I invited, for private discussion, anyone whose personal problems were unduly troublesome. Of men attending courses there were always a few who got drunk and stayed out all night, but they were easily dealt with. My chief concern was with my old regulars, many of them reservists who had been disabled at Dunkirk, or wounded in some later engagement, and come home to find grievous trouble under their own roof. A son, or a couple of sons, had grown up in their absence, and their mother could no longer control them; or sometimes the mother needed control.

At my confessional I would listen to a man's story, and then say, perhaps, 'Well, you're not entitled to leave, but if I give you a pass for Saturday and Sunday, will you promise to be back again for first parade on Monday?'

'Give you my word, sir.'

'And you'll take the opportunity to have a serious talk with that boy of yours?'

233

'Ay, and with his mother too.'

'Well, that's your business, and I'm not going to enquire into it. But I'm going to trust you – '

'There's just one other thing, sir.'

'What's that?'

'It's just a matter of money, sir. I haven't got the fare.'

Bus-fare or train-fare seldom came to more than a few shillings, and I usually got my money back next pay-day. Never – not once – did a man whom I sent on illicit leave fail to return at the promised time, and while many small boys, and sometimes their mothers, suffered a week-end whipping crime in my company was reduced to a comfortable level.

I fell out with my Colonel, however, which made life slightly uncomfortable. He required – or so it seemed to me – a standard of drill which was clearly too high for a depot battalion. It was only on Sundays that he saw his four companies together, but he made the most of his weekly opportunity. A long time had elapsed since I last appeared on battalion parade, and infantry drill was an elusive memory; but I had a loud voice, a good Company Sergeant-Major, and I performed without grievous blundering. My marching, however, had lost snap and precision, and my fellow company commanders were no better; one of them limped badly. No one was really smart except a fine, upstanding woman who commanded a company of A.T.S. She, we pretended to believe, slept with the Regimental Sergeant-Major, for she had exactly copied the measured, formal *panache* with which he moved, and in her voice there sounded a contralto echo of his stentorian tone.

Our Colonel praised her, and insisted that we, her male companions, should attend drill parades – with her on the right flank – under his direction in the gymnasium. His attempts to improve our carriage and step were, however, frustrated by the officer whose shattered knee made him limp – by a youngish man whose limbs were poorly co-ordinated – by me, who gently explained that I was more used to hill-walking – and by the stalwart commander of the A.T.S. company, who always finished three paces in front of us.

The School of Military Engineering had lost the grandeur that still marked and coloured it in 1940 – guest-nights were fewer, no longer did one wait for the grave procession of port, sherry and madeira – but it was much busier and more realistic. I found a few friends with one of whom – we ate a late breakfast and decided to take a day's holiday – I walked exactly thirty miles before tea-time; but that, I think, was my only excursion into the good country which lies north of Ripon. For six or eight weeks routine and recurrent crises occupied most of my time, but then, before returning to the War Office with a certificate of legitimacy, I was rewarded for my efforts.

I got on well with my Company Sergeant-Major, a regular with eight or ten years' service. Neither of us was fond of punishment, and we avoided, whenever possible, the harsh ritual of sending a man to be sentenced by the Colonel. My own powers, as a company commander, were limited, but could be stretched. My Sergeant-Major might say, 'Well, he knows the regulations, sir – a proper old soldier, he is – and he's entitled to go before the Colonel if he wants to. But I've had a word with him, and I don't think he'll insist. I think he'll take your punishment, sir.'

Or I, reading a charge-sheet, would say, 'There's not much in this, is there, Sergeant-Major? And he's a nice chap too.'

'Yes, sir. Headstrong and a bit careless with his language: that's all that's wrong with him. If I were you, sir – if you don't mind my saying so – I'd just give him a good talking-to. And rub it in a bit, perhaps.'

'I'm sure you're right, Sergeant-Major. Well, tear up the charge, dismiss the escort and bring him in.'

We saved ourselves a lot of paper-work, we kept a lot of men out of trouble, and, when I had packed and was ready to leave, my Sergeant-Major pleased me by saying, 'I'm sorry you're going, sir. You're a nice, *understanding* man.' I knew exactly what he meant. We had, to a large extent, gone about things in our own way, and we had managed to keep ourselves, as well as many others, out of trouble.

Then, or a little while later, I had ten days' leave, and

flew to Orkney. Marjorie and my mother had long since returned from their exile on the Borders, and my family was larger than it had been: my son Magnus was born in February 1942, and his godfathers were Compton Mackenzie and General Kemp, of whom we had been so frightened. Orkney was still full of soldiers and airmen, but there was little tension now. There was, indeed, a good deal of conviviality, and at a party one evening I was persuaded to join the umpires who, on the following day, were to watch a major amphibious exercise. Orkney, at last, was about to be invaded; but we had been warned what to expect, and defensive troops were in position.

Our defences were not – as it happened – seriously tested. There was a choppy sea in Scapa Flow, the attacking soldiers had been sitting too long in their landing-craft, and many were casualties before they reached the beaches: they came ashore to vomit again, and we who were umpires looked the other way. We did not, however, dissociate ourselves from the exercise, for the King had come to see it, and, no matter what happened elsewhere, we wanted to see him. It was a pity that we encountered him when Tom Howarth and I appeared to be bridesmaids rather than umpires.

Tom Howarth, who is now the High Master of St Paul's, was then a very young brigade-major. We were walking with the C.R.E.,* a colonel who in mind and manner was as much like a don as a soldier: a gentle, most amiable man with a lively, whimsical spirit and a donnish carelessness about his clothes. He was wearing breeches and puttees, and simultaneously we saw that the royal party was rapidly approaching, and the long tape of the Colonel's right-leg puttee was drifting behind him. 'Quickly!' we said. 'Round that corner and you'll have time to do it up.' But as the Colonel accelerated the tape of his left-leg puttee began to unwind; and the royal party was gaining on us. 'Never mind my damned puttees,' said the Colonel. 'Halt, face front, and salute as they pass.'

* Commandant Royal Engineers.

But Tom and I – anxious to prevent worse from happening, for both puttees were now falling fast – had stooped to pick up the trailing tapes, and as we turned right and stood to attention – one on either side of the Colonel – we still held them. We saluted with grave precision, and the King revealed his admirable self-control. He showed a certain interest in the spectacle we presented – we looked very like bridesmaids, holding up the Colonel's train – but he did not laugh. Not until, having returned our salute, he was three yards farther on and looked round to see if we still held our pose. 'Well,' said the Colonel, 'it was a more interesting exercise than we expected.'

I returned to duty and my impossible task of explaining the constitution and whole practice of the Army, from Pioneers to the Chaplain-General's department, and finished the first draft, of formidable length, by early October. Then I was rewarded for my labour by the offer of more interesting employment than I had lately had.

𝔐 Twenty-Two

GIBRALTAR, it seemed, was like the Army in that the general populace knew too little about it. Its garrison, moreover, had had an uncommonly dull time: the war had swept past them, into the Mediterranean and North Africa, and they, bored and stationary, had watched it go, and wakened to another static day. It would be good for their morale if the importance of what they had been doing could be demonstrated and brought home to them; and to that end the proper means might be a good documentary film. If I, said my masters, thought I could find material for such a film, and perhaps suggest a design for it, the Admiralty was prepared to release Lieutenant-Commander Ralph Richardson, of the Fleet Air Arm, and let him collaborate with me: a prospect that gave me much pleasure.

As a pilot, I think, Ralph's training had proved a little too expensive, and he had, at that time, no flying duties. But though the Admiralty might have little use for him, there were others eager to employ him, of whom the most influential was Sir Alexander Korda. He, when he heard what was proposed, declared it a monstrous waste of talent to use Ralph in a meagre, expository role, and offered to produce a film for audiences of the largest sort if a suitable story could be concocted. Our departure was delayed, but Korda's offer was tentatively accepted, and his brother Vincent added to our party as a technical adviser.

Late one night we joined a darkling throng at Paddington, the wartime flowing tide of laden soldiers and sailors in a loathsome gloom, and an hour or two later at an unknown station – security withheld all names – were haled from our carriage and led through a dark tunnel to a waiting car in which we drove, by narrow tall-hedged roads, to an aerodrome whose mazy paths were all untenanted beneath a shapeless moon. An aeroplane was waiting, a Dakota stuffed with sacks of mail, but in its cargo three holes had been left, into which we squeezed, and were given some sandwiches and three or four blankets apiece. The door was closed, and we sat for a long time, sealed off from humankind, in a dim aquarium light. The roof was painted green, and from it depended a single small electric globe. That was extinguished when we took off, and for some hours we shared, encoffined in that long steel tube, the darkness of a tomb with thousands upon thousands of letters from the women of Britain to their absent men.

Then a startling change from darkness: the aerodrome at Lisbon seemed to be lighted by reflexion from polished silver, and we drove through new-washed streets past country carts all crammed with greenery, to a hotel where we ate eggs and fruit, drank coffee and brandy, and after sleeping for an hour or two woke in the brisk and irresponsible air of holiday. Another two or three hours of flying, and we landed, as if on the deck of a gigantic carrier, on the long new-made runway between Spanish territory and the Rock. A hundred yards away, nodding in a gentle sea, floated a buoy that commemorated the recent death of General Sikorski: there, in the innocent greenish water, his aeroplane had mysteriously fallen, and he and his companions drowned.

We stayed at the Convent – Government House, that is – where our host was a man who had been built, as it seemed, to his own design. General Mason-Macfarlane was a martinet, and looked it. His ponderously handsome rather Roman head was carried slightly askew by reason of some misadventure in which he had broken his neck. He had broken many bones, at one time or another, but refused to admit any disability from his fractures. The weather was bitingly cold in the early morning, but till evening came he wore nothing except khaki shorts and an open-necked drill

239

shirt. Late in the day – when evening was ripening to midnight – he might join us again in the library, and settle down on the high fender to talk until two in the morning, and talk by choice of the theatre, and opera singers, and Moscow's ballerinas, many of whom he knew by the little names that were private to their friends.

Though much of his service had been spent in diplomatic or quasi-diplomatic duties, he was very decidedly a soldier, and of the soldiers under his command, and the problems of their absurdly confined life, he had a profound understanding. To them the Rock was little better than a prison. Between the Spanish lines and the great cliff that rises above the Mediterranean, that stands ragged and proud as a gigantic cockscomb, an army of men lived in a little area that might with decency have accommodated the population of a mountain village. Gibraltar was teeming-full, as crowded as an Indian bazaar in a shoulder-rubbing closeness of bodies; and nearly all were men's bodies. They were as straitly confined as if in a prison-yard, and almost as nakedly under scrutiny.

We climbed, by a road tilted steeply against the sky, to Rock Gun, the tall crest that overlooks the Spanish mainland, and peered through the aged telescope mounted there: staring back from a roof-top in La Linea, and from the Queen of Spain's Chair, were the Spanish sentries. When the light was good we could see that they were careless about shaving, and for their better observation they had fine long glasses made in Germany. We had worn plain clothes for our journey through Lisbon, and were allowed to cross no-man's-land into Algeciras; there, in its seaside villas, we saw other observers watching patiently, through great binoculars, all that happened on the Rock.

The soldiers suffered confinement and exposure too. It was a busy ant-hill on which they lived, and they were constantly at work. They trained for active war, they laboured on the aerodrome, they excavated long white tunnels in the rock. The tunnels, that cut through deep clouds of chalky dust to channel the whole mountain with a blind and pallid labyrinth, were strangely beautiful. We were led deeper and deeper into the bowels of the fortress, past ghostly working-parties drilling the rock in a pearly haze; down endless perspectives drawn in silver-point, and Chinese white, and coffin-gloom; past caverns big as a parish church but housing squat machines and oily steel; and so to a little window and a narrow balcony in the rock that looked along the coast towards Malaga. The tunnels, we thought, would provide some unusual and distinguished scenery for the film we meditated, and presently we boarded a curious vessel that might pack a story with authentic drama.

Rusty and desolate, the shell of an Italian tanker called *Olterra* lay in the harbour. She had taken refuge in Algeciras, and been interned, in 1942. Seemingly innocent, and most melancholy, she had lain for a long time opposite the Naval Signal Station, and about six miles away from it. Then one night a ship at anchor in the outer harbour, one of a merchant fleet waiting to join its convoy, was damaged by a submarine explosion that could not easily be explained. There were other 'incidents' – to use a pleasant meiosis of the time – and the *Olterra* was regarded with darkening suspicion. But she lay in Spanish waters, and, though Spanish neutrality was not unbiased, it had to be respected, and *Olterra* could not be searched.

Early in December, on a cold night, calm and moonless, a battleship, an aircraft carrier and a tanker lay alongside the Detached Mole that makes an outer wharf for Gibraltar; and Gunner Perry did his turn of look-out duty, and still felt wideawake when he was relieved. He was a fisherman, and taking his rod to the north end of the Mole, he cast his float into the water. Time passed, and by and by he observed something much larger than he had ever dreamed of catching. Ten yards from the Mole, gleaming below the surface, something long and vaguely cylindrical in shape was slowly moving: moving against the tide. Gunner Perry shouted an alarm, searchlights leapt against the water, and in a pale-green and silver-freakt translucency Gunner Perry saw a midget submarine and muffled riders straddling it. It turned sharply away, diving quickly out of the light, and he threw hand-charges at it. The Duty Watch turned out to throw more, and from a projector a heavier charge was lobbed into the bright sea. A motor-launch put out to search the bay, and four hundred yards away an American ship picked up two disconsolate wet Italians. Three-quarters of an hour after the alarm had been given, all was quiet again; and Gunner Perry resumed his fishing.

Seven days later two more Italian bodies were found floating in the harbour. They had been dead for at least a week, and had been killed by concussion: of a depth-charge, presumably. The submarine that Gunner Perry saw may have been one of a pair that set out that night to hunt in company.

When Italy surrendered the *Olterra* was handed over to the Royal Navy, and in her rusty hold – dark slimy-seeming water lapping against her scaling plates – we saw the iron vault, blocks and tackle hanging still, where the little submarines had been assembled and from which, by a flap-door in the side, they had been launched in darkness.

Balanced over that still, oily surface we looked thoughtfully down, and in imagination saw reflected in it a tense, cinematic scene. But the story, of course, could not be confined to Gibraltar, and in the freedom of our plain clothes we crossed again to Algeciras, through a horde of Spanish soldiers in diverse uniforms.

We spent a day or two in a fine hotel, where we lived in luxury, eating richly, drinking Tio Pepe and Spanish brandy, and felt blackly ashamed of ourselves; for beyond the gardens of the hotel were stark hunger and thin-ribbed poverty. Armless men and one-legged men, in cold sunlight, stood by the waterfront, and here and there we stumbled over a dead rat in the street. There was no lack of soldiers in uniform, shabby priests, and wineshops. We felt less ashamed of drinking our Tio Pepe and our Fundador when we realised how many, and how deep and full, were the wine cellars of Spain. But there was neither corn nor oil; the olives were being squeezed for Germany.

In a small ship whose cabin was full of Spanish officers and their families, whose deck was crowded with soldiers – and all grew pale and thoughtful, yawned and lay down to doze, when we rose and fell to a lop in the Straits – we crossed to Tangier, and landed in an evil fairyland. Flower-stalls filled the broad square of the market-place with fierce and delicate hues, with pointed and coronary shapes, with buds among their leaves and indolently open petals, milk-white and coral and red – but a rose was the price of a meal and brandy was cheaper than the azaleas. The little streets and lanes of the old town were quiet and lifeless, the shops with their pretty trifles of beadwork and leatherwork and jewellery were empty, their shopkeepers depressed: no tourists came to Tangier now. Here were sellers, but no buyers. The Spaniards, they said, had ruined the place, and the Gestapo ruled it. The tall square Rif Hotel was the Gestapo headquarters, and everybody told tales of intrigue, spies and mysterious disappearances. We were picked up by native agents of the Gestapo within an hour of landing, but all the good they got from us was fresh air and exercise. We took them for a country walk, and then kept them waiting at street corners.

We met some charming, almost anonymous English and American people who were doing their strange duty with a gentle hardihood; and twice they took us to the most agreeable night-club that could be imagined. On each occasion it was empty except for our party of some eight or ten; half a dozen pretty Hungarian girls who were said to have come from Budapest to Tangier by way of Khartoum, an improbable journey; and a dance-band of fugitive musicians from respectable European orchestras. The musicians were delighted to play a little Brahms between dances, and there was a beautiful broad-fronted barmaid with gap-teeth – but white as the white of an oyster-shell, in a florid and generous mouth – whose laughter was like the bass notes of a 'cello echoing from a crystal vase. The Hungarian dancing-partners had perfect manners and showed no smallest sign of resentment when we left one and took up with another.

'They daren't complain,' we were told, 'or they'd get the sack.'

'How strict the management must be,' we said.

'The Gestapo.'

'Really? I had no idea it was so efficient. But this sort of thing can't, of course, continue very long. If there are never more customers than this, the place will go bankrupt in no time.'

'There's not much fear of that. It has plenty of financial backing.'

'Some international syndicate, I suppose?'

'Oh no. The Gestapo.'

But the night-club was a guilty holiday from work, and contributed nothing to the film. Some jewellers' shops seemed more helpful. In all their windows hung row upon row of wrist-watches, and in the circumstances of the time we were much attracted by such richness. In England, and most of Europe, it had become hardly possible to buy a watch. Watches were famine-scarce in the embattled countries, and wrist-watches were a black-market currency of the highest value. With a dozen good watches, and a few thousand cigarettes for small change, one could buy one's passage – or so it was said – from Cadiz to the Baltic. Could I confect a story, with Gibraltar as its hub, in which Ralph, suitably disguised, purchased freedom of movement with a capital borrowed from a watchmaker's shop in Tangier?

We returned to the Rock, and Ralph's insomnia grew worse. It did not so much appear to be inability to sleep as a great unwillingness to begin; and as I shared a room with him at the Convent he would seek in my presence some excuse for postponing the dead nullity of going to bed. 'Let us play chess,' he would say, 'One game only – or perhaps the best of three?'

At fourteen or so my father had given me a set of chess-men – he regarded the game as part of a reasonable education – but, being indolent, I had never learnt more than how to move the several pieces. But Ralph would rather play with a booby than go to sleep, and, as he himself was impatient of the ordinary gambits, and regarded every game as a fine adventure in which – as in war – some unforeseen accident might change the whole face of battle, he was often lenient to my ignorance. But one night, being uncommonly sleepy, I refused to play, and quickly and churlishly went to bed.

He walked up and down, forlorn and woebegone. It was a long chamber and he had room to pace impressively, to sigh on the turn, and halt half-way to conjure some new device. With a more decisive step he came to the foot of my bed. 'You remember', he exclaimed, 'what we were talking about this morning? Whether the actor's part in a play is creative, or should be simple interpretation?'

'It depends on the play,' I muttered. 'We agreed about that.'

'Yes, yes. But I've just thought of a good instance.' He spoke quickly, his eyebrows rose high on his forehead as if he were already thunderstruck by the marvel of what he remembered, and across the great plain of his face there seemed to flicker small delicate tremors of excitement as when a breeze passes over ripening wheat. 'Something interesting, something relevant,' he said. 'Did you ever see Irving?'

'No.'

'But you know the story of *The Lyons Mail*? The scene in the garret of the inn, Dubosc alone, but outside the noise of the people who've captured his brother, and are torturing him, putting him to death? ... Well, this is how Irving played it.

'The stage was almost empty – dark, shadowy, a cobweb look about the rafters – and Dubosc sitting on a wooden stool. Like this. Not a movement. Just brooding. Then, as if the noise outside were sinking into his consciousness very slowly, so that he took a long time to understand it, he raised and turned his head – but little by little, very slowly – and when he had made up his mind to go to the window and look out he moved cautiously and suspiciously. Like this.

'Then he looked out, and his curiosity grew impatient. Gradually, as though it were being carved on his face, an appalling, diabolical glee changed his whole appearance. . . .'

I was sitting up by this time, watching him. I have never cultivated terror, or sought to be frightened – I much prefer comedy – but now terror was coming closely to my ribs. They were protected only by pyjamas; and the lineaments of Ralph's face were twisted in unholy design.

'Then,' he said, 'with an expression very hard to analyse, but there was arrogance in it, Irving came downstage towards the wooden stool, and with a sudden burst of anger – a lordly anger, you might think, a violent scorn of all crude material things – he kicked it. The stool turned over, and lay on its back with its legs in the air. Three legs, all pointing into the air.

'This was unexpected, and Irving retreated from it. It was unnatural, it was horrible. There was the stool on its back, with its legs in the air. You could see the pride and the anger disappear from his face, and stark terror come creeping on. But more than that, you could feel, as the terror grew in him, a cold and horrid fear spreading like an arctic fog over the audience. And all because a wooden stool lay on its back with its legs in the air, and Irving saw it as something – oh, something deadly and insane. . . .'

Sitting up in bed – my body feeling narrower and more transparent than it really is – I had seen Irving and felt the chill draught he blew across his audience. I had seen the dreadful unnatural stool with its vile legs in the air – and now Ralph, with the kindest look in his eyes, all the kindness in the world, and his round face a map for the tenderest expressions of hope and solicitude, was saying, 'Well, you see what I mean, don't you?'

'Ralph,' I said shakily, 'let us play a game of chess. I don't feel nearly as sleepy as I did. I think a game of chess would be an excellent thing.'

'Splendid,' he said. 'Splendid! I'm so glad. Which will you take – the white pieces?'

A thought occurred to me in the second game, and with my remaining castle in my hand I paused and asked, 'When and where did you see Irving?'

'Irving?' he said, astonished. 'I never saw Irving, dear boy. I'm younger than you. . . .'

I felt a little tired when morning came, but we talked about the film, we talked to more of the soldiers who endured their rigorous, dull and exacting servitude on the Rock, and believed in some cause that they could not express, though they knew it in their hearts like the street they had lived in. The soldiers of the garrison must be the solid background of the story, for theirs was the achievement; but their life was dull, and they themselves were often bored and sometimes more certainly resentful. How could I combine the long heroic boredom of the soldiers with some moving excitement that should meet – where they had met indeed, when the great invasion of North Africa was being prosecuted – in the midnight hours of Gunner Perry's fishing on the Detached Mole?

We watched the morning flood and the evening ebb of the thousands of Spanish labourers who came into the dockyard, and went out again with loaves of bread for their hungry friends. We watched the searching of suspected spies and smugglers. We explored the quiet untidy court-yards of Irish Town, and further reaches of the romantic tunnels: drills madly chattering, little tubes of polar gelignite being thrust into holes in the rock, the tangle of wires, the insane glare of arc-lights in a chalky fog, the sturdy common sense of the soldier-miners eating their bread and bully between the honeycomb of the Rock and the silver popple of the sea.

We saw the bay one night dazzled by searchlights, then filled by them when they poured in their radiance like hoses filling a huge cauldron with streams of transparent incande-scence. We saw the dainty little village at Catalan Bay, we were introduced to the monkeys who must never desert the Rock, we met the diligent Wrens who worked with such precise attention to their duties in cells dug deeply under-ground. We talked to the lonely gunners high on Spyglass Hill, and mingled with the shouldering noisy throng of soldiers and sailors and airmen who at night crowded the main street and filled its noisy shabby little cafés. We spent an evening with a squadron of the Royal Air Force when they were celebrating a successful assault on a submarine pack in the Atlantic west of Cape Spartel: the usual poor wooden furniture with dartboards and mugs of beer for ornament, the usual gallantry singing the usual songs, and two young flying-officers deep in liquor and a metaphysical argument. Flying their Wellington by night, they had killed a marauding U-boat, and now, to the accompaniment of breaking glass, their debate interrupted by monotonous repetition to the barman – 'Same again, Charlie' – they were exploring life's casual mystery. Another glass was swept from the bar, but whether to illustrate their tactics or the world's unreason I do not know. Its fellow crashed a moment later. 'Same again, Charlie.'

We saw what there was to be seen, and much of it was heroical and good, and some of it fantastic, some dreadful as a sentence to penal servitude, and some comical. We flew home again, and landed on a morning of shouting wind and wild bright sunlight on the outermost part of Cornwall.

🏶 Twenty-Three

1944 began badly. Strong disapproval had greeted my tedious long account of the Army, though I had done only what I was told to do. My instructions had been to start with an introductory chapter in which I could say something of Britain – of its troubled state of mind in 1938 and 1939 – to explain a process of rearmament so tardy and ineffectual that when we were committed to war the Army, though larger on paper, had had no time to train its new recruits, and was still calamitously short of modern weapons. Dramatically, of course, it was a good beginning: it would let me show our final achievement as a miraculous release of latent strength almost comparable with Moses' discovery of water in the desert of Sinai. But I wrote too harshly of the sterile years, and gave offence.

I diagnosed our national distemper as *accidie*, which – I thoughtfully explained –

means sloth or torpor, and used to be regarded as one of the Seven Deadly Sins. It was this disease which prevented us, during the middle thirties, from recognising the increasing danger in which we lived, and in the late thirties, when danger could no longer be denied, left us incapable of making any serious effort to defend ourselves. In 1936, when Italy, Germany, and Japan were all threatening various parts of the world with war, we owned a solitary Tank Brigade which, had it been at full strength, would have numbered two hundred tanks. But only on paper was it up to strength, and the tanks which it did possess were either obsolete or obsolescent. A year later we began to re-arm, but our re-armament programme was only impressive as another symptom of *accidie*: income tax was raised by threepence in the pound, and it was announced that neither marriage nor a few false teeth would be a bar to enlistment in the Army.

I added other examples of a policy which lived on pretences rather than practice – there was no lack of them – and commented, without sympathy, on those – and they were many – who during the war in Spain had warmly advocated intervention, and warmly denied the necessity of protecting ourselves against the possible consequences of intervention. I may, indeed, have gone too far and said too much, for I was, as a result, summoned to the presence of Lord Croft, then Under-Secretary of State for War. He, with some anger, rebuked me – for insolence, I think – and said I must rewrite the offensive chapter.

That I refused to do, but covered my stubbornness with a cloak of thick civility. If there was any value in what I had previously written, I said, it was due to the fact that I had never suffered dictation, nor been asked to. I had been allowed a great deal of freedom, and to freedom I had no other title than a modest, unassuming honesty. Thus, or in some such manner, I defended my intransigence, but Lord Croft – for many years a Member of Parliament for Bournemouth – was not impressed, and I was dismissed with acrimony.

A few days later I was sent for by P. J. Grigg, the Secretary of State for War, who had risen to high office, not out of Parliament, but from the Civil Service. Standing before him I felt some anxiety about my future, but he was unexpectedly sympathetic; and when I repeated my defence said quietly – a little wearily, perhaps – 'Yes, I thought you'd say that.' I think now that I behaved rather foolishly. At the time, however, I felt that I was defending a principle, and in the defence of principles it is always difficult to avoid pomposity and self-righteousness. In the quietism of old age I regret my intransigence, and marvel that I escaped reprimand. My tedious long report was jettisoned, and that, at least, was judiciously done.

More trouble followed, for my film-script on Gibraltar was heartily disliked by the brigadier to whom it had been submitted for criticism. 'Do you think this is the proper way to represent the Army?' he demanded. 'There's a man in this play of yours, a corporal or a sergeant, who gets a girl with child – '

'He marries her in the end,' I said.

'You seem to pretend that he's typical of the Army, typical of the Gibraltar garrison, and when he's refused compassionate leave – well, what does he do? He gets drunk. Fighting drunk!'

'It does happen,' I said.

'Well, it's not going to happen in a play that gets our approval,' said the brigadier.

I had, I thought, invented a story that was full of brooding excitement – too wildly plotted, perhaps – and deeply sympathetic with the sturdy patience of the soldiers on the Rock. But it failed to find approval, and I had to swallow my disappointment.

That was easier to do – easier than it might have been – because I had been writing other things as well, and I have always found that disappointment, in such-and-such a sector, loses most of its bitterness when one's attention has moved elsewhere. Failure may be reported in the south, but in the north new enterprise is on the stocks, and one is naturally more interested in the thing half-made than in the thing that's finished, polished, signed and gone out of control. A writer who hopes to enjoy some semblance of equanimity should always start a new book before the last one is in proof.

I had written two more conversation-pieces – during my regimental employment at Ripon I had had many long, uninterrupted evenings – and one of them, *The Great Ship*, received unusual favour when Val Gielgud persuaded his brother John to play the principal part, and three times sent it out upon the air. The other, *Rabelais Replies*, was less popular. The need for education – for prolonged and continuing education – was its theme, and to my cast I added Bishop Grundtvig, the creator of the Danish Folk High Schools. But in England few people knew who Grundtvig was, and education – as a source of entertainment – has little appeal.

I was, moreover, rewriting *Don Quixote*, with some free-dom, as a serial for broadcasting: Ralph Richardson had promised to play Quixote, and George Robey was studying the part of Sancho Panza. I wrote six episodes, I think, and with Ralph recorded an introduction; but I heard nothing of what I had written, for I was under orders, before the first episode was broadcast, to proceed to the Mediterranean.

The war in Italy had come to a standstill: or so it seemed. The Italian campaign had always suffered from divided counsel and divided interests. The Americans had never been whole-heartedly behind it, and hardly had it begun be-fore General Alexander was told to send home seven divisions and most of his landing-craft to feed and fatten the army that was being gathered for the invasion of Normandy in the following year. Now, after a bitter winter and months of grim fighting, the Allies appeared to have been decisively halted under the pale menace of Monte Cassino and before the many-gunned, thickly mined banks of the Garigliano. If, as it seemed, the campaign had been aborted, then I might be allowed to write about it; I would be writing history, not news, and I could not be accused of poaching on Fleet Street's preserves.

I was to go by sea as far as Gibraltar – the Navy had offered to carry me – and from there cross over to Algiers, where the documents essential to my task had already been gathered and catalogued and usefully indexed; or so I was told. Having exhausted the Algerian sources of information, I should then proceed to Italy, by whatever means I found convenient, and in Italy – well, it was hardly possible to give me specific instructions, and I must use my own judgment. I had my brief, and should act accordingly. Initiative one day and discretion the next? Something of that sort, I gathered.

In Liverpool a black rain was falling when I reported to the appropriate naval authority, and the draggled skirts of the sky were harried by a rising gale. *When the rain's before the wind.* . . . 'These are your instructions,' said the Com-mander. 'You're proceeding to the Mediterranean in *Flint Castle*.'. . . *Then your sheets and tops'ls mind.*

252

'A big ship?' I asked.

'No, I wouldn't say that. She's a corvette.'

I felt, for a moment, that curious sort of unhappiness which seems to find an abdominal centre. A corvette, a mere cockle-shell, and a gale of wind was blowing up. With some difficulty I concealed my dismay, pretended a fine indifference, and a very beautiful Wren served her country by driving me to the docks.

The gale increased as darkness fell. The whole sky was howling, and the Irish Sea, tormented by its violence, rose savagely against it. It was a vile crossing, but I had a bed for my unhappiness; most of the young sailors were also sea-sick, and much less comfortable. Then in Lough Foyle I moved from the corvette that had brought me so far, into her sister-ship the *Flint Castle*, and presented myself to her Captain. He was a tall, fair-haired, good-looking young man of twenty-four or so, called William Sitwell. His experience of life, as I discovered a little later, was larger than one could gather from the evidence of his voice and manner; which were conventionally polite and a little shy. His First Lieutenant – Liggins, a Western Australian – was a brown-faced laughing man, a yachtsman, hard-working but unperturbed by his work. The other officers, by their appearance, were not long out of school.

The weather improved, and for three days we did anti-submarine exercises and some gunnery practice. Star-shells hung on the darkness like the star of Bethlehem on a Christmas card, the Asdic whined and warbled. Then, under a black moonless sky with a spring-tide beneath us, we had to find again the narrow entrance to Lough Foyle, thinly lighted, with rocks on the one hand and sandy spits and bars on the other. Morning and April sun showed the white cottages, the green turf and yellow gorse of Donegal, and over against them the rough dark hills above Coleraine. The morning breeze blew stronger, and with warning of a full gale our Escort Group put out in line ahead to meet a convoy west of Islay: destroyers leading, then corvettes, and a trawler astern. I looked back and saw, between obscure and savage rain-storms, Inishowen white and gold and green under a vanishing patch of wild blue sky. Everybody was a little tense that morning, and inclined to grim or gloomy reminiscence.

Here was someone who had left Freetown with a convoy of twenty-one ships, and brought only four of them into Derry. Someone else had seen fifteen ships out of twenty lost to Stukas in the Channel in 1940. But the Chief Boatswain's Mate, contemplating profits rather than loss, claimed to have been in at the death of more than a dozen U-boats, including three in twenty minutes when the gallant Captain Walker's Group surprised a trio on the surface of the Bay, and sank them all.

About three in the afternoon we saw the merchantmen coming out of the mists of Islay, led by a furiously plunging trawler. We drew closer to the destroyer *Hesperus*, and passing a line received from the Senior Officer of the Group instructions for the convoy, which we had to deliver, like a marine postman, to every ship. We were by this time in a tidal race south-west of Islay, among overfalls in a very heavy sea patched with livid green, and the movement was so confused and violent that a great deal of patience and seamanship was necessary to bring us close enough to the merchantmen to pass their orders to them. A frigate of the Group lost a man overboard, and about midnight another corvette reported contact with a U-boat, and attacked; but to no purpose. We, of course, had no belief whatever in his report, for though your heart leaps with an assured faith when upon your own Asdic the echo cries *Ping!* you are utterly sceptical of another's claim.

When we were two or three days out, the ship's company presented a new appearance, very different from their trim, tidy, but rather subdued aspect in harbour. They wore now a hardy piratical look, and piratical garments: stocking-caps of red or dark blue wool drawn rakishly to one side of the head, coloured shirts, dirty towels or bright handkerchiefs knotted round their throats and sea-boots pulled over dungaree trousers. There is more liberty in a small ship than a big one – to compensate for less comfort – and having such liberty the sailors showed their dislike of uniform. And having disguised themselves as pirates they did their duty with the more zest; having disguised it a little too.

The weather moderated, and by the following day the sea was deep blue, no longer ragged but swelling smoothly into vast hills that slowly sank again; and the uncurtained sun shone from an empty sky. I talked with Sitwell, and when he told me that he thought South Shields the most romantic place in the world I grew inquisitive and persuaded him to tell me more.

Being about sixteen when his father died, he made up his mind that he could not remain a burden to his family, but would go to sea. Consulting no one about his decision, he left Harrow and in the Port of London found a shipmaster who signed him on for a voyage to the Baltic. Then for some years he sailed in ships that traded from South Shields, and there, in what some may think a dull or even a dismal town, he met so great a variety of men, such a lively company whose workshop was the whole round world, and heard such talk of faraway coasts and foreign cities, that he decided – and would defend his opinion warmly – that South Shields was not only a delightful place in which to live, but a harbour of true romance. At the other extreme in his regard was Igarka, the Siberian port two or three hundred miles from the sea on the river Yenisei; which he held to be the most detestable place he had ever seen.

There was a new moon at night, a mere rim of light on the circumference of the earth's shadow, and Sirius ahead of us shone bright and high. Morning came a clear grey, the swell subsiding but the wind freshening again.

I talked for a long while with a Naval Reservist about conditions in the Merchant Service. He was a good man, angry when he spoke of the hardships and unfairness of his life, but not, I think, embittered by them: not poisoned by remembrance. His pay as an A.B. in peacetime had been £8 2s a month, out of which he allowed his wife, with two children, thirty shillings a week. Often, he said, he had come ashore from a seven-weeks' voyage, not with money in his pocket, but a few shillings in debt to the ship; and going home had found his wife quite penniless. Once, on a voyage from New York in a ship badly undermanned – there were only four A.B.s who stood watch and watch – the seas had been so wild that for days they had been unable to get forward to their fo'c'sle, and had had to sleep on the engine-room gratings; and his first necessity after reaching home, with no money in the house, had been to go to 'the Guardians' for meal-tickets.

Most of the officers had stories, too, of the Admiralty's meanness. From boats and rafts they had picked up survivors of torpedoed ships – all of them, I think, had had such an experience – and given the poor sea-waifs what clothes they could spare. But would the Admiralty pay them for what they had given? They laughed a little coarsely. Not likely, they said. At the best they might get a third of the estimated value of their impulsive charity.

Story followed story. The Gunnery Officer had been in a small ship off Freetown, and surprising a U-boat on the surface they had rammed it. Then drawn off, and rammed again. Engaged it with gunfire, and finished it, when it submerged, with depth-charges. And the Coxswain, a man with a twinkle in his eye, a soldier's son born in Quetta, was full of curious anecdotes. 'Full of flannel,' said Liggins.

Then came a morning of such cerulean perfection, the sea a deep wrinkled blue and the sky cloudless but for a few pale shadows on the horizon, that it was bliss to be alive and breathing it. We were astern of the convoy, and because the leading escort-vessels were nearly hull-down, we had a pretty illusion of seeing the convexity of the world, and the ships of the convoy – painted a light grey, all in trim parallel lines, their smoke neatly brushed behind their right shoulders – looked as though they were steaming over the edge of it.

While we were admiring this handsome sight, there came a curious noise from somewhere above the bridge, and the men working there, painting and scrubbing, looked up in surprise. Alone, aloft, in simple happiness, the look-out in the crow's-nest was singing. There was rude laughter, and someone shouted, 'Shut your mouth and keep your eyes open! You're looking for destroyers aren't you?'

News had come from the cipher-room that six German destroyers were out in the Bay, and had been attacked by one of our aircraft. The aircraft was damaged, but a destroyer was on fire. Every day small items of news from the still-continuing Battle of the Atlantic came at intervals, and on slips of pink paper we read that a lone ship far to the westward was being pursued by a U-boat; that a straggler from a convoy had been torpedoed and was sinking; that an aircraft had attacked a submarine and the submarine was fighting back.

At noon a Sunderland flew over and reported that a raft was floating a few miles away. We searched for it and found it empty, overgrown with weed and barnacles, so old a denizen of the sea that it might have floated from the Flying Dutchman's waist when some great darkling wave swept over his bulwarks. Not far away a whale was blowing, and a lost swallow fluttered about our deck.

Sitwell and I played a game of chess after tea, and when I had his Queen in difficulties there came the alarm: Action Stations. We hurried out into a headlong rush of men, laughing and eager. A moment later came a profound explosion, and from end to end the whole ship shuddered – 'That'll shake the wax out of your ears,' said the Coxswain – as at slow speed we dropped a depth-charge over the stern to foil the U-boat's initial gambit. The Asdic was talking confidently. Its *Ping* had the accent of truth and we attacked immediately with our principal weapon: a projector which threw a heavy charge that could be timed to explode at given depths.

As we came on to the bridge, Sitwell was wearing slippers, flannel trousers, a khaki shirt, a fur-lined leather flying-jacket, and a blue beret. He exchanged his beret for a steel helmet. He threw off his leather jacket, and rolled up his shirt-sleeves as if he were going to engage the U-boat with his fists. He turned to me, laughing, and like Roland at

Roncesvalles cried 'Ha!' Then settling himself on his tall stool, gave his orders.

The heavy charges thrown by the projector exploded with a fearful detonation. They threw up huge fountains of water when set for a relatively shallow depth, but after a deeper explosion the surface of the sea quivered violently and flung a light spray, as if sweating in the agitation of utter panic, and presently green whirlpools or water-blisters would appear. We made two or three attacks at medium depth, then one at maximum depth. Three explosions seemed to reverberate in some tremendous chasm, with a profound effect upon the mind as well as on the body, and three minutes after the charges had been fired there was a strange and far-spread disturbance in the sea.

An oval smoothness appeared. It was about a hundred and fifty feet long, and it was surrounded by a clearly visible rim. It looked like a huge pale green ulcer encircled by a writhing lip of proud flesh. The smoothness heaved and pulsated. We waited in a most painful breathless excitement. It was going to split and give birth to something huge and broken. We watched, and saw the rim of proud flesh subside. The smoothness disappeared, and the area became indistinguishable from the surrounding sea. Nothing solid broke the surface.

The destroyer *Hesperus* joined us, was sceptical at first of our claim – no one believes in another man's *Ping* – but then got a strong contact, and after attacking with a multiple projector that threw up a quincunx of fountains, ordered us to stand clear while he made an attack at speed. 'Coming to take the credit,' we said, and sullenly hauled off. *Hesperus* set his course, and at full speed, a great arc of sunlit water at his bow, ploughed a straight furrow in the sea and dropped behind his lethal seeds, that flowered with immediate thunder to great petals and plumes of white spray.

Here and there we saw patches of oil, but not enough to be good evidence. *Hesperus* claimed to have seen a periscope, and attacked again. We in our turn grew sceptical of his assertions, but when he left us, to rejoin and lead the now vanished convoy, we got another good contact. While advancing slowly to attack we observed an oily white line that seemed to be moving at equal speed between us and the sun. We attacked ahead, swung hard to starboard, and getting a contact near the white line, discharged upon that also. Could there be a second submarine, or had we filled the ocean, two thousand fathoms deep, so full of whirlpools and wandering vapours that our own depth-charges were haunting and mocking us?

It was past eight o'clock, and Sitwell, turning on his stool, perceived that his bridge was untidy. 'Who', he shouted, 'has been eating hard-boiled eggs on my bridge?'

'We have!' answered the sailors on duty there. 'All of us, sir.'

Four hours had gone since the affair began, but we had been unconscious of time. Sailors' stomachs, however, are less emotional and require orderly attention no matter what is happening; so a kind of picnic feast, of gigantic sandwiches and eggs and mugs of tea, had been carried round the ship. Now it was growing dark, and orders came from *Hesperus* to rejoin the convoy. We had to leave our battlefield without a trophy.

Sitwell sent for his First Lieutenant. Liggins came onto the bridge, and went to starboard round the Asdic house. Sitwell, to meet him, took the port side. The sailors laughed happily and said, 'Look at the Skipper and Jimmy the One playing ring-o'-roses!'

In the morning, a fine fresh morning, being roughly in the latitude of Brest, we led the right wing of the convoy, and when an aeroplane was seen, that could not be identified, the belief became current – but I could not determine whether it was wishful thinking or dreadful thinking – that its purpose was to direct against us a fleet of U-boats, torpedo-bombers, glider-bombers, or all of them together.

I discovered that two of our stokers had in civil life – if that is the proper word for it – been prize-fighters; one of whom used to challenge all comers for £1 a time in a travelling booth. There was a seaman who had been a bookmaker's tick-tack man, another a professional dancer. We had a stoker who took part in the River Plate battle, and one who was in the submarine *Truant* when she lay on the bottom with a live bomb aboard. A telegraphist had served ashore, as a gun-spotter with the Royal Horse Artillery, during General Dick O'Connor's advance into Cyrenaica; and the Yeoman of Signals was at the Salerno landing. He had seen the explosion of so many sea-mines that he thought nothing of the white splashes by which the ship, lying off the beach, was surrounded, until someone on the bridge said, 'That was a close one.' Then, realising at last that the white splashes were caused by plunging shells, he suddenly became frightened. . . . If experience of life could be gathered and weighed and valued, the *Flint Castle* would have been entitled to a lot of prize-money.

After a clear sunset the young moon was delicately bright, and still so thin that its convexity was like the muscular bending of a bow – and there to the left of it, a looted diamond on the invisible archer's finger, shone Jupiter. The stars were few and magnificent; and Orion's Belt hung a hand's breadth above the southern horizon. But even the most splendid of stars do little to mitigate the feeling of loneliness, of a desolate shrinking, when night falls upon the sea.

Day returned with a sunny strong breeze and wind-clouds in the sky, fine thin streamers bent across the zenith with frail and lovely wool-combings flying from them. On a pink slip of paper came the news that survivors of a lost ship were floating on a raft some hundreds of miles to the south-west; and several of our sloops were inviting battle at the northern entrance of the Bay. One of the ships in the convoy was anxiously enquiring the proper treatment for a badly scalded stoker.

Dudgeon, an engineer-officer, was small, very young, white-faced and extremely polite. You would not think, to look at him, that his history had been remarkable. Perhaps in our contemporary scale of values, it had not been outstanding; but it compelled my respect. It included long months of patrolling off the South American coast – four weeks at sea, twenty-four hours in harbour – and the Mediterranean in the bad time when we did not make known our losses, though the people of Alexandria could see the *Queen Elizabeth* and the *Valiant* disabled in their harbour. Then he was torpedoed in a desperate small convoy of seven ships protected by as many cruisers and a score of destroyers. Going stern-first through villainous weather his wounded ship had reached Aden, and been patched with concrete; then to Bombay, to be patched again, and from there to the Brooklyn Navy Yard. Dudgeon's Chief had been in the cruiser *York*, lost off Crete, and after that in an ancient Greek tramp on the Tobruk run; and when she grounded and was lost, he had gone to the *Medway*, a submarine depot-ship, which was torpedoed. Whenever the ship rolls, I thought, and I stumble against a passing seaman, I am rubbing shoulders with history.

A little before dusk we began to fuel from an oiler. We took aboard a cable and a pipe-line, and thereafter, keeping station on the pipe-line, had to follow exactly in the oiler's wake. From a cloud glowing like honey pale sun-shafts struck the western rim of the darkening ocean.

Sunday was grey-skied and clear, four hundred and fifty miles off Finisterre. In obedience to the Articles of War, which command 'the public worship of Almighty God to be solemnly, orderly, and reverently performed', we descended through a hole in steel to a lower mess-deck where, swaying slightly, we sang 'For those in peril on the sea'; and then, 'Lay hold on life and it shall be Thy joy and crown eternally'.

Sitwell stood between a pumping-engine and a heap of neatly rolled hammocks, against a background of cheap suitcases very trimly arranged. He read the sixth chapter of Genesis, the building of the Ark: 'There were giants in those days.' But really, I thought, they are no pigmies who serve today. When he came to the description of pitching the Ark, of pitching it within and without with pitch, there were nudges and sidelong looks among the seamen, for they realised that Noah was a man of the same kidney as their own

Number One. Liggins had kept them hard at work, painting within and without with paint. The sailors grumbled at his strictness, made wry jokes, and were devoted to him.

In recognition of Sunday the wardroom table-cloth was turned. It had become very dirty indeed with its accumulation of gravy-smears, the stain of patent sauces, fragments of cabbage, and the ruddling of spilt jam; but the under side was appreciably cleaner.

The first of May came calm but overcast, clearing to sunlight in the afternoon. I had some conversation with an engineer who had served in *Rodney*, sailed in three Malta convoys, shared the chase of the *Bismarck* and the bombardment of Italy from the Messina Straits. A messmate, he said, having been hit by several shell-splinters, mysteriously began to swell. As the swelling increased, very quickly and quite monstrously, he started to choke and was expected to die of asphyxia at any moment. But tracheotomy relieved him almost on the instant, and the strange intumescence of his body rapidly subsided. Another mate of his had been under an armour-plated deck when the *Rodney* was hit by a bomb, and being dragged into daylight, looked like a mere cinder; but he too recovered. *Rodney*, he told me, had fired three hundred and fifty heavy shells against the *Bismarck*, and the German ship had turned over before the cruiser *Dorsetshire* sent the finishing torpedoes into her.

We changed course to the south-east before dark, and learnt that four U-boats were in the vicinity: presumably to contest our passage through the Straits. But on the following day domestic news held the air, for one of the destroyers had a case of acute appendicitis, and arrangements had to be made to put the man aboard the convoy rescue-ship for immediate operation; while a surgeon, having visited the engineer who had lately been scalded aboard one of the merchantmen, reported that he was now quite comfortable.

The next morning, a hundred and sixty miles north of Madeira, we were in a heavenly climate, warm and with far visibility, treading a wrinkled calm sea and softly buffeted by mild airs. There is no luxury like good days at sea.

Nothing happened to break the calm, and after a gentle night, rain-showers in a grey morning sprinkled the pale lawn of the Atlantic. The smoke of all the ships in the convoy hung together in one huge brown canopy.

In the evening some escort-vessels from Freetown met us, and eight of the ships in our convoy passed to their care.

A rough night brought another calm morning, and we approached the Straits of Gibraltar on a course about East by North. 'Channel fever' set in with reports of an unidentified aircraft, and two Spanish trawlers were vaguely suspect. In the late afternoon the sky looked like a grey Shetland shawl, and when the darkness turned it to a black ram's fleece – but lighted now by a nearly full moon – a sister corvette reported a contact, the ships of the convoy turned this way and that in the zig-zag agitation of evasive action, and we went to Stations with loud ridicule of our neighbour's *Ping*. He himself confessed, a little later, that he had been mistaken, and at the order 'Secure Action Stations' our steel decks resounded the tramp of scornful boots. Then echoed them again at midnight when a Catalina discovered a U-boat and gave its course. More zig-zag for the merchantmen, and swift hunting for us; but to no purpose.

In the morning, Trafalgar – and a doubt about the geography of Browning's 'Home Thoughts from the Sea'. How, with Cape St Vincent to the north-west, Gibraltar to the north-east, and Trafalgar full in face, could he see a blood-red sunset running into Cadiz Bay?

Spain in the early light was dark blue and grey, the Rock magnificent but gaunt, as though history had clawed it to the bone. History is a tale of lacerations, and much of it is therefore a gloomy tale. But in the making, before the gloom has settled, there may be pleasant lights upon it, if you happen to be in the proper place to see them. I had been very fortunate. I had seen the young captain of one of His Majesty's ships of war roll up his sleeves to engage a U-boat in personal conflict; and I had heard such a valedictory address, to his sailors after action, as no historian has ever set on paper. No historian has recorded, after battle, such homely indignation as: 'Who's been eating hard-boiled eggs on my bridge?'

I had been sixteen days aboard the *Flint Castle*, and the unwillingness with which I had boarded her was loudly mocked by the reluctance with which I left her.

✤ Twenty-Four

In Algiers I lived for some time in a shabby small hotel which housed a shifting population of war correspondents, photographers, and a few people whose status and identity remained doubtful. It had a bruised and battered appearance, but was tolerably clean. There was an inexhaustible supply of dark red wine, and of gossip as boldly flavoured.

Occasionally I shared a bottle with a man who bore the dry scars of torture. He was, I believe, an Alsatian, and certainly a man of stubborn temper; he was blind of one eye in consequence, and through his hair ran thin white lines to show where the Gestapo men had burnt him with incandescent wires. Sometimes, of his own volition, he would speak of the sensations, both physical and mental, of being tortured, and the curious, unpredictable effects of prolonged, insistent pain; but he never replied to questions. It was known that he had a friend, living somewhere in Algiers, who had suffered more grievously than he; but no one had ever seen the friend.

Then, as I was walking home one night – I had been at a party, it was very late – I met the Alsatian, and recognised him before he saw me. He stood behind a baby's push-cart – but a push-cart almost as long as a coffin – and he was leaning forward to speak to the creature who lay, blanketed, beneath its hood. He was not pleased to see me, but said, 'You knew I had a friend who was hurt by the Gestapo? He does not like to be seen, so it is only at night that I take him out for a walk. Speak to him, but do not try to shake hands.'

There would be no profit in recalling – even if I could – the emotion excited by that encounter. There was more of

hatred in it than pity. To look at the Gestapo's victim induced a numb despair; but to think of the men who had
done this thing roused a hatred that was both impersonal
and extreme. I wanted to be judge and hangman; grave-
digger too. There was no cure for gangrene, moral or
physical: lop off the offending members, and put them out
of sight. . . .

With great relief I returned to my simple duty and the
tasks of investigation in a Nissen hut that stood in the
grounds of a large French villa on the hill above Algiers.
There was, in fact, not much to investigate. An American
professor, from one of the south-western colleges, had
assembled a great deal of information about the taking of
Sicily, which he was so generous as to share with me; and
opposite him sat Major John Counsell, late of the Theatre
Royal, Windsor, who had – if I remember rightly – a
unique collection of what were called 'situation reports', but
not much to supplement them and explain the significance
of the situations described. In addition to them there was an
amiable Scotch corporal, and there were two young
W.A.A.C.s, the American equivalent of our A.T.S.

With zeal and persistence I worked on the Sicilian
campaign, until my attention was diverted by an invading
swarm of locusts. For a day or two they were merely a
nuisance: walking back to my hotel in the evening, they
struck me with a small, blind impact, and with revulsion I
trod on their fallen bodies. But then came a morning when,
on our hill-top, they clouded the sky, and with one of the
W.A.A.C.s – a slim and amiable girl from Oklahoma –
I went out to breathe the agitated air and marvel at the
rushing multitude of their wings. I carried my little
swagger-cane – two feet of polished malacca, thick as a
thumb – and with an idle swing I struck a locust to the
ground. Another swing, and another fell.

'Say, that's kinda fun!' exclaimed the girl from Oklahoma, and running into the hut returned with John Counsell's swagger-cane. Then, before competition began, we
elaborated rules – we could play only in an agreed sequence

of strokes: forehand, back-hand, volley and lob – and the pile of our victims mounted before we tired of the exercise and went to lunch. She was a friendly, communicative girl, and in a khaki blouse that was always freshly laundered she made our A.T.S. look very shabby: the Government of the United States presented its uniformed females with a rich trousseau for foreign service, and underclothes of lavish variety.

The locust-storm coincided with exciting news from Italy: the war had begun to move again, and my work in Algiers lost its savour. I was conscientious, however, and worked for a little while longer, then flew to Naples and reported to the vast military bureaucracy that was housed in the baroque palace of Caserta: on the one side the cascades of its enormous artificial waterfall, on the other a marble staircase rising incongruously from the middle of a court-yard, and in between a busy tedium, punctuated by incessant saluting, and inadequately sustained by American rations devised, as it seemed, for the women's dining-hall of some refined New England seminary. I disliked Caserta, but did what work I could as hastily as possible, and took the first opportunity that offered of joining the advancing Eighth Army as a camp-follower.

That, of course, was the proper decision, for the war I had been sent to describe had ceased to be. The static war had become fluid and expansive, and if I was to write any-thing of value about its renewed purpose I must see some-thing of it before action had been dried and sieved and reduced to dead words in war-diaries and situation reports.

I was handicapped by the fact that I did not belong to any field formation. I 'belonged' to the War Office and in Italy the War Office had no more authority than the Pope of Rome in a convocation of Presbyterian pastors in Edin-burgh. I had no transport, no assurance of food and accom-modation other than the amiability of my uniformed neighbours. As I made my way forward my difficulties diminished, for hospitality increases in inverse ratio to one's distance from the enemy; but it was exasperating to have to beg for favour, even though favour came half-way to meet one. For some weeks I followed the war with the fortuitous navigation of a hitch-hiker; I moved in approximately the right direction, but seldom by the shortest way.

I saw the muddy battlefield of the Garigliano. I saw the Poles who had been fighting in the last of the battles for Monte Cassino come down from those terrifying, haunted heights; and as slowly they marched away they all appeared to be images of the same man. They all looked alike. Their faces grey, and under that uniform hue there was bone — pressing hard on starved skin — that came from the same matrix. Death at close quarters, and contempt for death, had stamped upon their faces a heroical identity.

In the Liri valley the Canadians were fighting at Ponte-corvo, and for a day or two I had some conversation with them. I woke one morning to find they had gone — the battle had moved on — and I was alone beside a pool of the river that babbled invitingly. I stripped and went in; but only for a moment. Here and there a darkness floated in the water, and I splashed ashore to vomit blood; not my own, but German or Canadian. Then — but I forget where — I met Philip Jordan, who between Kuibyshev and North Africa had seen many aspects of the war, and still retained a look of quizzical disbelief in what he saw. The fall of Rome was imminent, and Philip had decided to approach it from the Anzio bridgehead. He, more richly endowed than I, had transport of his own, so we returned to Naples and took ship for a short night-voyage to Nettuno.

Of our entry into Rome, and the careful modulations of Roman enthusiasm, I have written in *A Year of Space*; but I said nothing, in that account, of her who may be the unsung heroine of a momentous night. If my memory serves, we first heard the story — Philip and I — when we sat down to lunch in the Piazza del Popolo a few hours after driving in, and on a later occasion I heard it again; but I cannot swear to the truth of it.

On 4 June, when the Americans were on the outskirts of the city, there was still some doubt about the Germans' intention, a lingering fear that they might blow the bridges on the Tiber and fight a delaying action from the Porta San Giovanni to Monti Parioli and the road to Viterbo. In the event they pulled quietly out when darkness fell, but still the Americans advanced slowly and cautiously. Heedful of surprise their infantry moved warily, reconnoitring every corner. Rome was not built in a day, and might not have been taken in the course of a single night but for the loud encouragement of a female voice that broke the silence of the streets.

'Come on, boys!' the great voice commanded. 'Old Ma Reynolds is here, she'll look after you. Come on, come on! You and me, together, boys. Old Ma Reynolds knows the way!'

There were many American war correspondents in the field, but few were better known than Quentin Reynolds and his wife. He had a voice that seemed unnaturally loud even when reduced to print, and she, I believe, was a woman of exuberant temper. Warm and impulsive, said her friends; noisy and truculent, said those who liked her less. Perhaps she grew impatient, and marched boldly into the darkness. The story may be true, and I hope it is. I like to think of that voice re-echoing in the empty streets, and Ma Reynolds taking possession of the Forum.

The battle for the capital was less successful than it should have been. If Mark Clark, commanding the American Fifth Army, had maintained the direction and impetus of his initial advance – if he had fought for a strategic rather than a political objective – he could have cut the retreat of Kesselring's army while the mass of it was still in the Liri valley; but he turned aside to pluck fame and the golden fruit of Rome – was punished heavily for untimely ambition – and let Kesselring hold the Via Casilina until his threatened divisions had pulled out. The consequence was that a German army, which might have been confined in prisoner-of-war cages, was skilfully regrouped, and when the weather broke stood ready to oppose our further advance.

For a couple of weeks the Eighth Army moved swiftly,

and many in it were surprised by sudden, unexpected school-room memories as they drove into Viterbo or Chiusi – from forgotten pages came Tarquin and the milk-wolf and Lars Porsena – and on the green hill above Lake Trasimene stood Hannibal counting the prisoners he had taken from the defeated army of the consul Flaminius. But between the southern shore of Trasimene and the little lake of Chiusi the Germans found a defensive line, and when low skies loosed their hoarded rain the earth dissolved under the weight of our tanks and guns, the advance slid glumly to a halt, and the enemy industriously improved a good position. Antici-pating a change of weather, I had snatched a chance to visit Orvieto, and after admiring the cathedral and the view – yellow marble and blue-green profundities – I bought half a dozen flasks of excellent white wine. With me was a young man in the Rifle Brigade, and he had the good fortune to be friendly with the officer who commanded and administered Caledon Camp; where we intended to sleep.

Caledon was General Alexander's private demesne: his retreat and sanctuary. It consisted of a couple of caravans and a few small tents. It was mobile, its staff was very small, its custodian discreet; and he was allowed to entertain passers-by, whose discretion he could trust, when the Commander-in-Chief was unlikely to require accommodation for himself. The wine I had bought was a present for Cedric Yates, our *de facto* host, and he seemed to approve my choice. We had begun to dine – we had opened, I think, our second fiasco – when, without warning or ceremony, there entered General Alexander and General Harding, his Chief of Staff.

It is always embarrassing to be caught trespassing, and few acts of trespass can be more blatant, or aggravated, than to be found seated at a general's private table and eating his dinner. Our discomfort was increased, moreover, by the fact that we had been talking about the several mishaps which had robbed, or were robbing, General Alex of the triumph he deserved: Mark Clark had taken the wrong turning, the Americans were moving seven divisions out of Italy to mount a pointless assault on the Riviera, and now the rain had come – it drummed in frenzy on the roof of the caravan – to bog down an advance which, by rapid continuance, might have regained something of what had been lost. He might, we had thought – playing lightly on a dark idea – be in a difficult mood.

But General Alexander was in a most genial temper. He and Harding appeared to be unmoved by their ill luck, and they showed no displeasure at the sight of uninvited guests. With apparent goodwill, indeed, they shared our Orvieto wine, and I recognised equanimity, not only as one of the heroic virtues, but as a heroic grace; and was duly thankful for it. I fell asleep to the ceaseless drumming of rain on the taut canvas of my tent, but in the morning the sun shone warm and clear, and young jays were busy in a nearby hedge. Birds – but only birds – had cause to be grateful for the war. In the years of peace there had been no mercy for larks and linnets – not in Italy – but war brought them immunity and they flourished in their unaccustomed freedom. Nightingales made the dark melodious, and a great dawn-chorus woke one before the sun was up.

West of the Trasimene lake there was lush, richly growing country, cut by a long canal and many irrigation channels; north of it bare hills rose steeply. For a week, and longer, there was infantry fighting at close quarters, every day a punctual payment to death, and a gradual advance. When I found myself going forward in a company attack – fortunately it aborted: we ran into heavy fire – I realised that I was becoming too emotionally involved, and a day or two later retired to the salutary boredom of paper-work in Rome. I had, by that time, established my claim to a chair and part of a table in a small room whose other occupants were two Polish officers. Though quite untrammelled by discipline I was – I insist on this – remarkably obedient to conscience, and constantly I did what I could to construct a sort of growing framework, or moving picture, of the campaign, that I patched or coloured with the profits of my own observation. Several years later, when I wrote a semi-official history of the war in Italy, my notes added little to the final account, but were of real value in that they gave me a remembered background for the events I then had to plot and measure.

I went north again before Arezzo was taken, in mid-July, and I have an engaging memory of being mocked by a company of Scots Guards who, newly relieved, were emerging from the scene of recent battle that I was approaching. They were in high spirits, and loudly they exclaimed, 'You're going the wrong way! There's Jerries down there, you don't want to get mixed up with them! You come along with us and you'll be all right!' I was alone on the bare hillside, and I had to run the gauntlet of their mockery. But what good fortune to see and hear such boisterous geniality as the immediate aftermath of battle! I walked on, and an hour or so later was in a part of the town which appeared to be quite deserted. Then I felt uneasily alone, but was saved from serious disquiet by a spectacle of such blatant impropriety as almost denied belief.

In that campaign looting was not unknown, but such looting as I had previously seen was modest in scale and venial in kind: a fat goose, a few bottles of wine, nothing more serious. But now, on a street half-blocked by fallen houses, I saw a three-ton lorry halt, to let its driver measure the remaining clearance, and as it lurched slowly forward its cargo was revealed. As if it were a furniture-remover's van it was packed with chairs and tables, bedsteads and ornate cupboards and pictures in large, elaborate frames. Some rich and possibly noble house had been stripped of all it held, but for what purpose? There were four or five men in the lorry – one of them waved gaily to me – but I shall identify neither the arm of the service to which they belonged, nor the dominion from which they had come. There was no black market for their cargo, they could neither sell it nor ship it home. Their purpose, I assumed, was to furnish their mess in unexampled splendour, and give a party – perhaps to sergeants from another dominion – that would excite the envy of their guests and long be remembered for its dignity and riches.

From Arezzo the war advanced towards Florence over the roof-tops of the Chianti hills. I had by then acquired great freedom of movement, and I enjoyed some healthy walking there. Nowadays it is strange, almost beyond belief, to remember the friendship established between soldiers of the Pretoria Armoured Regiment and the tall Coldstreamers with whom they lived in the 24th Guards Brigade. The sight of tanks on those steep green hills was marvellously improbable, and friendly, teasing conversation between Cockney and throaty Afrikaner voices now seems quite impossible. But friendly they were, and it wasn't Cockney nationalism that spoiled their friendship.

My increased freedom was the consequence of a summons to attend General Oliver Leese, commanding the Eighth Army. He was encamped high on the hills above Arezzo, and in the space of time proper for the comfortable drinking of two large whiskies and soda – comfortable because I sat in the sunny shelter of a caravan and some tall trees – I executed the first of his commands, which was to compose, in suitable language, an Order of the Day to announce the King's impending visit. That was approved, and after dinner the General said he wanted me to broadcast, over some far expansion of the B.B.C'.s wartime network, occasional reports of his army's progress and successes. That, I thought, would give me no great difficulty, and I was surprised, as well as pleased, when he added, 'Now if you're going to do that for me, what can I do for you?'

'Will you, sir, give me a *laissez-passer* to cover all your territory?'

'But of course. And for a start, perhaps, you would like to follow the King for a day or two, and see what he's going to see?'

It was in blazing heat that the King set out to inspect his troops. Under a brassy sun and a shimmering sky he stood, lean and brown, in his jeep, and was driven mile after mile past rank upon rank of his soldiers from India and New Zealand, from Canada and South Africa, as well as our familiar domestic regiments. More than one of the beautifully accoutred young men in the royal entourage collapsed under the cloudless heat of the Italian sky, but the King – grave and forever attentive to all he saw – sustained without wilting the stare of the sun, and the intensive stare, the abrasive applause, of a seemingly innumerable army; and at the end of it all he was given a treat – a juvenile treat – that no one had intended.

He was taken, with great regard for security, to watch a demonstration of gunfire against a German battery or batteries, that were not expected to reply. For a few minutes our guns fired without response, but then, for another few minutes, the enemy replied with some vigour, and angry shells came down about the royal party with a violent assertion of acrid, dust-clouded and persistent hostility. The duel was concluded, and walking back among senior officers, who looked pale and shaken, came the King in widely grinning, loud-spoken delight. He had come to Italy to inspect his soldiers; for a little while he had shared their danger; and he was manifestly pleased by the bonus he had been given. On the following morning, in the cool of the morning, I was among those who were presented to him, and that was the preamble to my major experience in the Italian campaign.

❧ Twenty-Five

T HE movement that was to culminate in so joyful an occasion began badly. We had been shelled in camp during the night, and now, when we were breaking camp to go forward, I found myself without transport. Despite my enlarged freedom I was still dependent on charity for my passages, and my expected host for the day failed to appear. I had to travel in a slow, rattling, grossly overburdened Dodge truck, and as traffic on the road from Arezzo to Siena was heavy the immediate prospect was a very tedious hot day in convoy in a cloud of thick white dust. But my luck turned and showed its promise before we reached San Savino.

A figure, white as flour, in a jeep coming swiftly from the west waved as he passed, and came alongside again a few minutes later. It was Wynford Vaughan Thomas, then a war correspondent for the B.B.C., whom I had last seen dancing on a road a few miles south of Rome, on the day before we went in. He had spent four months with the beleaguered garrison at Anzio and, newly released from that long confine-ment, had no patience to talk about it but danced in the joy of freedom. Now he was looking for the Eighth Army's Press Camp, and could not learn where it had gone.

'San Donato in Poggio,' I said, 'but it's very difficult to find. I know the way, so you had better take me with you.'

Then, travelling fast and nimbly overtaking the several hundred tanks and tank-transporters, command vehicles, light trucks and three-tonners and ambulances ahead of us, the road became tolerable despite its dust. It follows a curving ridge, and where the fog of travel was not too thick there were pleasant views of the nearby woods or wrinkled mountains to the north. Near Siena the country goes bald. There are widely rolling downs, pale in colour, with naked limestone staring through. At a hamlet called Poggio al Vento there is a view of the Cathedral's black and white tower and the slender high stem of the Campanile.

The first time I went to Siena the streets were deserted, for the *goums* were in town, the thin-faced Moroccan irregulars, whose fierceness and savage legend kept the inhabitants behind locked doors and shuttered windows; and black soldiers from Senegal had set up their cots and were washing their shirts in the court of the Palazzo Pubblico under the great hall where Simone Martini painted his frescoes. There had been a stillness in the narrow streets as if they were holding their breath and listening. But now they were cheerfully crowded, for the *goums* and the Senegalese had gone, and instead there were sight-seeing Americans and Afrikaans-speaking soldiers from Pretoria and the Cape.

From Siena we drove north, on the main road to Florence, through the shattered little towns of Poggibonsi and Tavernelle, then turning into a network of dusty lanes found our new camp-site in an olive grove. Ahead of us the Germans were fighting a desperate tenacious battle to hold Florence, and there was acute anxiety about the city's fate. Would they abandon it, when they were driven from their present positions, or would they contest it street by street?

I wanted to visit the 8th Indian Division, and persuaded Vaughan Thomas that he could spend a profitable day by taking me to it. I had lately met one of its officers in Rome, Captain Nayar of the Mahratta Light Infantry, and I had promised to visit him as soon as I could find an opportunity.

We called on the Indians on 30 July. At Divisional Headquarters we had lunch with Unni Nayar and a Punjabi friend of his called Quereshi, a gentle good-looking young man with luminous brown eyes. The afternoon was warm and bright, the olive trees on the higher slopes turned their leaves in the wind like a shoal of silver fish. We were in a comfortable mood when we set off, now climbing to some enormous view, now going slowly through a shell-torn village, then descending to the lowland heat again. Nayar pointed across a valley to the house in which his battalion had established its headquarters.

It was a union of little castle and large villa, an ancient tower rising among cypresses on a small hillside above the plain high walls of a sixteenth-century building. It was, we discovered, the Castello di Montegufoni, the property of Sir Osbert Sitwell. In recent years incongruities have been as common as violent death, but, unless the mind has been numbed by too much exposure, the latter still dismays and the former continue to excite a curious pleasure. If it was engaging to find the Mahratta Light Infantry in residence in a Tuscan castle, it was delightful to learn that it belonged to Sir Osbert: the Indian soldiers looked like new images, domiciled as urbanely as their many divers predecessors, in the Sitwells' eclectic hospitality; and we may have been fractionally prepared for the greater, the superb, the enchanting surprise that awaited us within the walls.

We could not immediately see the Colonel, we were told, because he was asleep. He had spent the previous night in active prosecution of the war, and had earned his rest. We were about two thousand yards from the German's forward positions on the ridge that runs through San Michele and La Romola, but the afternoon was quiet except for the occasional intervention of our medium artillery in the valley behind us, and the infrequent passage of a German shell, like a lonely migrant, from the hill in front.

Idly we looked into a courtyard, and within a minor entrance to the house discovered to our surprise three or four pictures propped against a wall. Elderly dark paint on wooden panels, and some tarnished gold: a Virgin, the Child and the Virgin, a painted Crucifix. The yellow faces were drawn with the severe and melancholy stare of the earliest Florentine painting.

We sat on our heels to examine them more closely. One of us said with astonishment, 'But they're very good!'

'They must be copies,' said another.

I answered like an auctioneer, with the conviction of faith rather than of knowledge: 'Genuine Italian primitives!'

We went into a room where many more pictures were stacked against the walls, some in wooden cases, some in brown paper, and others naked in their frames. Two or three of those that were exposed to view aroused in us the dishonest pretence of recognition so common in visitors to an art gallery. 'Why,' we said, 'surely that's by So-and-so. Not Lippo Lippi, of course, but — oh, what's his name?'

We were not the only occupants of the room, however. Half a dozen soldiers were rummaging in a large desk which seemed to have been roughly opened. It would be altogether too harsh to accuse them of looting, they were only looking for small souvenirs. But they may have been careless, for there was broken glass on the floor and books which had been tidily stacked were scattered about in some confusion. I looked at some neatly tied bundles of yellowish paper, and saw that they were legal documents of Sir George Sitwell's time. I found a copy of *Before the Bombardment* inscribed by Osbert to his mother, and some invitation cards which announced that Lady Ida Sitwell would be At Home on such-and-such a date, when there would be Dancing.

Presuming on the slightest sort of acquaintanceship — I had met Osbert once or twice — I said to the soldiers, very mildly, 'I don't think you should take anything from here. I know the owner of the house.'

A genial well-fed sergeant at once replied, 'Oh well, sir, that makes all the difference, doesn't it? If we'd known that, we wouldn't have touched a thing. Not a thing,' he repeated, as though shocked by the very idea.

Nayar and Quereshi and Vaughan Thomas had gone to explore the farther rooms, and now Vaughan Thomas, his rosy face tense with excitement, reappeared. 'The whole house is full of pictures,' he exclaimed, 'and some of the cases are labelled. They've come from the Uffizi and the Pitti Palace!'

Hastily I followed him into the next room, where a score

278

of wooden cases stood against the walls, and then to the room beyond. There a very large picture lay upon trestles. It was spattered with little squares of semi-transparent paper, stuck for protection over imperilled areas where the paint was cracking or threatening to flake. On the near side there were cherubs, or angel-young, with delicate full lips, firm chins, and candid eyes wide open over well-defined cheek-bones. Against a pale blue sky the Virgin floated in splendour. Two reverent, benign and bearded figures held a crown above her head.

We failed to recognise it. We knew now that we were in the presence of greatness, and a bewildered excitement was rising in our minds. Recognition could not yet speak plainly, but baffled by the vast improbability merely stammered. Stupidly we exclaimed, 'But that must be ...'

'Of course, and yet ...'

'Do you think it is?'

By this time we had gathered a few spectators. Some refugees had been sleeping in the castello – their dark bedding lay on the floor – and now, cheerfully perceiving our excitement, they were making sounds of lively approval, and a couple of men began noisily to open the shutters that darkened the last of the suite of rooms. This was a great chamber that might have served for a banquet or a ball, and as we went in the light swept superbly over a scene of battle: over the magnificent rotundities of heroic war-horses, knight tumbling knight with point of lance – and beside it, immensely tall, an austere and tragic Madonna in dark raiment upon gold.

Vaughan Thomas shouted, 'Uccello!'

I, in the same instant, cried, 'Giotto!'

For a moment we stood there, quite still, held in the double grip of amazement and delight. Giotto's Madonna and Uccello's Battle of San Romano, leaning negligently against the wall, were now like exiled royalty on the common level. They had been reduced by the circumstance of war from their own place and proper height; and they were a little dusty. We went nearer, and the refugees came round us and proudly exclaimed, 'È vero, è vero! Uccello! Giotto! Molto bello, molto antico!'

Now Vaughan Thomas is a Welshman, more volatile than I, quicker off the mark, swifter in movement, and while I remained in a pleasant stupefaction before the gaunt Virgin and the broad-bottomed cavalry, he was off in search of other treasures. A stack of pictures in the middle of the room divided it in two, and he, with Nayar and Quereshi, was on the other side when a helpful Italian took down the shutters from the far end, and let in more light. Then I heard a sudden clamour of voices, a yell of shrill delight from Nayar, and Vaughan Thomas shouting 'Botticelli!' as if he were a fox-hunter view-halloing on a hill. I ran to see what they had found, and came to a halt before the Primavera.

I do not believe that stout Cortez, when he first saw the Pacific, stood silent on a peak in Darien. I believe he shouted in wordless joy, and his men with waving arms made about him a chorus of babbling congratulation. We, before the Primavera, were certainly not mute, and the refugees – some had been sleeping side by side with Botticelli – were as loudly vocal as ourselves. They had a fine sense of occasion, and our own feeling that this was a moment in history was vigorously supported by the applause they gave to our exclamation and delight.

Then at the proper dramatic moment the hero of the piece arrived, and the Italians introduced him proudly: 'Il Professore, il Professore!'

The Professor was a small brisk man of middle age, dark-skinned and lean. He wore gleaming spectacles and a grey tweed knickerbocker-suit of sporting cut: he had been an Alpine climber, he later told us. Had we landed upon a desert island he could scarcely have given us a warmer or more vivacious welcome, and soon we perceived that we were more than discoverers. We were the rescue-party that he had anxiously been waiting for.

It took us some little time to unravel his story, for he spoke no English, none of us had any real command of French, and my Italian was enough to buy a bottle of

Chianti but little more. Vaughan Thomas, however, proved himself to be a remarkable linguist. His formal knowledge of Italian was small, but he had a Celtic way with words, he could invent what he did not know, both syntax and vocabulary, and his conversations with the Professor became contests in volubility, Celt playing Latin on equal terms, in what was often a brilliant improvisation of language.

The Professor, it appeared, was not really a professor. The title had been given him, *honoris causa*, by the neighbouring *contadini*. His name was Cesare Fasola, and he held some appointment in the Uffizi Gallery. Most of the pictures and some of the statuary in the Uffizi, the Pitti Palace, the Accademia, and other collections had been dispersed, for safety's sake, in March 1944, after the Allied Air Force had bombed the railway station in Florence. The Republican Fascists, then in power, believed that this attack was preliminary to a systematic destruction of their city, and in panic mood decided to remove its treasures to various country houses in the neighbourhood. The German Army lent them transport, and the removal was so hastily done that many of the pictures — as we had seen — were brought out naked and unprotected. The galleries stood empty, and never another bomb came near them.

Then the tide of war set northward, and the Eighth Army drove its way up the Liri Valley. The beleaguered men of Anzio broke out, and Rome fell. Savage fighting followed, but the advance continued and presently the noise of battle echoed in the Tuscan hills. Now the treasures of the Uffizi and San Marco and the Pitti Palace were in real danger, and the Fascists, unhappy and flustered, thought they would be safer within their own walls. Again they asked the German Army for transport, and the Germans promised they should have it. But the Eighth Army was moving more rapidly now, the ring was closing upon Florence, and though the Germans fought with the desperation of the manifestly damned they could neither hold their ground nor gain the time they hoped for. The great Madonnas and the Primavera and the Coronation of the Virgin were left behind in a perilous no-man's-land, and only the Professor remained to guard them.

When it became evident that the pictures were in danger, the Professor persuaded the German authorities to give him a pass; and mounted his bicycle. The chief treasures were at Montegufoni, but there were other pictures of great value in three nearby houses, at Montagnana and Poppiano, and all this area became his parish.

Day after day he bicycled from house to house, and so long as the Germans were in occupation his pass was respected and he could go in and talk to whatever troops were quartered in them, look at his pictures, and preach the necessity of treating them with all possible respect. His parish, during this period, was under fire from the guns of the Eighth Army, but the Professor was undeterred by shells. He had his duty to do.

Then the Germans departed, in something of a hurry, and the leading troops of liberation appeared. The Professor found them less sympathetic than the *Tedeschi*. His German pass meant nothing to them, and they could not understand why he, a mere Italian and lately an enemy, should demand the right of entry to buildings which had been newly won in battle and were still in the forefront of battle. They listened impatiently, and waved him away. Sadly the Professor remounted his bicycle, and now he had to beware of shells and mortar-bombs descending from the north. His parish was now under fire from the German artillery, and his new parishioners refused to recognise him. With what hope and patience he could muster, he waited for the rescue-party.

That was his story, and now the responsibility was ours. Nayar went to wake the Colonel, and I went with him.

Commanding officers who have lately been engaged in battle and are roused from their entitled sleep are sometimes difficult; but fortunately for us Colonel Leeming of the Mahrattas was a good-humoured man. He listened politely, then with growing attention to what I told him. He knew there were some pictures in the house, but he had had no time to look at them, he said, and he had supposed they belonged to the family. The castello was the property of the Sitwells, who were artistic people, weren't they?

To describe the wealth of treasure that lay below him, I used all the superlatives I could put my tongue to – and still the Colonel listened, unprotesting. To the north we could hear the noise of war, and so much concern for a few yards of paint may have seemed excessive to him, whose care was men; but he was very patient. He admitted that he knew little about art, and wistfully added that if his wife were there she would be more impressed. She took a great interest in pictures, he said.

He put on his shoes and came down to look at the Primavera. He stood silent for some time, and still without comment walked slowly past the other pictures, into the adjoining rooms and back again, as though he were making his rounds of a Sunday morning after church parade. He was evidently pleased with what he saw, and now permitted himself – with a decent restraint – to be infected by our enthusiasm. He would do everything in his power to keep the pictures safe, he promised.

Several other officers had appeared, and to one of them he said: 'Have all these rooms put out of bounds, and get a guard mounted. You'll have to find somewhere else for the refugees to sleep; there's plenty of room in the place.'

We explained to the Professor that his pictures were now under official protection – Mahratta bayonets would guard them night and day, we told him – and at once he grew boisterously happy, and danced about thanking everyone in turn.

Vaughan Thomas and I had decided that, while he told the world of our discovery, I must find a smaller executive audience, and inform the military authorities; so he returned to the Press Camp to write and broadcast the story, and I went with Nayar to the headquarters of the Indian Division to call on General Russell.

The General was out walking. His caravan stood on the edge of a wooded deep ravine, and from its depths came the occasional echo of a revolver shot. We listened – and decided that the reports were growing louder. 'He won't be long now,' said his A.D.C. 'He walks very quickly.'

It was his custom, I gathered, to take daily exercise in the roughest country he could conveniently find; and to practise revolver-shooting *en route*. Presently, gleaming with sweat, he came out of the ravine: a heavily built, heavily moustached jovial man. I had to wait until he had had a bath, but as soon as I had told my story he telephoned to the brigadier within whose sector Montegufoni lay, and then to Tactical Headquarters of the Eighth Army; and on each occasion spoke with impressive vigour, and very heartily informed them both of the large responsibility that now lay upon them. Then we dined, and both Nayar and I, exulting over our discovery and immensely relieved by the knowledge that we had done all that was immediately possible to safeguard the pictures, found it a little difficult to behave with the quiet decorum proper to a Senior Officers' mess.

In the morning we returned to Montegufoni, and found dark sentries, grave of feature and dignified in their bearing, outside the doors. Then the Professor appeared with one of the Mahrattas' English officers, and we went inside. The Colonel's orders had been strictly obeyed, and the rooms had now the untenanted peace of a museum on a fine morning. We opened the shutters, and with more leisure made further discoveries. Many pictures that we had scarcely noticed in our first excitement now appeared like distinguished guests at a party, obscured by numbers to begin with, who, when at last you meet them, are so dignified or decorative that it seems impossible they could have remained unrecognised even though their backs were turned and a multitude surrounded them. Lippo Lippis came forward smiling, a Bronzino was heartily acknowledged, Andrea del Sartos met our eyes and were more coolly received.

Beside the Giotto Madonna stood a huge equestrian portrait of Philip IV of Spain – by Rubens or Velasquez? I do not know which – and peering round Philip's shoulder, absurdly coy, was the stern and antique countenance of another great Virgin. With some difficulty we moved the King and revealed a Madonna of Cimabue. In a room on the other side of the courtyard, that we had not visited before, we found Duccio's Sienese Madonna, the Rucellai Madonna. Here also were many altar-pieces, triptychs in lavish gold, and painted crucifixes of great rarity in long-darkened colours with mouths down-drawn in Byzantine pain.

Then, privily, I returned to the great room and Botticelli's Primavera. I was alone with his enchanting ladies, and standing tiptoe I was tall enough, I kissed the pregnant Venus, the Flowery Girl, and the loveliest of the Graces: her on the right. I was tempted to salute them all, but feared to be caught in vulgar promiscuity. Some day, I said, I shall see you again, aloft and remote on your proper wall in the Uffizi, and while with a decently hidden condescension I listen to the remarks of my fellow-tourists, I shall regard you with a certain intimacy: with a lonely, proud and wistful memory. The officials, I thought sadly, will certainly not allow me to take a ladder into the gallery.

It was time now to visit the neighbouring houses of Montagnana and Poppiano, and to remind us that we were treasure-hunting only by grace of the troops in front a low-flying shell whistled over the roofs of Montegufoni a minute or two before we left, and exploded in a field below.

Montagnana was being used as an artillery observation post, and approaching it discreetly we entered with some caution to find a scene of ragged untidiness and petty destruction. German soldiers had lived there before British troops came in, and who was to blame it was impossible to say. Some rooms had been pillaged, and others were in dismal confusion. But most of the pictures were in wooden cases, and none had been damaged so far as we could see. We found nothing of the first importance there.

At Poppiano, two or three miles to the south, pictures had been stored in a castle of the Guicciardinis and a nearby villa. The castle had not been disturbed, but a shell had entered the villa by an upstairs window, burst on a bedroom floor, and made havoc of the room beneath where many uncased pictures were lodged. A big one lay, face up, beneath a strange heap of oddments: plaster and torn curtains, splinters of wood, and shawls and tumbled pictures, and a lot of revolver ammunition. Vaughan Thomas incited us to clear the mess, and when that had been done we saw that the picture below was Pontormo's Visitation of St Anne. It was badly scarred, but the lovely pale faces of the Virgin and her mother were unhurt.

On our return to camp we met a tall, eager, bespectacled, wildly excited American lieutenant, an expert in the fine arts, who had been sent forward by the Allied Military Government to take charge of the pictures. He had brought no camp-kit with him, but as he was too agitated to sleep much he did not suffer unduly from the lack of it. We took him to Montegufoni on the following day, and found that the military guard which A.M.G. had undertaken to provide was not there. A few Italian policemen in plain clothes stood about, but the troops ignored them. The doughty Mahrattas, who now were guarding the Primavera and the great Madonnas with the most jealous respect – they had already, one felt, become part of the Mahratta tradition, a rosette upon their colours – the Mahrattas were moving forward at night, and the pictures would again be unprotected. Already in the villa at Poppiano, there had been a sad and sordid little case of vandalism. Two busts, of no value, of Caesar Augustus and Dante had been knocked off their pedestals and broken, and a couple of bad pictures slashed across and across with a knife. Two or three unknown soldiers, a tearful housekeeper told us, had broken in the night before, and stolen all her blankets and a frying-pan. But that, though brutal and improper, was comprehensible, for the nights were cold and soldiers sleep out of doors. Less easy to admit, and shuddering in the mind when the admission had been made, was the knowledge that soldiers, going forward into battle, may be possessed by such a hatred of the world that its harmless and pretty adornments become a mockery to them, intolerable to their eyes. Over, then, go the poor busts of Dante and Caesar, out come the jack-knives and a painted canvas is ripped across to show their loathing and contempt of life and its silly arts. At Poppiano hatred had been satisfied cheaply enough – but what if it visited Montegufoni?

Our art expert, in despair, returned to some rearward area to seek more assistance, and Vaughan Thomas and I, angry and afraid, went to the Eighth Army's Tactical Headquarters where we described the situation with some vehemence. There, after one abortive interview, we were given a guard from General Leese's Defence Company which we took to Montegufoni, and having seen it properly posted, there and at Poppiano and Montagnana, returned at last to our proper work; which was to pursue and observe the fighting. For three days the Primavera, the Madonnas and Uccello's plump war-horses had filled our thoughts and we had been concerned only with our own campaign for their protection; but the larger battle, a very stern and bloody contest, had been moving slowly forward.

The New Zealanders, solid men with pride in every fibre of their muscles, had been fighting grimly on the ridge from San Michele to La Romola, and from one of their observation posts beyond San Casciano I saw Florence lying in its bowl of the hills, Giotto's Campanile standing firm, the burnt-orange Duomo, Fiesole on the slope beyond, while in the foreground on the ridge the battle for it was still violent. Then the ridge was taken, our line went swiftly forward, and early in the morning of 4 August – just thirty years after we first declared war on Germany – we went into that part of Florence which lies south of the Arno. The South African Armoured Division, the New Zealanders, the 24th Guards Brigade, and the 4th Infantry Division had made a race for the city, and the South Africans, I think, had won by a head.

The Florentines of the South Bank, poor people for the most part, gave us a warmer welcome than the Romans. Tears streaked their faces while they cheered, and for an hour or two their affection had almost the peril of a cannibal's. At one moment my companion of the day – Vaughan Thomas was no longer with me – was mercilessly embraced by a bristle-bearded labourer while I, with my left arm clutched to an unseen but young and palpitating bosom, was being heartily kissed by a pair of the plainest old trots in Tuscany; but then the crowd broke and scattered as snipers opened fire from a window or a roof, and our partisans replied. The partisans were hotly enthusiastic, and for some time my jeep carried half a dozen of them, armed with strange weapons, through narrow streets where the crowds gathered tightly or swiftly fled, where frightened faces peered from doorways, then lightened and grew jubilant, and followed — with their attendant bodies — our slow progress.

We went through the Boboli Gardens to the south entrance of the Pitti Palace, and saw that it had become a vast caravansary. Its courtyards and lower rooms were full of refugees, hazy with their cooking-fires, fluttering with their spare shirts, noisy with their countless children. We met a curator of the gallery, and to put him in a good mood I told him that the Uffizi pictures were safe, and that his colleague Cesare Fasola had bravely done his duty and was well. We were rewarded, for he gave us the gossip of the city and presently conducted us, through a horde of amiable and voluble people, to a concrete shelter where, in large crates and packing cases, lay much Florentine statuary. Here we could see an arm by Donatello, and there, anatomised, something of the strength of Michelangelo. Deep in the pile were Ghiberti's bronze doors from the Baptistery: those green miracles were safe, and to know that was a comfort when the smoke of ruined buildings was still rising beyond the Ponte Vecchio, and bursts of machine-gun fire echoed along the river bank. The Germans and the Fascists still held the northern part of the city, and no one knew what its fate would be. All the bridges were down but the Ponte Vecchio, and that was grievously damaged. The lovely Santa Trinità had vanished utterly, and dusty ruins lay on both sides of the river. Florence was divided again, as if between more savage Guelphs and Ghibellines.

In an ornamental pond in the Boboli Gardens, in thick

green water, five little boys were swimming and diving and ducking each other. Machine-guns chattered and stammered near by, and shells whined overhead, some coming from the north and some from the south. The little boys climbed to the top of a rocky pedestal in the pond and dived into the green scum. When they perceived that they had spectators their antics became wild, and they showed-off with noisy glee.

In the late afternoon rain drove the people indoors, and all the flowers they had thrown lay wetly trampled on empty streets. Few of our troops were in the town itself, but a Provost Company had set up its headquarters, and there I went to beg some rations. Standing at the door was a man red from head to foot. He was a Fascist who had been caught and beaten by some virtuous Democrats – he was a spy, he was a Guelph or a Ghibelline, no one could properly discover – but he was still bleeding slowly from his bruised head and face and hands, and the rain had soaked his torn shirt and thin trousers with his diluted blood till he was total gules.

With two American war-correspondents I decided to spend the night among the refugees in the Pitti Palace; for now the Germans were shelling the road beyond the Porta Romana, by which we had entered, and we could not get out again. The curator whom we had met offered us a suite of rooms in one of which hung a large painting of the Holy Family – by Luini? We could not be sure, and grew earnest in our discussion of probabilities. The noises of battle were louder at night.

Now Montegufoni was quiet and peaceful, and the Primavera and the great Madonnas stood in a stillness very like that of an art gallery when the bell has rung and the last reluctant visitor has gone. But Florence, their native place, was darkly turbulent and fierce as the age in which they were painted. Someone began to argue that although the history of mankind is full of achievement, there is no evidence of progress; but we were too tired to undertake so heavy a debate.

The Provost Company had given me a generous parcel of rations, and I went out and found a young woman who was very pleased to exchange a flask of wine for a tin of bully beef. By the light of half a candle we sat down to supper in our room in the Pitti Place.

❧ Twenty-Six

In Rome, to my great advantage, I had become friendly with Nigel Dugdale. Somewhere on the roof of Africa he had been badly wounded – he was in the 17th Lancers – and in lieu of a squadron of tanks he commanded a comfortable hotel not far from the Piazza di Spagna. Most of his lodgers were American war-correspondents – there were times when the hotel overflowed with them – and with great skill Nigel kept them reasonably happy: he controlled the entire output of a gifted man who confected, from unknown ingredients, a dark brown, rather syrupy brandy, which the lodgers drank with pleasure. Usually, too, he was able to give me a room from which I enjoyed a broad, honey-coloured view of Rome, and there, soon after kissing Botticelli's flower-girls, I began to write the novel which became *Private Angelo*.

Since leaving London I had had no instructions from the War Office, but I had gathered fragments of the material necessary for a history of the campaign – if a history of the whole campaign should be demanded from me – and between Naples and Florence I had seen much of the ground on which the Eighth Army had been fighting. The Americans had a competently manned Historical Section that was busily collecting, assessing and indexing documents of every sort; and we had the nucelus of a similar organisation that was so small as to be barely visible, and amateur rather than professional in character. In Rome, then – as well as writing a chapter or two of *Private Angelo* – I composed a long memorandum in which I pointed to the folly or imprudence of letting the Americans assert, over the Mediterranean, a monopoly of its history. The Eighth Army would have no future unless its guardians were appointed now, and I made suggestions, in some detail, for the establishment of an historical unit large enough to make immediate preparation for what would be its eventual task. A copy of my memorandum I sent to the War Office, and another – scrupulously directed through 'the proper channels' – to General Alexander; who had asked me my purpose in Italy when he caught me trespassing in Caledon Camp.

Rome offered many diversions, and I enjoyed the conversation of the Polish officers whose workroom I shared. They – the men without a country, whose valour seemed indifferent to circumstance – were great gossips, and knew every scrap of sidelong talk that blew about the streets, or through the doors of black-market restaurants. 'You see her?' they might say. 'She is of good family but has no money. So now she is sleeping with Colonel So-and-so, who is very rich. You can always buy petrol from him, if you have the money. When the Germans were here she slept with General Such-and-such, but an American colonel has more money than a German general. Her husband is in Naples. He lived in good style before the war, and did not collaborate, so for a long time he was poor. But now, with American money, she can keep him in the style he was accustomed to. She is a beautiful woman, don't you think? And honest too.' It was, perhaps, a full-hearted involvement in the life about them that absolved the Poles from self-pity, and let them shrug off their country's tragedy.

The outstanding event of my Roman season was the arrival, from the Vatican, of Winston Churchill. The Prime Minister had come to Italy to talk strategy with General Alexander and Mark Clark, and he had agreed to meet and address an assembly of war correspondents. The meeting had been arranged – in part, at least – by Nigel Dugdale, who offered me a ringside seat. The floor would be crowded, but discreetly situated on either side of the platform there would be two or three chairs reserved, so to speak, for the management. Punctually we assembled, and waited idly for half an hour or more. We knew that the Prime Minister was to have an audience of the Pope, but had not expected the audience to be so protracted. The war correspondents, most of them American, grew impatient but briskly applauded when Winston at last appeared. Then silence fell, and they were staring in astonishment at what they saw. It was towards the end of August, and Rome was like a baker's oven in the morning. The heat was like prison walls, but the Prime Minister wore formal clothes – black jacket, striped trousers – and showed no sign of discomfort. He walked, as it seemed, in his own climate. He brought with him, from the Vatican, an atmosphere of other-worldliness. He looked young and freshly plump. It was hardly possible to suppose that he had been breathing the stale and sultry air of the streets.

There was a hushed attention when he began to speak. His voice was gentle, conversational in tone – there was no oratorical boom in it – but men of little sensibility respected its authority, and emotion lay close beneath its quietness. He spoke of war, and its heroism, its horror. Twice he was moved to tears, and without embarrassment wiped them away with an enormous white handkerchief, and went on speaking with a simple candour that lighted all he said. I was no more than eight or ten feet away from him – a little behind his right ear – and the admiring wonder with which I watched him became, perhaps absurdly, a deep affection. He was smaller than I had expected, and when he sat down, and the war reporters were allowed to ask questions, I grew anxious about him, I wanted to protect him against any roughness or unfriendliness.

Some of the questions were crude and silly, but he answered them with courtesy and patience. Once he made a simple joke – some fool had asked him how many cigars he smoked – but the aura he had brought with him from the Vatican remained unbroken; and as he left us – his hand raised in that familiar gesture – I heard someone say, 'Is that V for Victory or Pax Vobiscum?' He was still calm and composed, as though insulated against the heat of the day, and it was not until later that one wondered if he, in the

Vatican, had left an impression as deep as that which the Vatican had made on him.

It was then – a week or two before, a week or two later – that I met Evelyn Waugh again, and was shocked to see his frail and shrunken look, so different from his ordinary compact and hardy appearance. He had escaped, with a few seconds to spare, from the blazing wreckage of an aeroplane that crashed somewhere in Yugoslavia. With him, and fortunate as he, were Philip Jordan and Randolph Churchill, but most of their company – I forget how many – had died in the flames. Now invalids in general show a gentle, rather wistful optimism about their condition, and submit to their doctors with a touching faith. But Evelyn did neither. He was physically weak, but his temper was unsubdued. With indignation in his voice – faint though it was, there was room in it for indignation – he insisted that he was very ill indeed, and had no faith in the treatment he was receiving. He demanded to see the Commandant of the hospital where he lay, and the Commandant had to listen to some harsh and cogent criticism of his doctors, his nurses, and the whole administration of his hospital. I listened too – I was cited as a witness to the fact that a patient was complaining of faulty treatment and indifferent attention – and when next I went to see him Evelyn was in another ward and already feeling much better in consequence of the different treatment that he himself had prescribed. I shall not pretend that Evelyn was a better diagnostician than the Commandant, but he knew what he wanted, and – from the minimal authority of a hospital pillow – he got it.

He regained his health, and when I returned to Rome we dined together at a very good black-market restaurant, called The Bear, which he had discovered; he was no longer combative, he was purring with content. In the apricot light of Roman afternoons and the bland exuberance of its architecture he had found the ambience necessary for his convalescence.

The small, the barely visible historical unit with which I had a tenuous connexion had been given a new and manifest

importance – I cannot remember when – by the appointment
to it of a young lieutenant-colonel called Raymond Kittoe,
who enjoyed, among other useful qualities, the advantage of
knowing by their Christian names a number of officers who
lived on or within the fringes of authority. It was by his
adroit steering, I think, that my memorandum got some
attention, and early in September he and I were commanded
to dine with General Alexander at his Advanced Headquarters in a wood just south of Siena.

Darkness enfolded the wood, there was wind in the
branches, and rain on the skirts of the wind. Then, where
the trees grew thickly, a subdued light poured thinly from
the Commander-in-Chief's mess, and we went into a large,
square tent furnished with rather shabby chairs and tables –
they had, conspicuously, a cast-off look: not loot but salvage
– with here a tray of bottles and glasses, and there, incongruously formal, a display of tidily arranged magazines and
newspapers carefully folded but apparently never read.
The grey canvas walls of the anteroom were rain-sodden
and shuddered with the wind, but formality triumphed over
circumstance, and out of the wood and into the warmth
came General Harding and a couple of A.D.C.s, Oliver
Lyttelton and his two sons, one of them from the Adriatic
front, the other from the hills beyond Florence; and then
General Alex. At dinner I sat beside him, and he told me
that in a broad and general way he approved of my memorandum, and he wanted me to go home and argue my case
with his authority behind me: though 'goodwill' may be a
more accurate word than 'authority'.

It was Oliver Lyttelton – then Minister of Production
and a member of the War Cabinet – who dominated conversation during most of the meal, and the stories he told left
broad, creaming wakes of laughter. But General Alex
gathered everyone's attention when he began to speak of the
battle the Americans were fighting near the Futa Pass, on
the mountain road between Florence and Bologna. He
asked me if I had been to see them lately, and promptly
added, 'Well, you must go as soon as possible. They've been

doing very well indeed. They're fighting a remarkable battle in quite extraordinary country, and if you go at once you'll see the detail of it.'

He spoke across the table to Oliver Lyttelton, whose memories of the first war were almost as extensive as his own: 'You remember the astonishing litter of a battlefield? But you have to see it immediately after the ground has been won, or the impression gets blurred. I was there, in the mountains today, and it's a very interesting scene. There's been a lot of shell-fire, the Americans are lavish with their artillery, and as well as all the usual débris, the paper – as much paper as if there'd been a Bank Holiday instead of a battle – there were the twigs and branches that had been lopped off the trees. There was quite a big wood in front of the guns, or where the guns had been. So you could see little branches with the broken ends still white, and twigs with the leaves on them, not wilted yet. And any quantity of Germans. They've killed a lot of Germans. They're lying about in curious attitudes. Some of them in very curious attitudes.'

He turned to me again: 'But you'll have to go quickly if you want to see it properly. A battlefield loses its look of reality very soon. A night's rain will spoil it completely.'

To observe upon the battlefield the white wood of a newly broken branch, the short-lived freshness of leaves that shells have lately pruned, is a faculty of the artist's eye; and when he spoke of the curious attitudes of the German dead there was certainly more of the artist than of the soldier in his voice and mind. It is the soldier's duty to kill and discomfit his country's enemies. The soldier, as the scapegoat of a silly flock, must take upon himself that burden, and is therefore entitled to a professional gratification when he counts the slain. But in the General's voice there had been but a single note of that sort, a light and passing exclamation of satisfaction, and then a much livelier disclosure of aesthetic interest: of the artist's concern with life and death, who with a more than common humanity is equally interested in the dispositions and significance of both. The lines of a sprawling leg, of a head twisted below the weight of a dead body, were

296

clearly remembered, and there may have been in his mind a little regret that he had not had time to sit down with a sketch-book and make drawings of them. As an amateur artist he was unusually gifted, and in the work of the masters – the Italian masters in whose country he was fighting – he showed an interest both profound and helpful.

In popular esteem Alexander's reputation as a soldier never approached that established, so assiduously, by Montgomery; and the reasons are not hard to discern. Montgomery appeared on the African stage at a critical period in the drama, and by force of personality – a force that appeared to combine, by genius itself, the actor's gift with the dramatist's own authority – he re-created, in an army whose confidence had withered under doubt and defeat, a spirit not only emulous of victory but assured that victory was within its grasp; and victory was its reward. No one, and no argument, can deny Montgomery the triumph he earned at what should, perhaps, be called the second battle of El Alamein; but no one, so far as I remember, has made sufficiently clear the fact that during his long preparation for that battle Montgomery had behind him the un-stinted support of Alexander, his superior officer. Alexander claimed no credit for the help he had certainly given, and Montgomery, I think, made no particular effort to show gratitude for it.

Alexander, of course, had none of Montgomery's popular appeal or theatrical ability. He could never, even at the darkest moment which may justify theatrical appeal, have cried in the fashion of Henry V – if Shakespeare can be trusted, about which there may be difference of opinion – 'Now God for Alex, England, and St George!' One can see him, quite often, behaving as Wellington did, but never as Henry V or Montgomery. He was an aristocrat – that species so nearly and so lamentably defunct – and his aristocracy was so perfectly articulated, so evenly distributed, that he carried it without effort. By breeding a patrician, he hap-pened also to have an artist's eye, an artist's sympathy and the practical gifts of a very great soldier.

I am not writing military history – that I may have said before – but in the course of trying to write, with such truth as one can encompass, some fragments of autobiography I cannot avoid the environment of war in which, for a few years, I laboured inconspicuously; and I should be guilty of grievous falsification if I omitted, from my tale of events in Italy, the fact that I met there a man of outstanding character whose ability and achievement, in his own profession, seem to have been curiously undervalued. Alexander's victory at Tunis, in May 1943, lacked the dramatic impact of El Alamein, but his battle brought in 267,000 prisoners – more than half of them German – and on his initial strategy his tactics wrote a pattern of success which looks very like the design of an artist in full control of a medium more difficult by far than the oils and pigments with which masterpieces of a more permanent impact have been created. A year later the battle for Rome was planned in a comparable fashion, to a comparable design, and might well have achieved a like success if Mark Clark had not been diverted to what seemed a richer, readier prize than strategic victory. But General Alex uttered no protest, made no complaint, nor told the newspapers what he intended to have done, and would have done if everyone had followed his advice. Though a man infinitely more amiable than Coriolanus, he had, perhaps, no greater liking for popular applause.

I saw him first near Caserta. A fugitive from that unholy mixture of overblown baroque and American bureaucracy, I was walking in the fields a few miles away when I encountered, to my embarrassment, a figure as solitary as I was, and infinitely better dressed. He was wearing a well-tailored bush-shirt of pale blue-grey flannel – the Indian Army called it 'greyback' – with admirably cut breeches and a service cap curiously flattened in front, so that it carried – slanted lightly over the left eye – a mildly Muscovite *panache*. He was, without affectation, a military dandy; and two or three miles from Caserta – in the hinterland of a lively war – he was walking utterly alone, unarmed, so far as I could see, in the natural security of a squire in his demesne.

In 1945, when the war in Italy was newly over, he celebrated victory by a parade, in Siena, not of troops but of pictures. During the war they had lain hidden in monasteries and deep castle-cellars. Then, by his direction, they were brought together and hung in exhibition for the pleasure of his soldiers. The art of Siena's four great centuries, from the thirteenth to the sixteenth, from Byzantine gold and Duccio to Sodoma and the sinful elegance of Matteo di Giovanni, was displayed in a procession of growth. Simone Martini, the two Lorenzettis, delicate Sassetta, and the enchanted Giovanni di Paolo hung out in triumph the wealth of their spirits' conquest for the delectation of the soldiers who had suffered for a cause that not all of them comprehended; and in surprising numbers the soldiers came to stand, and stare, and wonder.

In the summer of 1944, when news of the taking of Rome was dimmed by the invasion of Normandy, there was a story, current in Italy, of a signal that General Alexander had sent to General Montgomery. In the previous September, while Montgomery with some difficulty was advancing northward out of the Toe of Italy, General Clark had landed at Salerno. Montgomery sent him a signal: 'Well done! Hold on, I am coming.' This was received with varying emotions, but carefully remembered by all who treasured the anecdotes and *obiter dicta* of Montgomery. Then in June came the invasion of Normandy. General Alex was somewhere in the vicinity of Rome. He sent a signal to Montgomery on the Norman beach: 'Well done! Hold on, I am coming.'

It is a story that accords nicely, I think, with my memory of General Alex walking, like a squire in his demesne, through the vineyards behind Caserta in his carefully tailored bush-shirt of Indian greyback.

🌸 Twenty-Seven

Before going home – to some almost wasted but very
agreeable months in London and Edinburgh – I threw away
a story that would have brought me rich and vulgar success.

I spent some weeks on the Adriatic front, where General
Leese had committed the greater part of the Eighth Army
to assault on the eastern bastions of the Gothic Line. Nature
had given the Apennines a grimly frowning aspect, and
German engineers had armed and armoured them with
Teutonic efficiency. But Oliver Leese was rewarded, at the
start, with immediate success. The outer defences were
cracked and opened, and for a moment or two optimism rose
almost as high as the hills that stand hugely before San
Marino. Then came disappointment, the mountain slopes
grew more formidable, and once again the weather broke:
the Germans, it seemed, could always call on rain to help
them.

I had never seen that side of Italy before, and when for
the first time I drove through ancient Umbria to an Adriatic
beach I was assailed, yet again, by feelings more proper to
the eighteenth century, when writers, without shame or
the impediment of self-consciousness, could show their
response to natural beauty and the grandeur of distant hills.
I had already given much of my heart to Italy, and now –
though the local wine was bad – I renewed my dedication. I
had also acquired a deep affection – born of admiration,
nurtured by wide friendship – for the Eighth Army; and
that also, in the weeks to come, was reinforced. I lived,
indeed, in a state of idealistic adultery, and of that union, of
course, *Private Angelo* was born. My emotions were taut as

fiddle-strings, and the sober, stone-walled charm of little towns, the romantic enmity of the hills, and the insoluble virtues of our rain-drenched soldiers vibrated on them in a discordance I could not regret.

I went forward into the hills one day to call on an armoured regiment, some of whose officers I knew, and found them unusually glum. Their circumstances were uncomfortable, but that was not enough to account for their mood. Somewhere ahead of us loomed the horrid, hotly defended ridge called Gemmano – Croce and Coriano were other nearby names, almost as unfriendly – and the regiment I was visiting had failed to make the progress expected of it.

I went a little farther, and met a general whom I warmly liked and deeply respected; and he too was in a sombre frame of mind. I told him with whom I had been talking, and he asked if they had had anything to say about him. No, I answered.

'Well, if they've any sense they'll keep their mouths shut,' he said, 'and I hope to God they do. But some people nowadays are too fond of talking – and these war correspondents get about, don't they? There was a woman up here the other day.'

'What did you say to them?'

'They made a balls of things yesterday. They were supposed to take Point XXX, and they made a start all right, but they didn't get very far. Well, I had a talk with their colonel this morning, and he told me about their difficulties, of course, but when I asked what casualties he'd had, he said, "We were lucky, in fact. We had a lot of mechanical trouble, but casualties – well, we only had five." '

'And you said?'

'I said, "Go out and get some more!" It would make a nice headline in the *Mirror*, wouldn't it?'

I went back to the small press camp where I was living – I had long since assumed that my *laissez-passer* entitled me to the hospitality of press camps, and I preferred them to more formal accommodation – but I felt ashamed when I contemplated the comfort that awaited me, and compared it with the horrible conditions to which the soldiers on those gun-pelted hills were condemned. In a material sense my comfort was small enough – a canvas roof, a canvas bucket to wash in, a bottle of sour wine – but there was a beach across the road, the sea was mild and blue, and one could swim in the very early morning and again before dusk. Though there was always rain on the hills, the beaches had their own climate.

That evening, moreover, the village was uncommonly lively. A company – perhaps the remains of a battalion – of an Indian Division had been sent down for a couple of days' rest, and the villagers were delighted to have such strange-looking but well-behaved visitors. There were no young men in the village – no young men native to it – but only women and children, slow-moving grandfathers and a few cripples; and at first sight of them the women and children had pretended to be afraid of their guests. But the Gurkhas were so plump and jolly, so friendly, generous with their rations and manifestly well mannered, that all pretence of fear had gone within an hour or two, and children sat fascinated while the thickly built little highlanders told them stories – which apparently they understood – in Gurkhali.

The following morning I returned to the unfriendly hills – Coriano, Croce, somewhere like that – and by evening, as it seemed, the Gurkhas had been accepted as a long-absent, far-wandering tribe of Old Umbria that had at last come home again. But very early the next morning, long before it was light, I was wakened by a confused disturbance in the village, and went out to find a most dismal scene of weeping and consternation, of outraged innocence on the one side, outraged virtue on the other. A girl had been raped – very roughly raped – and between sobs that shook her and hysteria that appalled the ears she declared that a Gurkha was the villain.

She could not, of course, identify him. But her assailant was someone whom she did not know, and, because the Gurkhas were the most obviously foreign of the many strangers in the village, it was natural for her to remember an initial fear and accuse a Nepali Rifleman of the outrage. Not for a moment do I believe her charge was justified. The Gurkhas were bewildered, indignant and filled with gloom. Severally and in unison they denied the charge, and no one who knows anything of the discipline of the Indian Army, of the ingrained, habitual good conduct of its soldiers, will think the poor girl's story credible. In all the unsettled parts of Italy there were wandering men, refugees and deserters — German and American deserters among them — and her assailant, beyond doubt, was a homeless, anonymous vagrant. All that could positively be said, however, was that rape had been committed, and ultimately to blame for it — leaving aside the matter of original sin — was the war.

There, then, poised against an idyllic landscape — ancient Umbria descending to the milk-mild sea — was my story depending, as it were, from three cruel hooks: the regiment that had failed in its allotted task, and may or may not have had good reason for its failure; the brutal general — so by malice he could be portrayed — who had told its colonel to go out and get casualties to prove his competence; and the girl, innocent and pious, who had been outraged by a savage stranger. I knew enough to make my battle-talk convincing; I felt deeply enough about Italy and the soldiers to let a controlled emotion carry the tale; and over the years I had acquired a certain competence in the use of words and the management of narrative. About 50,000 words would be enough, I thought — keep it short and keep it strong — and how utterly, how shamefully false my story might have been! But if I had written it, and published it in 1946 or 1947, how successful it would have been!

I had no difficulty in discarding the monstrous idea, but I saw it clearly, in all its falsity, and to throw it away was like drowning a sturdy, well-shaped bastard before he could speak and denounce my fatherhood.

My orders came, for new activity, and I flew to Algiers *en route* to London and conferences for which I was ill-fitted. At Algiers — idling at the airport — I saw thirty or forty men of strange appearance emerge from a sleekly fashioned machine which had flown direct from New York. The United States, I thought, was deporting some prominent members of the Mafia to their homeland; but when I made enquiry I was told, 'Oh, dear me, no! They represent American business, at its highest levels, and are about to re-establish commercial relations – profitable to all, we must hope – in the land they know best.'

I flew on, very comfortably though the route was indirect, and in London went to see, in succession, the Director of Public Relations at the War Office; Brendan Bracken, then Minister of Information; and – of most importance, I think – Sir Edward Bridges, Secretary to the Cabinet. I had a good case to argue, but I argued it poorly. American newspapers and magazines were presenting the war in Italy as an American campaign in which a small British army played – if there was room for it – a minor part at the foot of a column on an inner page; and history as well as the Eighth Army required another view, more balanced judgment. Of that I was convinced, but my conviction was lamed and weakened – when it came to argument – by the apparent fact that I was arguing on my own behalf. The better my case, the more it looked as if I were contending for advancement in the larger establishment which would have to be created. That was not what I wanted – I had lived in khaki for nearly six years, and I was tired of the colour – but it was difficult to stress the urgent need for the expansion of Kittoe's organisation without seeming to put forward my own claim to a promotion for which I had no appetite. I did little, I fear, to further the scheme which my own memorandum had originally defined – of which General Alexander had approved – and to this day I do not know if my advocacy had any effect, though Sir Edward Bridges listened to me with courtesy and exemplary patience.

I was, I think, given employment of some sort under Scottish Command – though what it was I cannot remember – and that suited me very well indeed, for Marjorie had taken a furnished flat in Edinburgh in preparation for her next lying-in; and I was within easy call when my second son was born in early December. Our parental score was then two girls and two boys; and though two pairs is a poor poker hand we decided to stay on it.

I did little, I think, to justify existence between October 1944 and March of the following year, when I returned to Italy. I wrote, I know, several chapters of *Private Angelo*, but for that I was not commissioned by the War Office. I had a curious assignment – which may have occupied several weeks – to examine and analyse the recorded conversation of some forty or fifty German generals whom, at one time or another, we had captured; and whose intimate or casual talk had been overheard and taped. I did not relish the task, but curiosity was stronger than distaste, and soon led to a remarkable discovery: our prisoners – or most of them – were doing what was expected of them by an audience of their own sort. They were playing in character.

Some of them affected to believe – or may in fact have believed – that Russia, already beaten, was on the point of collapse. Those whom General Alexander had captured in Tunis – there were dozens of them – looked forward to the eradication of Hitler and his vulgar associates, after which there would, inevitably, be a resurrection of healthy faith in Prussian militarism, and they, as representatives of an old, soundly established tradition, would again find honourable employment. They were, so far as I remember, most happily untroubled by self-criticism – the arrogance of Hitler, the ineptitude of their Italian allies were blamed for all their misfortune – and in comparison with their stubborn conservatism many of our own senior officers appeared to be dangerously infected with the heresies of progressive thought and the Left Wing.

For some time I lived again, very contentedly, at the Savile, and with persistent pleasure I recall two theatrical performances so fashioned by art, so illuminated by genius, as to be unsurpassed in my experience. There was a Wednesday or a Saturday on which I saw both parts of *Henry IV*, in which Ralph Richardson and Laurence Olivier gave acting the imaginative coherence, the complete expression, of

Figaro or Henry Moore's poised royalties. Olivier playing Hotspur with stammering intensity – Ralph, paunchy and short of breath, coming into the Boar's Head to exclaim 'A plague of all cowards' and escape retribution with the witty valiance of a fox – there was the very gold of Shakespeare, the ineffable gleam of the true metal coined again. And a few nights later Ralph played Peer Gynt and brought to life the coltishness, the moon-crazed doltishness, the peasant's cunning, the tenderness, the poetry of a haunted country-side, the affectations of success, the knowledge of defeat: all the vision of Ibsen's most intricate and deepest genius. That was the man who, in Gibraltar, had kept me awake – because he himself could not sleep – to show me how Irving, whom he had never seen, used to play Dubosc in *The Lyons Mail*.

Would it be indiscreet to recall another evening, at the Savile, when I sat, too late for prudence, with Michael Ayrton, a man whose character, like a true diamond, has many facets? There was a time when he walked beside a shadow that looked uncomfortably like St Antony of Egypt; another time when the ghost of Icarus hardly left his side; and lately, emulating Daedalus, he has built – for a mil-lionaire in Connecticut, I think – a labyrinth more solid and elaborate than anything commissioned since the age of Minos. On the evening of which I am speaking – it was, perhaps, a Sunday – we discovered, too late, that we were alone in the club. We were alarmed by the explosion of a V2, most terrifying of rockets, not very far away, and with a clouded memory of an earlier period in the war, when fire-watching was a recurrent duty, we found our way, not without difficulty, to the roof of the Savile.

The night was lurid with a fearful blaze – in Oxford Street? Perhaps farther off, but near enough and hot enough to convince us of its danger; so zealously we searched for the scoops and ladles that used to lie about in readiness for incendiaries. We could not find them, and then it dawned upon us – in the light of war's latest and most dreadful dawn – that scoops and ladles would be of no great help against a V2. It was late at night or early in the morning – we may have been talking about Daedalus – but marvellously we kept our balance when, leaning over the edge of the roof, we looked down at Brook Street far below. Here, in my house in Easter Ross, I have two of those bronze acrobats that Michael sculptured and poised trembling on tall, thin tulip-stems: we kept our balance as cleverly as they, and there is no truth in the story that we could not find our way down again till daylight showed us a trap-door in the roof.

My return to Italy was more ostentatious than is the usual habit of my life, and for that Nigel Dugdale was to blame. He in Rome had many friends, Italian as well as British and American, and some of them, who in happier times had been polo-players, now thought it possible to start the game again. But they were short of sticks, and I was asked to bring some with me. Nigel, of course, would supply them, and all I had to do was carry them. Never in my life had I held a polo-stick, but in an aeroplane, I thought, my ignorance of the proper grip might not be apparent; and I found, indeed, no difficulty at all. At the airport there waited for me a very smart soldier, of Nigel's old regiment, who carried two long, tidily wrapped bundles – four sticks in each – and as soon as he attached himself to me I became a person of uncommon importance. I had a Number 2 Priority warrant – very good going for a major – but I was accorded attention, treated with deference, far in excess of that to which I was entitled. There was a group of brigadiers, red-tabbed colonels, a major-general or two – aloof, until then, in their own dignity – but past them I was escorted, with Trooper Surcingle bearing polo-sticks at my side, to make room for which some exalted luggage had to be shifted, and before my superiors came aboard I was given a rearward seat – near the door, just in case – and my own suitcase was put down beside me, 'So that you won't be disturbed, sir.'

Gravely I thanked those who had helped me, and almost as soon as we were airborne a brigadier and a couple of colonels, in no way offended by the preferential treatment

I had been given, came aft to talk to me and tell me how glad they were to see that we were about to get the game going again. 'Just what we need in Rome,' they said. In future, I thought, when I shall have to pay my own fare again, I shall always carry, as part of my luggage, a couple of polo-sticks: I need say nothing, I shall immediately be recognised as a V.I.P. and treated accordingly.

I wasted no time in Rome, however, but hurried to catch up with the now rapidly advancing war, and in Ferrara, with an operatic intensity proper to the surroundings, I was quickly brought face to face with its realities. A German rearguard had retreated an hour or two before we went in, and their last vengeance for defeat had been to shoot five partisans; or young men alleged to have been partisans. We were taken, by an angry and excited throng, to see them where they lay. They had been tidily disposed, side by side, on a pavement near the moated Este castle. It was lightly raining, and the blood on their faces and their chests was still wet. About them – an inner circle of the surrounding crowd – crouched or sat eight or ten women, wives and mothers, who in their unrestrained grief wept with high-pitched, heart-breaking voices, and tore their dishevelled hair. It was tragedy on its own stage, played by amateurs who had no need to learn their parts; and on the following morning I saw them again. Now in the great romanesque cathedral the dead men lay in black-sheeted deal boxes, and in front of them sat their women, as black as their coffins; but now they were silent, bowed and motionless, like little monuments to the grief they had cried so piercingly the day before. Their grief was almost tangible, a pain to witness, but inescapable was recognition of the perfection with which they showed it: in violence and wild recrimination under the rain, in mute submission, still as death, under the high roof of San Giorgio.

Of the last phase of the war, as I saw it, I have written in other places, but I cannot resist the temptation to recall a voyage through Venice that was most memorable for its silence. I had seen – somewhere on the Adige, I think – the massed surrender of what remained there of a German army, and in the very early morning of the following day, prompted by sheer curiosity, I drove on to Venice. Somewhere *en route* I picked up two young officers, one English and the other American, who had lost their units or their way, and crossing the causeway we found a gondola. I remembered, from a brief visit many years before, that Danieli's lay pretty far to the east, and told the gondolier to go there. Now what was remarkable about our journey was that the city appeared to be dead or profoundly sleeping. The canals were blackly vacant, their waters mirror-calm. Nothing, except our intrusive boat, broke their ebony surface, and the silence was daunting until we came within shouting distance of Danieli's – where they who shouted had the friendly but unmusical accents of Auckland, Wellington and Dunedin. The New Zealanders were there, unabashed and noisy while all the rest of Venice, the native Venetians, lay quiet and apprehensive in the lowest depths of their houses or *palazzi*: there were German guns on the Lido, and no one knew if their gunners were going to surrender or die in a last Wagnerian fury of destruction. Fortunately for themselves, and everyone else, they decided to surrender, and immediately Venice came to life again.

Ashore, however, and especially perhaps in Danieli's, life became unexpectedly dangerous. The rich Italian families who had been living there – *embusqués* from the northern cities – were being ousted, decisively but without rudeness, to make room for the visitors from Auckland and Christchurch; and they in their turn were pushed about by a swarm of red-mufflered young partisans from the poorer parts of the town, who in relays took advantage of the hour to inspect the occupants and the furnishings of a fashionable hotel. Until then the *partigiani* had not been conspicuously active, but now they all appeared carrying rifles or tommy-guns slung on their shoulders, and from their belts, or safety-pinned to their shirts, depended small grenades. Everyone drew his breath in fear, and shrank his waistline to its smallest circumference, as they pushed their way through the crowd. Their bombs were so lightly attached that inadvertently one might brush them off – oh, like pollen. But everywhere it was the same. None of the soldiers carried weapons, but every civilian was armed to the teeth.

Now the canals were busy indeed, and all the gondolas were full of soldiers. Most of them were New Zealanders, and many had hired a couple of minstrels to accompany their voyage with music. A general and his A.D.C., sitting primly upright between their rowers, passed two sable vessels deep-laden with a sprawl of soldiers who shouted and waved friendly bottles at them. From another gondola a B.B.C. war correspondent was broadcasting his description of the scene. The gondoliers demanded exorbitant wages but, remembering their local duty to strangers, never failed to point out the Palazzo Rezzonico where Robert Browning died.

I returned to Florence, and stayed there for a day or two because I wanted to look at the Villino Medici in Fiesole, where my daughter Sally was born, and then pay my respects to Bernard Berenson. The big house, the Villa Medici, was a lamentable sight, with great holes in its roof where shells had plunged or bombs fallen, and the long garden wall, that divided the upper grounds from our own pleasance, had lost nearly all the stately urns that used to decorate it. I did not stay long in surroundings so melancholy – much of the library had been plundered, and the three sets of Henry James were rudely scattered – but drove on to Settignano to see Berenson.

In the summer of 1944 he had become a romantic, almost legendary figure. Few of the young officers in the caravans of the Eighth Army's Advanced Headquarters knew much about him, but his name was known and a youthful major boasted of an elderly aunt who at one time had been his friend. He was, they agreed, an expert of some sort, either scholar or connoisseur. 'He knows everything about Italian painting,' said one. 'About the Florentine and Sienese artists,' said another. And when it became known that he had 'gone underground', there was much speculation about his probable fate. He was an old man, and his age was pleasantly exaggerated. 'He must be eighty at least,' thought some. 'Nearer ninety,' said others.

He survived his adventures, however, and in Settignano I found him living in a house agreeably spacious and very tidily ordered like a mansion in Connecticut. He was a little tiny man, spruce and grey, so formally and neatly dressed that he looked like a miniature banker in Wall Street; though his voice was gentler. His voice was soft and charming, but lively too, and his eyes within circles of aged white were very much alive. But his teeth betrayed his years. They were uncommonly large, and somehow they suggested mammoth ivory. He was very friendly, and almost immediately uttered a warning.

'I refuse to be heroised,' he said. 'Many kind but mistaken people have sympathised with me – even admired me! – because, for rather more than a year, I had to go underground, as they say. But the truth is that I spent one of the pleasantest years of my life in concealment. I was unable to work, so I had time to read. That was a state of affairs I had long been hoping for, but had never had the strength of mind to bring about, until circumstance brought it about for me. And then I took advantage of it. I reread the classics. I read Shakespeare again, and Homer and Goethe and Dante and Schiller. With the greatest pleasure! Yes, I was very fortunate. And when the Germans came? No, that didn't improve things. They were, eventually, on all sides, about two or three miles from where I was hiding, and to be surrounded by them. . . .' He hesitated, and then admitted, 'Yes, it felt slightly eerie!'

I asked why the Republican Fascists had sought him – a critic of art, not of politics – for one of their victims. Had he encouraged resistance to them?

'It was well known that our sympathy was with the Allies,' he said, 'but that, I think, had very little to do with it. It was a personal matter. I had offended one of their leaders.

'I suppose', he said calmly, 'it had something to do with a woman.'

This was in 1945; and Mr Berenson was born in 1865.

My reverence increased, and I perceived that the Berenson legend had its roots in a good deal of ground. 'And you were able to read Homer and Goethe,' I asked, 'with Germans all round you?'

'What else was there to do?'

'You have achieved a workmanlike philosophy,' I said.

'If a man hasn't become a philosopher at my age,' he answered sharply, 'it's most unlikely that he ever will.'

His library was magnificent, and beautifully arranged in a wing of the house, built for it, that was heated to a luxury of warmth uncommon in Europe in 1945. The American Army, he said, had been very kind to him, and had given him enough fuel to heat the working part of his home. 'The working part only,' he said; and his work had more and more closely become a comparative study of religion.

I made the mistake of referring to his noble array of books as a collection. 'No, no!' he exclaimed. 'You mustn't say that! I have never *collected* books! I could never afford to, even if I had wanted to, which I certainly didn't. This is a working library, a workman's library, and nothing else.'

His little gallery of pictures was part also of the warm quarter of the house, and in it were pictures in the charmingly mannered elegance of Siena. There was a Bellini, there were two Simone Martinis: it was a gallery of *les grands vins* of painting, undiluted by anything that suggested a mere beverage.

'But you must see my garden too,' said Mr Berenson, and though the morning sun was warm he put on a muffler, a tweed overcoat, and a hat before leading me out of doors. The dimensions of the garden were generous: about fifty acres, I think. It was a little neglected and pleasantly informal except for a lovely down-sloping cypress avenue. 'This is the part of it', he said, 'that Logan Pearsall Smith admired. He used to say it was the only civilised arrangement in my garden, but I think the olive-grove is more truly civilised. These olives of the north are by far the best. They grow fatter in the south, but they are greasy there. They are at their finest in the most northerly limits of their growth – as, indeed, are so many things. Wine, for example. There are no vineyards north of the valley of the Rhine – no vineyards of any consequence – and the Rhine wines are the best in the world. Before the war, not this war, of course, but the last one – before 1914 there was wine in Cologne, for which you had to pay, perhaps, twenty-eight or thirty marks a bottle, and that you could drink with real pleasure.'

'And after drinking Rhenish at thirty marks a bottle,' I said, 'at thirty marks a bottle before 1914, have you really been able to live contentedly in Italy and be satisfied with Orvieto and Chianti?'

'You get used to the growth of the country you live in,' he answered. 'It may not be the best, but as time passes you find it agreeable enough. Yes, I like the little wines of Italy.'

Under the olive trees he spoke again of books, and with some animation of the taste-buds, acquired after half a century of reading, that tell immediately whether a book deserves to be read, or merely consulted. I asked him, with a cautious reference to his length of experience, if at eighty he wanted to read less and less, or more and more.

'Oh, more and more!' he exclaimed. 'At my age books trouble a man – a man like me – as women do when you are twenty. They are always in my mind. No, not to amass them, not to gather a great and troublesome variety, but to learn and to know each one as it arrives. And I have so little time! I have no time to learn even the old books, let alone all the new ones that are being written! There are mornings when I wake up and think that I must go into Florence, and stand at the corner of a street like a beggar, and take off my hat' – he took off his hat, and as a suppliant held it towards me – 'and say to the people who pass me by, "Will you give me five minutes, please? You are quite young, you have so many minutes, and really you do nothing with them. Give me five!" For that is what a man of my age truly wants: a few more minutes! He wants time, because he has so little left, and there is so much to do, so much to learn.'

Does a fox suffer more than a lion? I do not know, but

you can see a fox shiver, and the emotions of a lion are invisible in its shaggy bulk. Berenson, holding out his hat, was tremulous with desire: desire of time, that to the commonage of the world is but a burden. Old lions are slow, there is more life in a fox.

'You must not heroise me,' he said. But should one refrain from lauding so lively and greedy and generous a pursuer of beauty, and the truth of its creation, and art's life everlasting? Those officers of the Eighth Army who discussed him and his fate, in the country south of Florence, were intuitively aware of his entitlement. They knew that somewhere beneath the name there was a man, who anchored it, who had loved his days and used them. 'Few and evil have the years of my life been,' said the patriarch Jacob, and so many poor miserable souls have echoed him that nervous travellers may sometimes wonder if the journey is worth while. 'But give me five minutes more,' said Mr Berenson, holding out his hat – and one stamped another visa on his legend.

Siena was now my destination. The ingenious and resourceful Raymond Kittoe had found, in that enchanting town, suitable headquarters for his Historical Section, now reinforced by an Irish historian of amiable temper and a sergeant with the calm assurance of a richly paid secretary. I settled down to work in a modest, redbrick villa, with cherries ripe for picking in the garden and the Pinacoteca within an easy walk: on its walls hung the great or delicate, masterful or exquisite pictures – Duccio and Sodoma and Lorenzetti – assembled by the inspired command of General Alex, and Simone Martini again dominated, without vulgar interference, the Palazzo Pubblico where, a year before, I had seen Senegalese infantry hang out their washing. In Siena the tourist's joy – where Pinturicchio showed how Frith could have painted his *Derby Day* had he lived a little earlier and under a brighter sky – I worked sedulously for a couple of months, and I can offer no greater proof of my virtue than that.

I resisted, however, Kittoe's invitation to stay with his

historians and go with them – as he had learnt they were to go, with the forces of occupation – to Klagenfurt in Austria. There was temptation in his offer, but insufficient to overcome my impulse to go home. I had a wife to whom I was still warmly attached; I had four children of whom I knew little; and I had a house in Orkney that stood on the edge of a good fishing-loch. I took advantage of the ruling that allowed early release from the Army to elderly persons who had served in it since the beginning of hostilities, and returning to London for the exhausting process of demobilisation I was rewarded with a suit of civilian clothing, that I promptly gave away, and thankfully boarded a train that took me to Inverness, Thurso, and the little steamer *St Ola* which carried me, yet again, across the Pentland Firth.

🌸 Twenty-Eight

I FINISHED *Private Angelo* in August 1945 – rather more than a year after beginning it in Rome – and it was published, I think, early in 1946; too soon, perhaps, for it to be immediately welcomed. I had written of war without apparent bitterness, without manifest anger and open denunciation of its folly; and in the aftermath of war it was obligatory to make one's disapproval of it obvious. My hero, indeed, was an Italian soldier who feared and hated war as intensely as the warmest pacifist could desire; but he was polite in speech, he had good manners, he became friendly with his country's declared enemies, and he suffered extreme humiliation with a hallowed patience. The subject of my novel was not only war and its capacity for destruction, but Italy and its genius for survival. War in Italy had a character all its own: it was tragical, as war inevitably is, but also ludicrous because its waste and folly were underlined, emphasised and thrown into toppling-high relief by the accumulated riches and beauty that Italy had created in the twenty-five centuries since an Etruscan crossed the Tiber and got a she-wolf with twins. War was hateful – anyone could see and say that – but war in Italy was also irrelevant because the forces of civilisation, and the benignities of art, were clearly so much stronger, more informative and more permanent. War, in Italy, was a drunken, destructive and impertinent clown; to deal justly and truthfully with it one had to keep one's temper cool, one's judgment clear, and write a comedy.

I created a hero typical of Italy's good sense and good temper. I wrote of him with kindliness because it would have been dishonest to conceal the love I had acquired for his country and its people; the other characters – the British soldiers who became his comrades – I drew with an accurate knowledge of their unobtrusive but innate decency. I have never found any difficulty in accepting the seeming paradox that while war is an abominable activity the soldiers who engage in it may be more agreeable companions – and more admirable against the strict scale of morality – than their compatriots who stay at home and proclaim their detestation of war.

I avoided, in my novel, what is colloquially known as 'realism': none of my characters used the sort of language which is commonly called 'realistic' because Italy so clearly advertised the fact that a pervading and persistent regard for form and order was the true reality of Tyrrhenian life and culture; and the speech of the actors – or so I thought – should be congruous with the scene of action. I did not deny the enormities of misconduct that war may release, but drew attention to humanity's ability to endure and survive them. When, for example, Angelo and his sweetheart Lucrezia are both raped by a Goum – one of France's fierce irregulars from the Atlas – Angelo consoles the weeping girl by telling her, 'We are not to blame, so the best we can do is to let bygones be bygones, and thank God we are still alive.' And when Angelo is distraught by the discovery that Lucrezia, while he was in Africa, had borne a child to the Englishman, Corporal Trivet, she is allowed to defend herself with the question, difficult to answer: 'Was it not more unnatural for you to become a soldier than for me to become a mother?'

'Liberation' was a word much in use. It was to liberate Italy that our armies had invaded it, and it was, of course, impossible to do so without a measure of destruction. Only by force could the Germans be expelled, and, though a British or American general could observe with satisfaction the demolition of ancient walls and domestic buildings that harboured their enemies, the Italians who lived in a town, thus doomed, watched the process with other feelings. Angelo, with pardonable exaggeration, describes the native view of 'liberation':

317

In the first place, before a town or village can be liberated it must be occupied by the Germans, and the Germans will rob it of everything they can find; but that is of no importance, that is merely the Overture. Liberation really begins when the Allied Air Forces bomb the town: that is the First Movement, *Allegro* so to speak. The Second Movement is often quite leisurely but full of caprice: it occurs when the Allied artillery opens fire to knock down what the bombers have missed, and may be called *Andante Capriccioso*. After that has gone on for some time the liberating infantry will rush in, that is the Third Movement, the *Scherzo*, and though the Allied soldiers do not loot, of course, they will find a number of things, such as geese and hens and wine, that apparently belong to no one – for the local inhabitants have taken to the hills or are hiding in their cellars – and to prevent the wine and the geese from being wasted the soldiers will naturally take care of them. Then comes the Last Movement, when the officials of the Allied Military Government arrive and say to the inhabitants, 'No, you cannot do that, you must not go there, you are not allowed to sell this, and you are forbidden to buy that. If you want to live here you must apply for our permission, and it is against the law for you to be domiciled anywhere else.' Yes, that is the *Finale*, and then you may say that the process of liberation is complete.

To my great pleasure the novel was favourably received by former members of the Eighth Army, who recognised its accuracy; and I was pleased again to learn that it was well liked in Italy. A few years ago, when I was lecturing there for the British Council, I fell into conversation with a professor in the University of Florence who insisted that we had met before. I could not remember him and at first he could not remember where we had met. Then, during luncheon, when there was some talk of our discovery of the Uffizi pictures at Montegufoni, he leaned towards me and excitedly declared, 'That is where we met! I was there when you arrived with an Indian officer and someone else!'

I remembered the dishevelled figures sleeping on straw and sacking under the great Madonnas, the plump war-horses of San Romano, and the Primavera; and said, 'But apart from the soldiers there was no one there except a couple of dozen refugees – '

'Yes, yes, and I was one of them!' He smiled most

charmingly and said, 'At that time, you see, I was another Private Angelo.'

Before the year was over I was elected Rector of Aberdeen University, and that requires explanation. The office, which is honorary, survives from the establishment of the continental universities which were taken as models when St Andrews, Glasgow and Aberdeen erected their own seats of learning; and until fairly recently it was reserved, almost exclusively, for politicians prominent and important in their generation. Balfour, for example, had been Rector of both St Andrews and Glasgow; Baldwin of Edinburgh and Glasgow; Asquith of Glasgow and Aberdeen. But then, in 1931, Compton Mackenzie became Rector of Glasgow, and though he stood as an advocate of Scottish Nationalism it was not primarily as a politician that he was elected, but rather as a man who had excited the imagination of the young by the daring and elegance of his writing and the independence of his views: he was not a member of what is now called 'the Establishment', but in some respects a rebel against it, and in all respects untrammelled by its conventions. His election was a tribute to his talents, a rebuff to the established order and its orthodoxies.

I was present, as a guest, at two notable Rectorial elections of the 1920s: that of Birkenhead in Glasgow, and of Kipling in St Andrews. Birkenhead delivered a scintillating speech that attracted much comment – most of it unfavourable – because he commended adventurous individualism to a world that already was beginning to distrust individualism, and reminded his audience that glittering prizes still awaited those who had sharp swords to win them. At a civic luncheon, an hour or two later, he gave more immediate offence by speaking, with equal brilliance, for fifty-five minutes when most of those present were waiting impatiently to go to a rugby football match – one of the matches of the year – between the select teams of Glasgow and Edinburgh.

There was a dance at night, and I was presented to Lady Birkenhead. 'You come from Aberdeen?' she said. 'Well, we have a grudge against your university because in 1914 both my husband and Winston Churchill were candidates for the Rectorship, and my husband withdrew because a political clash, at that time, would have been most unseemly. But it was understood – it was made quite clear to him – that at the next election he would go in unopposed. But that didn't happen. He wasn't even invited to stand! Now what have you to say to that?'

I made what excuses I could, and a little while later met Birkenhead himself. 'Aberdeen?' he said. 'Well, let me tell you this. I've got a grudge against Aberdeen. . . .' And out came the story again. I thought it odd that both should remember so clearly – should keep on the quick tongue of memory – an incident of such minute importance in a career both various and splendid; but the prestige then attached to a Scottish Rectorship was made very obvious, and when, a few years later, Compton Mackenzie put on the gown that Balfour and Birkenhead, Asquith and Baldwin had worn, the diminution of the politician in popular esteem made a menacing appearance.

It was in 1922 that Rudyard Kipling became Rector of St Andrews, and he, whom I had venerated from childhood, made a speech of arresting dullness. Beside him, however, sat his cousin Stanley Baldwin, to whom an honorary degree was given; and while Kipling very nearly sent one to sleep Baldwin kept one anxiously awake. He who had a reputation for placid, imperturbable strength was fidgety as a dog with fleas. A rock unshaken by storm – living testimony to the virtues of roast beef and green fields – placid as a ploughman, equable and sturdy, solid as the Malvern Hills – so one had thought him, but not for a moment could he sit still. He crossed his feet, he fiddled with his fingers, looked this way and that, played with his waistcoat buttons, and oddly grimaced. Alone in that large audience he was unaffected by the somnolence that Kipling diffused.

In Aberdeen, in 1945, the Rectorial candidates were Admiral Sir Robert Burnett, a dashing leader of destroyers; Tom Johnston, Secretary of State for Scotland, who had benignly dammed the Highlands to provide hydro-electric power; Sir John Anderson, sometime Governor of Bengal, later Lord Waverley; and myself. I was manifestly the outsider, but the others as clearly were pillars of the Establishment, and I won. I was pleased and flattered by my election, but not deluded. It was just twenty years since I had taken a belated degree, I had been something of a figure, something of a 'character' in my student days, and that was remembered. I had, more recently, made a small reputation for myself, and to those who sat where I had sat, and drank where I had drunk, that was gratifying and encouraging. But in 1945 there was already a mutter of resentment against the established order, a nascent contempt for tradition and its standards, and my election was basically a cry of dissent, a murmur of insurrection. I was put forward as a symbol of revolt – at the mature age of forty-six I was the protagonist of youth and its impatience with the old régime – and sadly I betrayed my supporters. I behaved with the utmost decorum, and my Rectorial address was a model of what should be said from the platform to which I had been elevated. But my election opened a breach in the ancient walls of custom.

My immediate successor was the second Lord Tweedsmuir, a son of John Buchan, but after him came that exuberant comedian Jimmy Edwards; and in Edinburgh, a few years later, the massive figure of James Robertson Justice, film actor and adventurer in the Spanish War, was elected and re-elected. Jimmy Edwards, bemedalled in the Royal Air Force, was a Master of Arts – no mere Bachelor – of the University of Cambridge; and James Justice, my friend and neighbour, could hold his own, as a linguist or field naturalist, with scholars professionally recognised as such. Let their virtues be admitted, but it was not for their virtues they were chosen. Neither could claim apostolic descent from the lineage of Balfour and Asquith – of Gladstone and the towering Victorians – but had to thank, for their elevation, the groundswell of dissatisfaction, with life and its leaders, on which Compton Mackenzie and I had been raised.

I delivered my address, I returned to Orkney, and in the summer of 1946 the good loch of Harray gave me the best trout-fishing I had ever had. But Orkney, we discovered, had lost its old compulsive attraction, and for that there were several reasons. It had, for a start, suffered grievous defacement in the war. Many parts of the world had been blackened and devastated by enemy action; Orkney, on the other hand, was a victim of friendly interference. Its native population, in 1939, was about 21,000; its garrison, when it was most nearly threatened, numbered more than that, and behind them, when they left, there remained acres of rusting barbed wire, brown slums of crumbling huts, irremovable concrete foundations for guns and searchlights, tank-traps and other barriers to invasion. The islanders had been greatly enriched by the war, but a gentle landscape – gentle despite the occasional violence of its weather – had been brutally scarred. Nowadays, after a quarter of a century, little or nothing can be seen of the soldiers' ungainly colonisation, but in 1946 it was woefully apparent. The Orkney I had known was an Orkney which – in common with much of the world – had changed for the worse.

We too – Marjorie and I – had changed. Not for the worse, perhaps, but the manner of our life had become more difficult. We had four children, and we had to think about ways and means of educating them. Already the two girls – Sally was twelve, Kristin two years younger – were going to a school in St Andrews, and six times a year they and Marjorie were made unhappy by the Pentland Firth. It was less hostile than they thought – often enough it was sunlit and placid – but they had convinced themselves of its brutality, and imagination, like the Atlantic, has formidable tides. It was a common problem that we faced – education is a grievous burden to parents as well as to children – but isolation, kindly though our island was, enlarged and aggravated it.

Unwillingly I said: 'If, above all things, you want to keep your children with you, we shall have to sell our house here, go to live in Edinburgh and enter the girls at St George's, the boys – when they are old enough – at the Academy.' I had no wish for that to happen, and good reason for hoping it would not. But I thought Marjorie should be given the larger share of decision, and she took her responsibility seriously. There was a difficult week or two, during which her temper was uncertain, and then she came, though unhappily, to the conclusion for which I hoped. She thought or felt – wisely, I believe – that it would be a mistake to return to the circumstances and environment of her own childhood, and I was thankful for her judgment.

Much though I liked Edinburgh, I did not want to live there under a roof which also sheltered a couple of adolescent girls and a pair of rapidly growing boys. I had been fortunate in having a father who spent his life at sea; I wanted to give my sons the equal advantage of a father who lived at home while they got their schooling abroad. Few parents, I think, are well qualified to oversee their children's upbringing, and in all the talk that goes on about the problems of education – about its true purpose and ideal mechanism – there is a lamentable silence about the policy to which we should be giving thought and enquiry: which is the provision of boarding schools for all our young. I can think of nothing that would so dramatically increase the happiness of both parents and children as limiting their association to the holidays.

No sooner had we solved one problem than another obtruded, and I was forced to reconsider the *peripeteia* which I had devised – before circumstances compelled me to find another – as the concluding chapter of *The Man on My Back*. In 1939 I had already discovered that Orkney – deeply though I loved its fluent hills and shining water – was not a sufficient environment for the sort of life which I had chosen or to which I had been committed. Early in 1939 I started to make plans for the following winter. In those days it was possible to live quite cheaply in the smaller islands of the Caribbean – the Windward Islands or the Leewards, I had no preference – and I felt, very strongly, a growing need for views and circumstances of extreme and staring difference from those about me. For a long time I had had no more persistent purpose than to make Orkney my habitation and circumference; I had succeeded in all I set out to do; and a major consequence was my discovery that I must go somewhere else. I had reached, not my destination, but a turnabout. The plot required a *peripeteia*.

In 1939, however, freedom fled from Hitler's manic gaze, and instead of the Windward Islands, or perhaps the Leewards, I went with our local Territorials to the little island of Flotta. But now, in 1946, the impulse and need of an earlier year returned, and again I grew dissatisfied with the house that my father built and I had so lovingly enlarged.

My emotional attachment had found a wider area. I still live in Scotland, and though, many years ago, my impulse to do so was obscured by a sense of duty – I felt that Scottish writers should live in the land to which they belonged – that sense has long since evaporated, and I live where I do in the pure light of self-indulgence. I have seen much of the world, but no part of it has so constantly and consistently pleased my eyes as the northern counties of Scotland; and throughout my life my eyes have been my primary instrument of pleasure.

In Orkney they gave me pleasure, but not pleasure enough. I wanted also the romantic aspects of Wester Ross and Sutherland, the generous landscape of Perthshire and the noble expanses of Aberdeenshire. I wanted to live in the midst of a larger beauty than the loch of Harray could reflect. I wanted to belong to the islands of the west as well as to the islands of the north.

My dissatisfaction with a narrow environment was aggravated, moreover, by a mishap whose magnitude can only be explained by the persistent influence of my peasant ancestry. As every peasant does, I wanted land. I wanted to own a few acres, and Merkister, my house in Orkney, had a meagre patch which did not satisfy me. But immediately to the north of Merkister was a little farm, of no great value, but its forty or fifty acres lay agreeably beside the northern-

most bay of the loch, and for many years I had been promised possession of them when their owner – an amiable but
idle farmer – should retire or die. And then, without notice
or warning to me, they were sold – for a good price, I hope –
and my long-cherished belief that I should ultimately
become their owner had to be discarded for ever.

It was then that I heard of a small estate in Easter Ross,
newly on the market, and when I went to see it I was
immediately taken captive by the noble view it offered: a bay
of the sea, broadly intrusive, lay under the slope of the land
and separated it from coloured fields and the bluff, battle-
mented ridge of Fyrish, over which soared Ben Wyvis
capped with snow. The house was too big for us, and I could
not afford the whole estate. But the sitting tenant was willing
to buy the home farm, and the view was irresistible. With
the house, moreover, I acquired a circumference of land, a
little wood, a small croft, and a long, narrow strip of fore-
shore: enough to satisfy my peasant appetite. I sold Merkister, and in the early spring of 1947 we moved into
Pitcalzean House in the county of Ross and Cromarty.

One of my earliest tasks here was to write my history of
the campaign in Italy. In Austria the Historical Section to
which I had been loosely attached completed its enormous
labour, and I was warned to expect a cargo of documents. I
drove to the railway station, and there found packages that
weighed, in all, two and a half hundredweight. They kept
me busy for more than a year, and in the history, which the
Stationery Office published, there are more than a quarter
of a million words. It is painstakingly accurate, and illuminating in parts; but much of it, when I look at it again,
reminds me of Kipling's poem about infantry columns in
the South African War:

> We're foot – slog – slog – slog – sloggin' over Africa –
> Foot – foot – foot – foot – sloggin' over Africa –
> (Boots – boots – boots – boots – movin' up and
>   down again!)
> There's no discharge in the war!

For the last twenty years I have, indeed, been decently industrious. I have written many books without spectacular success or total failure. Some of which I thought highly have done less well than I expected, but much that has been written by others, and found wide approval, has given me no pleasure at all: one writes in obedience to one's own will, and it is by chance that the individual will coincides with popular favour. I am very fond, for example, of a fable called *A Spell for Old Bones* which fell as unnoticed as a snowflake in Lapland: most people are, or lately have been, so obsessed by their own predicament – their own fears and problems – that a fable with no immediately apparent relation to common life is unlikely to attract interest unless it evokes a savage sexual excitement, or perhaps the current superstitions exploited by science fiction. I was more deeply disappointed by the indifference which attended the publication of *Position at Noon*: in conception, as well as in execution, it is the wittiest novel I have written, and wit is a quality that I value and expect to be valued.

My industry – my respectable industry – has not, however, made me desk-bound, and I have travelled widely enough to prevent imprisonment within a parochial ambit. But Scotland – northern and western Scotland – has remained the controlling focus of my life, and I have contentedly made my home in what must seem, to the majority, a remote and empty place. Some little time ago, when I was celebrating my seventieth birthday, an alert and ingenious young man called Raeburn Mackie, employed by the *Scotsman*, came to talk to me, and wrote a very friendly article which filled half a page. At some time during our conversation he must have asked me how I would describe myself, and I, as it seems, presented him with a phrase that he found good enough for a title. His article appeared under the banner, in thick black capital letters:

AN OLD PEASANT WITH A PEN

List of Books

By Eric Linklater

NOVELS
White-Maa's Saga
Poet's Pub
Juan in America
The Men of Ness
Magnus Merriman
Ripeness is All
Juan in China
The Sailor's Holiday
The Impregnable Women
Judas
Private Angelo
A Spell for Old Bones
Mr Byculla
Laxdale Hall
The House of Gair
The Faithful Ally
The Dark of Summer
Position at Noon
The Merry Muse
Roll of Honour
Husband of Delilah
A Man Over Forty
A Terrible Freedom

FOR CHILDREN
The Wind on the Moon
The Pirates in the Deep
    Green Sea
Karina with Love

SHORT STORIES
God Likes Them Plain
Sealskin Trousers
A Sociable Plover
The Stories of Eric Link-
    later

AUTOBIOGRAPHY
The Man on My Back
A Year of Space
Fanfare for a Tin Hat

BIOGRAPHY
Ben Jonson and King
    James
Mary Queen of Scots
Robert the Bruce
The Prince in the Heather

ESSAYS
The Lion and the Uni-
    corn
The Art of Adventure
The Ultimate Viking
Edinburgh
Orkney and Shetland

HISTORY
The Campaign in Italy
The Conquest of England

The Survival of Scotland
The Royal House of Scotland

VERSE
A Dragon Laughed

PLAYS
The Devil's in the News
Crisis in Heaven
To Meet the Macgregors
Love in Albania
The Mortimer Touch
Breakspear in Gascony

CONVERSATIONS
The Cornerstones
The Raft *and* Socrates
Asks Why
The Great Ship *and* Rabelais Replies

PAMPHLETS
The Northern Garrisons
The Defence of Calais
The Highland Divisions
Our Men in Korea
The Secret Larder